CW00540428

Please return this book on or before the due date below

WITHDRAWN

Cox's Navy

Cox's Navy

Salvaging the German High Seas Fleet at Scapa Flow 1924–1931

Tony Booth

Pen & Sword
MARITIME

First published in Great Britain in 2005
and reprinted in 2008 by
Pen & Sword Maritime
an imprint of
Pen & Sword Books Ltd,
47 Church Street, Barnsley, South Yorkshire, S70 2AS

ISBN 978 1 84415 181 3

A CIP catalogue record for this book is
available from the British Library

Typeset in 11/13 Sabon by
Kirsten Barber, Leeds, West Yorkshire

Printed and bound in Great Britain by Biddles Ltd, King's Lynn, Norfolk

Pen & Sword Books Ltd incorporates the Imprints of
Pen & Sword Aviation, Pen and Sword Maritime, Pen & Sword Military,
Wharncliffe Local History, Pen & Sword Select,
Pen & Sword Military Classics and Leo Cooper

For a complete list of Pen & Sword titles please contact
PEN & SWORD BOOKS LIMITED
47 Church Street, Barnsley, South Yorkshire, S70 2AS, England
E-mail: enquiries@pen-and-sword.co.uk
Website: www.pen-and-sword.co.uk

To John Appleby

for giving me the time to learn

'With ships the sea was sprinkled far and nigh.'
William Wordsworth

'Our ship, but three glasses since, we gave out split,
Is tight, and Yare, and bravely rigg'd, as when
We first put to sea.'
William Shakespeare, *The Tempest*

Contents

Acknowledgements

Although one person is usually acknowledged as being a book's author, their ability to source, collate and piece together events they were not privy to witness first-hand relies on many individuals and organizations who give freely of their time and expertise. *Cox's Navy* is no exception, and I would like to thank the following for their help, time and generosity, which were pivotal in ensuring this book's completion.

For their permission to use direct quotes, original dialogue and illustrations, I would like to thank: *The Orcadian* newspaper with their reporting of the whole salvage operation during the 1920s and 1930s; *The Illustrated London News* Picture Library and Archive; *The Times*; the *Daily Mail;* and ITN Archive/Stills. Many thanks are owed to Kim Foden at the Herald Print Shop, Kirkwall, Orkney, for permission to quote from *The Orkney Herald*; to the National Archives for permission to quote freely from their records; and to The United Kingdom Hydrographic Office. Extracts from *The Silent World* by Jacques-Yves Cousteau with Frédéric Dumas (Hamish Hamilton 1953, Penguin Books 1958), were reproduced by permission of Penguin Books Ltd (pp. 3, 129); from *Down to the Ships in the Sea* by Harry Grosset, published by Hutchinson, reprinted by permission of The Random House Group Ltd; and from *Scapa Flow* by Malcolm Brown & Patricia Meeham reproduced with the permission of BBC Worldwide Limited, Copyright © Malcolm Brown & Patricia Meeham 1967. Thanks to Birlinn publishers in Scotland, for permission to quote from *The Grand Scuttle* by Dan van der Vat; to BAE Systems, Submarine Division; to Eric Dobby Publishing Ltd in Kent for permission to quote from *The Man who Bought a Navy* by Gerald Bowman; and to Mr Lee Selisky, Minnesota, USA, for his permission to quote from *Deep Diving and Submarine Operations* by R. H. Davis,

Eighth Edition, Siebe Gorman, 1981. Quotes from Hansard appear by kind permission of the Clerk of Records at the House of Lords Record Office and are from Volume 175, Columns 49–50, 920–21 and from Volume 350, Columns 1448–49. For accurate calculations of currency value based on the Retail Price Index from the 1920s and 1930s to the present day, many thanks go to Mr John J. McCusker, 'Comparing the Purchasing Power of Money in Great Britain from 1264 to 2001', Economic History Services, www.eh.net/hmit/ppowerbp.

Many thanks to the Institution of Mechanical Engineers for the use of 'Eight years salvage work at Scapa Flow' by E. F. Cox, Thomas Lowe Gray Lecture, December 1932. I would also like to thank the Institution of Engineers and Shipbuilders in Scotland for use of 'Marine Salvage in Peace and War' by Thomas McKenzie CB, CBE (Paper Number 1122, 29 November 1949); the Orkney Museum and Archive for access to their records in Kirkwall and Stromness; Mr Lars Walder, Public Relations Manager at Smit Salvage, Rotterdam, for information on the *Kursk* recovery; and Tony Redding, Public Relations for the International Salvage Union, who gave valuable information regarding the state of modern marine salvage. Thanks must also go to the Exxonmobil Corporation for their information regarding the *Exxon Valdez* salvage operation.

Please note, despite prolonged and exhaustive enquiries with numerous publishers, tracking down certain copyright holders has proved impossible.

In addition my thanks go to Jane Westcott for her detailed drawings of Cox's floating pontoons and how they work; Anni Bichard at the Patisserie Café in St Peter Port, Guernsey; Stephen Furniss for his research assistance in London; Jennifer Cochrane for her editorial advice; to Vee for her patience; and to my son, Jack, for his pleasant distraction from the keyboard. I cannot thank enough Mr Jon Moore, one of Ernest Cox's two surviving grandsons who, along with his wife, Pat, made me feel so welcome in their home and shared freely what were at times personal memories of Cox and his work. Thanks are also due to Lewis Munro for all the help he gave me one freezing day in Lyness. Finally I must thank ex-salvage linesman and diver, Sandy Robertson. Ninety-five-year-old Sandy is one of the very few men alive today who actually worked alongside Ernest Cox. He moved to Lyness in 1927 and still lives in the same croft overlooking Lyness Pier where all the salvage work began.

Sandy invited me into his home, a typical Orkney croft with roof slates as big and thick as paving slabs, which in January 2004 were covered in deep snow. As we sipped whisky, sitting by Sandy's roaring fire, he was able to recall a great deal of information, filling in many gaps in the Scapa Flow salvage story. When the time came to leave, Sandy gave me some parting advice that I never forgot while writing this book. 'Just keep the comments down, and no ideas'; good advice for any writer whose job is to record non-fiction.

Introduction

On Midsummer's Day 1919, Rear Admiral Ludwig von Reuter seemed unusually distracted as he walked out on to the bridge wing of his interned flagship, *Emden*, in full battle uniform. He gazed out at more than seventy other interned German warships anchored in Scapa Flow, a remote Scottish inlet in Orkney. Behind him lay the light cruiser, *Brummer*, and to his left lay the battleships, *Bayern* and *Friedrich der Grosse*. The rising sun had just burnt off the last of the Saturday morning haze. The only sounds came from the water lapping against the *Emden*'s side and a low hum from a generator somewhere below decks. Von Reuter heard laughter coming from some crewmen unloading stores from a supply boat moored alongside and lent over the bridge's high rail to get a closer look.

Within minutes the rapid ringing of a ship's bell somewhere to the *Emden*'s left shattered the tranquil setting. The order had been given aboard *Friedrich der Grosse* to abandon ship. Von Reuter followed the sound, only to see her already heeling over and sinking within minutes. The ringing from other ships' bells around the Flow began sounding the same order as men clambered into lifeboats or jumped over the side as their ships went down. Von Reuter felt he had done his duty as the entire German Imperial High Seas Fleet began majestically sinking all around him – by the head, stern or completely upright – like some macabre steel water-ballet.

Scapa Flow is a large expanse of water surrounded by the Orkney islands of Graemsay and Pomona to the north. Hoy lies to the west and Flotta, South Walls, South Ronaldsay and Burray lie to the south and east. They surround the natural 80 square mile inlet, which offers all-round protection from the North Atlantic and the North Sea in all weather conditions.

On 4 June 1812, maritime surveyor Graeme Spence submitted a report to the Lord's Commissioners of the Admiralty proposing the establishment of a naval base at Scapa Flow. Spence said the Flow was 'admirably well adapted for a northern roadstead for a Fleet of Line-of-Battle-Ships; and it is doubtless the finest in Britain or Ireland, except Spithead, if all the qualities which constitute a good roadstead be considered. Even the Romans, so famed for their choice of eligible military stations, thought the Orkneys [sic] of so much importance that on the division of the empire among the sons of Constantine the Great, the Kingdom of the Orcades fell to the share of Constantine ... .' In 1588, part of Philip II's defeated Armada was known to have sheltered there after being chased around the North Sea by Sir Francis Drake. He only stopped his pursuit when the British fleet was out of ammunition. However, more than a century would pass before the Admiralty seriously considered Spence's 'northern roadstead' as a serious proposition for one of Britain's key naval bases.

On 5 June 1916 Lord Horatio Herbert Kitchener, Commander in Chief of the British Army at the beginning of the First World War, left from Scapa Flow aboard the cruiser HMS *Hampshire* for secret talks in Russia. She left Scapa Flow's protection to head northwards through a Force 9 gale. Three hours later, the *Hampshire* was steaming past Marwick Head on Pomona's north-west tip when she struck a German mine placed there only a few days before by *U-75*. The 11,000-ton cruiser sank rapidly. Lord Kitchener was among nearly 700 men who drowned or died of exposure in the freezing North Atlantic. Only twelve managed to survive.

Several Royal Navy vessels were lost within Scapa Flow's sheltered waters. Just before midnight on 9 July 1917 the 42,500-ton battleship HMS *Vanguard* exploded while at anchor, instantly killing more than 800 of her crew. A lurid glare loomed over the site and burning debris ignited moorland in the surrounding area. The blast was so immense that a 400-ton gun turret was blown off the *Vanguard*'s main deck and landed more than a mile away on the island of Flotta. Although Britain was still at war with Germany at the time, sabotage was unlikely. The cause of the blast has never really been confirmed, but the spontaneous detonation of cordite is the most plausible explanation. During the Second World War, Scapa Flow did suffer its worst casualty through enemy action. The 34,000-ton battleship HMS *Royal Oak* was torpedoed at her moorings by *U-47* in the early hours of 14 October 1939. Most of her complement were asleep at the time. More than 800 lives were lost within half a mile of the shore.

The First World War was really Scapa Flow's heyday. It was home to the larger part of Britain's expanding 'Grand Fleet'. In 1914 the Royal Navy was only slightly behind the Kaiser's Imperial High Seas Fleet, which was still the superior navy. By the time Germany invaded Belgium, their fleet posed the first real threat to British naval supremacy since Nelson fought the French at Trafalgar. But throughout the ensuing four bloody years of entrenched land battle, the two great navies only really clashed once, at the Battle of Jutland, Denmark, on 31 May 1916. Both sides still argue over who won. The Royal Navy lost more ships and men so technically victory went to the Germans, who to this day know it as the Battle of Skagerrak. But the High Seas Fleet steamed back to Germany and never entered into a major naval conflict again, leaving the Royal Navy to maintain control of the North Sea.

The next time both navies met was on 20 November 1918 – nine days after the armistice was signed and all hostilities had ceased. Berlin was forced to hand over its fleet as payment for the Allies lifting their blockade of Germany, and the Royal Navy escorted the ships into internment. Although the Allies insisted the fleet would remain in a 'neutral' port, Scapa Flow was eventually chosen, much to Germany's disgust. The decision was intended to stand until the Allies could decide how best to share the many cutting edge warships among themselves. However, the political infighting dragged on for seven long months as no one could agree on the division.

The United States had already suggested that all the ships should be towed out to the Atlantic and sunk to 'destroy the German ships in the shortest possible time', thus ending months of deadlock and solving the problem in one fatal blow. As early as mid-April 1919 even Britain considered that the German ships might be sunk in deep water should the need arise. But Atlantic Fleet Commander in Chief Admiral Sir Charles Madden was well aware that such a drastic course 'admittedly assists the United States to become the premier Naval Power with the least possible delay'.

The main problem had always been the division of the ships. Although France and Italy wanted the greatest share, Britain felt it necessary to press for splitting up the German fleet based on actual naval losses, namely to the Royal Navy. Britain was clearly determined to maintain her two-power standard, meaning that the Royal Navy was bigger than the next two navies below it. At the same time, rapid naval expansion in the United States was seen as a very real threat. Admiral of the Fleet Sir David Beaty believed that any reduction in strength would weaken Britannia's power worldwide and he was convinced that the United States was trying to undermine her naval lead. Madden, too, was convinced that Britain must maintain her supremacy 'even over an admittedly friendly power such as America'. Division on Britain's terms would prevent the United States from taking the lead for many years. Finally, on the day that a compromise was agreed, all their words amounted to nothing. Von Reuter out-manoeuvred them all and sent his own navy to the bottom.

Salvaging any of the sunken ships for their scrap value was deemed useless. They were far too big and too deep to even consider recovering, especially using methods available at the time. But within five years, the question of raising the German fleet was both addressed – and answered – by a Wolverhampton-born scrap dealer with no prior knowledge of marine salvage techniques.

Chapter 1

Muck and Brass

On the front of the Blakenhall Community Centre in Wolverhampton's Dudley Road, there is a blue plaque, which reads:

Ernest F. G. Cox
Engineer
And
Marine Salvage Expert
Educated Here
1890–1897

During the 1890s the community centre was known as the Dudley Road Free School, and the only formal education young Ernest received was the seven years he spent in its classrooms. Ernest Frank Guelph Cox was born on 12 March 1883, a spit away from the Free School, at 55 Pool Street, in a cramped Victorian terrace. The area was in the heart of Wolverhampton's industrial metalworking district, which Ernest saw every day as he walked to school. He would set off from his house at the end of Pool Street, past the Drayton tin plate works, then into Drayton Street itself, and finally past the Vulcan ironworks on his five-minute walk to the school gates.

Altogether his parents, Thomas and Eliza, raised eleven children – Ernest being their last. Thomas was a tailor by trade and he tried hard to provide for his large family, but could not manage without the help of his elder children. In true Victorian Black Country spirit Ernest was brought up thinking that earning was better than learning, and at the age of fourteen, he gave up the chance of higher education to help support his family. Thomas managed to find Ernest

1

a job as an errand boy for a draper friend, but he hated the toil. Whatever the weather, he was seen trudging around the streets of Wolverhampton between the different drapers' shops clutching packages, letters or samples of stock, or sweeping floors and dusting shelves. The monotony was smothering him slowly and, regardless of his parents' wishes, Ernest's ability to stick with the mind-numbing drudgery began to wilt.

Even when he was young, Ernest was drawn towards engineering. Its pragmatic approach to solving mechanical problems excited his imagination. Like all large cities at the close of the nineteenth century, Wolverhampton was lit by gas. In the early 1880s, Midlands' engineer Thomas Parker had been devising ways to exploit electricity, which he believed to have great potential both to power and to light commercial and domestic premises. His machinery would later appear throughout England's early power stations. Wolverhampton had its own power station by early 1895, which was based in Commercial Road. Its supply could only cover an area of about $5^{1}/_{2}$ square miles. The noisy dynamos with their spinning wheels and clacking motors fascinated Ernest. Stealing into the main generating house he stared at all the oily, noisy machinery needed to make the coal-fired generators produce their power.

The sight of men in dirty, sweat-grimed clothing, rushing around and wiping away oil leaks and checking gauges, made him want to be among them and not at the beck and call of a town draper. Although Wolverhampton residents tended to ridicule the new power source, Ernest, like Thomas Parker, intuitively felt that electricity would one day replace gas as the country's main lighting and perhaps even become its main power system. For another year he struggled on as an errand boy and spent every free moment reading all available material relating to electricity and its uses. When he felt confident that he knew his subject, Ernest approached the power station's Chief Engineer for work. The clean-looking boy stood before the Chief Engineer, with a face that had never even broken into a sweat, let alone seen the dirt of a hard day's work. Although Ernest came from a very modest background, even by late Victorian standards, Thomas and Eliza had instilled in him a sense of good speech and behaviour – a talent Ernest could and did turn on and off as needed throughout his life.

He looked up at the generators he had seen so many times before from the power station's doors and casually opened a conversation about the benefits of operating the station's triple dynamo system as opposed to others of the time. He commented on the subtleties of how they pushed out their 350 kilowatts to the small substations and how they, in turn, converted the power into smaller 200-volt units for domestic consumption. Cox soon had the Chief's full attention. Within twenty minutes Ernest convinced the Chief Engineer that he fully understood how electricity was generated, what could go wrong, and how to fix it. Ernest got the job. He also got a pay rise of a shilling a week more than his draper's employment. At last Ernest's mind would be stimulated. He was only seventeen years old.

The theory Cox had spent a year absorbing was now being put into full effect through practical application. He immersed himself in all aspects of the power station's operation and soaked up every facet of his new job with ease. Whatever difficulty arose, he doggedly worked at it until the problem was solved. But in less than a year, too much repetition had already crept into his daily work routine and the challenges became fewer. Cox had soon learnt all he could from the Wolverhampton power supply and began looking for a bigger challenge. Eventually a vacancy arose in Leamington for an assistant chief engineer. Cox wanted the post badly, but he was too young and lacked the necessary experience. He knew he could either let the chance go and stay where he no longer felt challenged – or he could lie. Against the advice of his friends and colleagues Cox decided to lie. He applied, saying he was much older and had several years' experience in electricity generating rather than just the one. He was summoned to Leamington for an interview and assessment of his skills. Once he arrived it was obvious to the interview board that Cox was far too young for the managerial post. However, Cox again applied his charm and wide knowledge of power-station engineering to defend his position. Despite his youth, and his attempt to deceive them, the interview board was sufficiently impressed by his knowledge and self-confidence.

Cox was soon living in Leamington, facing the new challenges of an assistant chief engineer. Two years later, he felt confident enough to apply for a chief engineer's post. A domestic power supply was to be built in Ryde, on the Isle of Wight. The post included designing and building the power station from the foundations upwards, as well as calculating usage and laying down every power line, generator and substation needed to make the project a commercial success. As the popularity of electricity spread, its application as a revolutionary energy source also grew. A supply was being planned in Hamilton, near Glasgow and was designed for industrial output. Cox leapt at the chance for another challenge, applied for the job and, predictably, got it. Such a post would have satisfied many in the electrical generating field for the rest of their working lives, but when the plant was running at full capacity, Cox was ready to move again, this time to the nearby town of Wishaw where another plant was to be built. He was by now only twenty-four years old and already renowned throughout the industry as a leading figure in changing the nation's gas supplies to electricity. But he knew he could go no further in seniority and began looking for a fresh stimulus.

Tension between Britain and Germany had been accelerating for some years as both countries were locked in a frenzied naval arms race. Cox saw steel as the next emerging market. Wishaw Councillor Robert Miller got to know Cox well as a widely respected and competent businessman. Miller owned a large steel works known as the Overton Forge, near Wishaw, and wanted Cox to run the business and develop its potential. Miller first asked Cox to put together a recovery plan and then invited him to dinner at his house for an informal meeting. While discussing the various problems and how to solve them, Cox met Miller's twenty-three-year-old daughter, Jenny Jack. Like many Midlands men of his day, Cox's Victorian upbringing had taught him that women must be respected at all costs, but belonged in their place, which was to be protected from the harsh realities of life. They became friends, a relationship that could go no other way but for the twenty-somethings to fall in love. Within the same year, 1907, Cox took over the Overton Forge and married his new boss's daughter. The following year the Coxes added their own baby girl to the family. She was named Euphemia Caldwell, but the dark-haired little girl was always affectionately known as Bunty or Bunts.

Cox was now nearly twenty-seven years old and wanted to open his own forge in the hope of supplying the growing military build-up, but like many young entrepreneurs he lacked investment capital. Jenny suggested that he approach her cousin, Tommy Danks, as a potential investor. Danks was a young man who had inherited a fortune and was systematically spending it all between London, Paris and the French Riviera. He readily agreed to back Cox as long as he did not have to work in the forge. Publicly, Cox always showed his appreciation for Danks having taken the chance to invest in his new business, but in reality he disliked the playboy. Cox's humble working class background had taught him to appreciate a hard day's work, and the pay a man gets for it. Danks's frivolous lifestyle, supported by inheritance, grated against his work ethic. But he needed an investor and was more than happy to have complete control over his new business venture. And so the firm Cox & Danks of Oldbury, near Wolverhampton, began trading in 1913.

Strong rumours were suggesting that war with Germany now looked imminent, and Whitehall was awarding munitions contracts. Cox won a contract to produce brass shell cases. The work was repetitive and gave no engineering challenges once the machinery was in place and his men trained. But the war, which both sides thought would end by Christmas 1914, meant that Cox & Danks went on stamping out shells, profitably feeding the Allied war machine for nearly four more years. Once the 1918 armistice was signed and the lucrative contracts began to dry up, metal foundries throughout Britain were laying off men or closing down. But Cox & Danks were in a very strong financial position when they finally lost their Government work. Cox had enough capital to buy out his playboy partner. Tommy Danks agreed. Now Cox was the sole owner of a foundry, albeit without any large contracts to employ his workers or keep him in business for much longer. The fields of France and Belgium, however, were strewn with twisted metal and war machinery, which now had to be cleared. To Cox, the war debris was gold, and he set up a new foundry in Sheffield to cope with the tons of metal collected and shipped back to England for reprocessing.

The Royal Navy was reducing operations to peacetime requirements and Cox made his first venture into shipbreaking when the two ageing battleships, HMS *Orion* and HMS *Erin*, were decommissioned and put out to tender for breaking. He bid for the two old warships and they became the property of Cox & Danks. Because his two foundries were inland, Cox had to open a yard at Queensborough on the Isle of Sheppey to handle the initial breaking before parts were delivered to Oldbury and Sheffield. After the purchase and full cost of breaking up were taken into account, Cox still doubled his money. But the glory days for the war scrap merchants were numbered. The Western Front was virtually cleared of the most lucrative metal and the military scale-down was also coming to an end, making the future of Cox & Danks look very bleak indeed. Cox needed scrap metal in large quantities – fast. Everywhere he looked the land had been picked clean. But five years before, on Midsummer's Day 1919, another man's actions were destined to play a major part in Cox's next, and certainly most ambitious, decision of his life.

Chapter 2

Coup de Grâce

Rear Admiral Ludwig von Reuter was from a solid Prussian aristocratic family and firmly believed that the honour of the Imperial High Seas Fleet and Germany went before everything. He had the outstanding naval career expected of an officer who reached admiral rank, but unlike most senior officers, von Reuter achieved success while remaining both respected and popular among his officers and men. When hostilities ceased along the Western Front, the Allies insisted that Germany hand over its entire fleet until the final peace negotiations could be settled. On 18 November 1918, with their guns disabled, all seventy-four warships left Wilhelmshaven in north-west Germany and were later met by the light cruiser HMS *Cardiff* to lead them to the waiting Allied armada.

Admiral Hugh Rodman of the United States Navy later recalled that the sight of the *Cardiff* reminded him of an old farm in his home state of Kentucky, 'where many times I saw a little child leading by the nose a herd of fearsome bullocks'. As the Allies surrounded the German fleet, with all guns loaded and pointing directly at them, many among the British crews hounded the Germans by banging every tin cup, ratchet, crowbar and any other metal object to show contempt for their enemy. Seaman Sydney Hunt remembered the sea-born nervous tension.

> We were allowed up one at a time from our action stations, and we could not believe our eyes. It was like a wild dream, just miles of ships. That day of course all leave was stopped. Officers and Petty Officers all got tight, and the crews got hold of anything they could and just bashed it to hell.

In return many German crews replied by mustering their bands and repeatedly playing military marching songs to goad their captors as the solemn procession crossed the North Sea in a black, acrid fog created by the smoke billowing from more than three hundred funnels.

Upon arrival at Scapa Flow, von Reuter was nothing more than a chief caretaker responsible for the administration and organization of maintenance, supplies, medical treatment and all other forms of shipboard routine needed to keep the fleet in serviceable condition. Steaming into the Flow aboard the battleship *Von der Tann*, he later wrote:

> The lower parts of the land showed signs of rude cultivation, trees and shrubs were nowhere to be seen. Most of it was covered in heather, villages were just in sight on the land in the far distance – apart from which here and there on the coast stood unfriendly-looking farmhouses built of grey local stone. Several military works, such as barracks, aeroplane sheds or balloon hangars, relieved the monotonous sameness; in ugliness they would beat even ours at a bet.

Von Reuter thought he would be relieved after delivering the fleet to Scapa Flow and then be allowed to return home. About six months later he was still there, reduced to commanding mutinous skeleton crews aboard rat-infested and by now unserviceable ships, on which rumours and boredom were the new enemies.

Admiral Sir Sydney Fremantle was responsible for guarding the High Seas Fleet with a squadron of six battleships, their accompanying destroyers and a patrol of armed drifters. These were fishing boats specifically designed to allow their nets to drift with the current, unlike trawlers, which pull their nets at deep levels beneath the sea. Fremantle's first directive was to order the lowering of all German ensigns, which could not be hoisted again without Admiralty permission. The German crews saw this as a gross insult. They were not prisoners under the terms of the armistice, only internees who still commanded their own vessels. As commander of the German fleet, von Reuter was allowed access to British newspapers that had to be delivered four days late lest he act on any fresh news. His officers and men then had to rely on information filtering down through the ranks, which, all too often, was laced with speculation and rumour as it travelled around the fleet. As time moved on, 'steel-plate sickness', a marine equivalent of the barbed wire fever known to have affected thousands of POWs during the First and Second World Wars, began to affect the officers and men. Their uncertain future also played a large part in low morale, as the Allies kept prevaricating over how the fleet should be divided.

Able Seaman Braunsberger aboard the battleship *Kaiser* kept a diary throughout his internment. As the situation worsened he recorded the general atmosphere within the High Seas Fleet.

> The further spring advanced, the more monotonous it became for us. We received little post, no newspapers and we could not receive news over the radio either. The reluctance to work got worse. Engine maintenance was no longer properly carried out, the water for the boilers turned salty. The power was often cut so we had to sit in the dark in the evening. Lunch was often cooked on the coal burner and the diet got worse. Always the same comrades round you, always the same view of land. On top of that the agitation of the Workers' and Soldiers' Council which sowed only hate and strife. Even though we still believed in a happy ending, all this turned us into psychopaths.

Later that same spring, news reached the German fleet that the Allies had finally decided their fate. A public statement indicated that Germany was to get a few token warships and the might of their fleet was to be divided up among the Allies and the United States. The news was a crushing blow and tempers flared as everyone argued over how Berlin would react to the ultimatum. Von Reuter knew his Government had three options: they could reject the terms; try to negotiate a better deal or, which was inconceivable, agree. If Berlin rejected the terms then hostilities would commence with immediate effect and von Reuter would scuttle the fleet before the Allies could storm his ships. His thinking was based on a standing order from the German leader, Kaiser Wilhelm II, that all ships must be scuttled if surrender or a takeover was likely.

A negotiation could reap better rewards for the German people because the fleet could possibly be sold rather than taken as a war prize. Von Reuter saw an outright agreement as impossible. On 29 May 1919, Reichstag Chancellor Philipp Scheidemann publicly announced that the German Government had rejected the Allied peace terms. The Allies replied by issuing a warning to Berlin demanding an acceptance of the terms – or at noon on 21 June the horror of the First World War would begin again.

As usual, the news hit Scapa Flow four days later and the shock wave travelled through the fleet like an enemy broadside. Von Reuter decided he had no option other than to obey his Kaiser and scuttle the fleet. After all, he reasoned, under any armistice a state of war *still* existed and the ships *remained* German property. But how could he orchestrate the synchronized scuttling of seventy-four warships with limited communications – and in front of Fremantle's battle squadron? Von Reuter spent more than two weeks hatching the plan, which ultimately hinged on the goodwill of the Royal Navy. By now the German fleet had been in Scapa Flow for seven months and although German and British personnel were strictly forbidden to fraternize, illicit trading had sprung up between the two sides. Destroyer Captain Friedrich Ruge recalled:

> Officially we were not allowed to have any contact with the British but of course in seven months that could not quite be carried out. We ourselves had quite a lot of contact with drifters. They were not only on guard, they carried mail around and our provisions.

Von Reuter's key was in the distribution of mail. He made seventy-four copies of his scuttling orders and asked the Royal Navy drifters to kindly deliver his envelopes to every interned ship while delivering supplies and other routine correspondence. It was an act of kindness he was to relish up to the day he died. On 17 June 1919 the Royal Navy innocently delivered von Reuter's *Coup de Grâce* around the entire German fleet. The twelve-paragraph letter ordered that all gangway, bunker and internal doors were to be opened immediately von Reuter's order was given, along with all ventilators and portholes. Provision was to be made to open and fix all sea valves at short notice and arrangements made to evacuate all personnel. Paragraph Eleven read:

> It is my intention to sink the ships only if the enemy attempts to seize them without the consent of our Government. Should our Government agree with the peace conditions, in which the

ships are to be surrendered, the ships will then be handed over, to the lasting shame of those who put us in this situation.

Upon von Reuter's direct signal for all ships to confirm Paragraph Eleven, they were to be scuttled immediately. He gave no definitive date, however, in case the Royal Navy discovered his plan. Four days later, on the morning of 21 June, von Reuter stood on the bridge of his new flagship the *Emden* and looked out over his fleet gently floating on an unusually calm, sunny day. His Chief of Staff, Commander Ivan Oldekop, informed him that most of the British Guard Fleet had surprisingly left the Flow on manoeuvres. Von Reuter immediately ordered the raising of the flag signal 'D. G.' which meant that all ships' bridge watches must look out for further signals. Ninety minutes before he thought hostilities would resume, von Reuter ordered the signal. 'To all C.O.s and the T.B. (torpedoboat) Leader. Paragraph Eleven, confirm. Acknowledge. Chief of the Interned Squadron.' The *Emden*'s signalmen fluttered the order around the fleet by lamp as well as by semaphore and Morse code.

While the signal was relaying from ship to ship, a Royal Navy drifter called the *Trust-on* was moored alongside the *Emden*, delivering stores. Her armed guard sat around on deck joking and smoking cigarettes while her crew passed stores up to the waiting German sailors. Von Reuter walked out on to the *Emden*'s bridge wing and stood calmly looking down at the men who were innocently unaware of what was now taking place. Neither the German sailors loading the stores nor the *Trust-on*'s crew noticed that von Reuter had changed into his full-dress uniform, hung his highest insignia of decorations around his neck, pinned his Iron Cross First Class to his frock coat and was standing there – waiting.

On that same morning, fifteen-year-old James Taylor was among a group of 160 excited schoolchildren from Stromness Higher Grade School who were boarding the water tender *Flying Kestrel* for a day's outing to cruise around the interned fleet. Above the playground-like din, the teachers tried hard to answer the children's usual endless questions, 'Why were the ships there?' 'Why don't the Germans shoot their big guns?' 'Why can't we meet them and talk about the war?' The teachers were more interested in settling the children down safely and comfortably before the *Flying Kestrel* set sail. All they could tell the children was that their hopes of seeing the British Fleet would be disappointed as the Royal Navy was out on exercise. Seeing the giant warships coming into view drew most children out on deck for the thirty-minute run down the Bring Deeps to the first anchorage by Cava where the battleships and light cruisers were grouped. The time was approximately 11.00 am – sixty minutes before von Reuter thought hostilities would resume.

When the *Flying Kestrel* reached the first and biggest of the warships, all was still quiet on the Flow. First the children were taken around the big battle cruisers, *Hindenburg*, *Kaiser*, *Von der Tann*, *Moltke* and *Seydlitz*. Well into old age, James Taylor vividly remembered the impression the towering rusty steel walls made on him and his school friends:

> At long last we came face to face with the German fleet, some of them huge battleships that made our own vessel look ridiculous. The sailors thumbed their noses. Our teacher tried anxiously to explain that perhaps we would do the same if we were prisoners of war being stared at by a crowd of gaping schoolchildren. We ought to feel sorry for those poor men who could no more help being German than we could help being Orcadians. Rognvald St Clair, who was always so smart, said he only felt sorry he hadn't brought his catapult.

Most of the children had calmed down and just stared in awe at the gigantic ships of mass destruction tethered by the nose.

Some of them noticed that many of the German ships began raising flags, but thought no more of it. One of the flags was the German ensign, which Admiral Fremantle forbade them to raise upon their arrival in the Flow. The other flag was the red code letter 'Z', which meant that battle was imminent. Shortly afterwards the *Flying Kestrel* received a radio call stating that the German fleet was sinking. But the Flow still looked calm. Her captain continued hesitantly as the *Flying Kestrel*'s crew looked out on the fleet. All they saw was an increase of activity aboard some of the ships, but as the minutes moved towards midday, the activity increased dramatically. Sailors in life-jackets began jumping off their decks into the water. Others were piling into boats or on to life rafts. Soon the *Flying Kestrel* was surrounded by ships that were heeling at odd angles. Slowly it dawned on the children that something extraordinary was happening and that the ships were, indeed, sinking.

The *Flying Kestrel* was advised to make for the depot ship, HMS *Victorious*, to receive orders. Mrs Peggy Gibson (née Matheson) was ten years old when she and her three sisters were aboard the *Flying Kestrel* for the school trip:

> Soon we were passing between two rows of destroyers. They lay in pairs and we were so near them that we could read their names and see the men on them, but we had been warned to make no sign to the men as we went. We continued on for some time until we met a trawler, which sent a message over to say that the German fleet was sinking. Some were upending. Some were settling in the water. Some were turning over.

Now the Flow was in chaos. Wooden crates, hammocks, sea chests, furniture and personal effects were bursting from the submerged ships and popping up everywhere. Several children described a boiling, swelling mass as air escaped from beneath the sea all around them, and metal could be heard tearing and grinding under the water. Many witnesses reported the strange sounds for hours after the fleet had disappeared. The children were far more thrilled than frightened by what was happening. Some of the younger ones cheered and clapped, thinking that the spectacle had been put on especially for their benefit.

The Admiralty had already drawn up plans should the need arise to take the ships by force. Vice Admiral Sir Henry Oliver had written a confidential memo to Admiral Madden clearly outlining the Royal Navy's attitude towards the interned men. Should there be resistance, Oliver wrote:

> Suppose the crews are detained in the transports and told they will be punished if the ships are found on inspection to be damaged. Damage is discovered and the question of punishment arises. What is it going to be? If a percentage are picked out and shot summarily, it is extremely doubtful if our Ministers would support the action of the Admiral. The Germans are not prisoners of war and cannot legally be tried as such, and they are not subject to our Naval Discipline Act. If they are summarily imprisoned, the legality might not be questioned, but it would place the cost of keeping them in prison on the taxpayer. In the event of a disturbance, no one

is likely to question what is done in hot blood to quell it, but I think we shall have to be extremely careful about what we do in cold blood.

The German fleet was now beyond simply 'damaged' and the surrendering German seamen were now legitimate POWs under Oliver's Naval Discipline Act. Only two days before von Reuter ordered Paragraph Eleven, Admiral Fremantle finalized what action should be taken. One plan was called Operation SA, which was to be implemented should the Germans surrender peacefully. The other, Operation SB, was to be implemented should there be any form of resistance, which meant Royal Navy personnel should be armed, 'Officers, revolvers; petty officers, revolvers and cutlasses; rank and file, rifles and sword bayonets.'

The key to the plan's success was immediate and simultaneous action to take all ships at once, which would require ten capital ships and twenty destroyers. The Admiralty accepted that if either plan was required, the German personnel would become legitimate POWs. Although in an advanced state of preparation, neither plan could be implemented. With the main British Guard Fleet out of the Flow, the few remaining guards aboard the drifters could not cope, their numbers falling well short of the shipping and manpower needed to control any sudden German insurrection.

The *Flying Kestrel* could not safely return to Stromness back through the sinking mass and had to be given an alternative route to avoid any possible danger to the children. Their new course took them on a wide arc around the German fleet, passing vessels which, having received their scuttling orders slightly later, were still in the early stages of sinking. German lifeboats were full to the gunwales with unarmed officers and men with their hands raised. Some were waving makeshift white flags when the children heard a rifle crack.

Some children saw German sailors surrendering on the stern of a ship when one of them was shot, his body crumpling and falling into the sea. Fifteen-year-old Katie Watt watched a string of lifeboats being towed by a Royal Navy drifter. She saw a sailor shot dead as he was trying to cut his launch free. The remaining Royal Navy personnel had lost control.

One lifeboat had cleared away from the destroyer *V.126* as a Royal Navy drifter closed in. The German sailors were ordered back to save their ship. When they refused, the Royal Navy opened

14

fire instantly killing three men and wounding four more. Aboard another lifeboat a stoker was shot in the stomach and died later. Von Reuter had previously received a letter from an officer's wife asking if her husband, Captain Walther Schumann, of the battleship *Markgraf*, could be repatriated because she was struggling to raise their four children. Von Reuter had passed the letter on to Schumann who threw the letter away, refusing to leave his ship. As the *Markgraf* was sinking, many of Schumann's officers and crew were already in her lifeboats and pulling away from their ship. He was standing on her middle deck with a petty officer, watching an approaching Royal Navy drifter. Neither man moved as the drifter steamed closer and closer. When the drifter was in range, a Royal Navy sniper opened fire, instantly felling Schumann and the petty officer standing next to him.

Chief Gunner Gunther Soormann tried to reach Schumann to see if he was still alive, but had to wait until the drifter was out of range. When he eventually got to his captain and the petty officer, they were both dead. The *Markgraf* was now settling deeper in the water and those left alive had to abandon ship. Soormann and his colleagues had to manhandle the two bodies into a lifeboat and get away as fast as they could, 'under fire from sea and land'. Soormann gave a full account of Schumann's murder to the British Authorities in a written deposition, hoping that appropriate action would be taken. His eyewitness account was never acted upon.

Schumann's body, along with all those slain on 21 June, was buried in Hoy's military cemetery on the outskirts of Lyness. The final killing took place later that same day when a German sailor, now a legitimate POW, was shot dead in front of a number of other prisoners, simply for refusing to follow a British order. When the other Germans protested, the Royal Navy blamed a crazed sailor for the death and made an arrest. The following year the case was dropped. The other killings were blamed on misunderstood orders and the atrocity has never been accounted for. Altogether nine men were killed and sixteen wounded throughout the Royal Navy's unofficial shoot-to-kill policy. All were unarmed. All were surrendering. And all were the last casualties of the First World War.

After receiving news that the fleet was being scuttled, Admiral Fremantle raced his squadron back to the Flow to save what he could. He was too late. The drifters only managed to tow a few destroyers and smaller warships towards the shore and beach them. Fremantle was furious. He had von Reuter delivered to his flagship, HMS *Revenge*, for the benefit of a hastily called press conference. Von Reuter was led out to the *Revenge*'s poop deck where he was positioned beneath her White Ensign as it rolled and snapped in the late afternoon breeze. Fremantle vented his impotent rage in a formal verbal rebuke. He accused von Reuter of cowardice and violating common honour as no officer in von Reuter's position had the legal right to scuttle his fleet. In his defence von Reuter insisted that the British four-day newspaper delay meant he did not know Germany's position had changed since earlier that week.

Chancellor Scheidemann had resigned, the German Government had voted to accept the peace terms without alteration and the deadline had been extended by another forty-eight hours. But neither the British nor the German Government formally notified von Reuter that such dramatic changes in the peace talks had occurred. The reason why von Reuter was never notified remains a mystery. Collectively, all the information at his disposal pointed to renewed hostilities and he was adamant that any senior officer of any navy would have done the same in his position. Von Reuter had legally carried out a standing order of his superiors in a time of war, which included the armistice period when the warships were still German property. Failure to do otherwise was tantamount to treason against his own people – facts of which both Berlin and Whitehall were fully aware. After the Royal Navy openly murdered nine surrendering German seamen, von Reuter ended up on the Allies' Atrocity List, usually reserved for savage crimes during time of war against military and civilian personnel. Fremantle was unmoved by von Reuter's defence. When the public dressing down was finished, von Reuter clicked his heels, turned, and went into captivity confidently feeling he had permanently placed the Imperial High Sea Fleet far beyond Allied reach.

Three days later the Admiralty appointed independent salvage experts to report on the viability of raising at least some of the 400,000 tons of shipping now littering the seabed. Their report stated that salvaging some of the lighter ships might be possible, although the Admiralty concluded, 'Where they rest, they will rust. There can be no question of raising them.'

Chapter 3

Arrogance or Genius

In April 1923, while Cox was trying to find more scrap metal to feed his business, the Admiralty invited the Shetland-based Scapa Flow Salvage and Shipbreaking Company Limited to make an offer for raising the sunken German ships. Its owner, Mr John W. Robertson was a diver with twenty-five years experience and had a sound knowledge of marine salvage. He was considered by many to be an expert in his field where Cox knew virtually nothing. Robertson initially bought four destroyers and planned to lift these ships using mostly established salvage methods. Two concrete barges measuring more than 90ft long were used, one being placed on each side of a wreck. The two barges were 30ft apart and were held together by eight steel girders. Their combined lifting power was 3,000 tons. Then he would adopt a classic 'tidal lift'. As the name implies, the action of a rising tide is exploited to gain natural lift while raising a sunken vessel.

Salvage operators prefer working with the monthly spring tides to maximize lifting potential. 'Spring' derives from the old English word *sprungum*, meaning flood tide. They occur when the gravitational pull of the sun and moon are in line and so exert a greater force on a normal tidal rhythm. At low tide, ropes or wires are secured from the sunken vessel to one or more pontoons on the surface, then as the rising water mass is literally pulled towards the sun and moon, a sunken vessel will easily lift off the seabed. It is the same principle as a normal ship in port, dropping and rising as the tide goes in and out. The sunken vessel is then towed, submerged, closer to the shore and the process repeated until it is well above the low tide mark.

The British Government demanded that Germany hand over marine and shore-side equipment equal to the warship tonnage scuttled at Scapa Flow. Part of this included a specially designed

17

floating dock used to test U-boats. The dock was the biggest of its kind and included a cylindrical chamber, 400ft long and 40ft in diameter, which could be sunk below sea level. Shortly after the Admiralty took possession, *The Illustrated London News* explained:

> Owing to the shallowness of the waters round their coasts, the Germans could not test their submarines at sea and so they constructed this special testing dock for the purpose. After being towed into the cylinder, a submarine is subjected to air pressure equal to that of any depth required. Men then descend into the submarine through connecting tubes and caulk any apparent leaks. The cylinder can receive three submarines at once, one for testing and two for docking and repairs.

Cox's search for large scrap volume was becoming desperate. He already knew through press coverage that the Government had ordered Germany to relinquish a tonnage of material to match the scuttled fleet. Perhaps, albeit briefly, there was a chance to extend the life of his scrap business. When the dock came up for sale by public tender he put in a bid for £20,000, which the Admiralty accepted.

The chamber itself was made entirely out of non-ferrous metal and Cox had the perfect buyer, Otto Willer-Petersen, who was a partner of Petersen & Albeck, a Danish scrap metal business based in Copenhagen. Otto's main interest was the purchase of non-ferrous metal, which had a considerable market in Denmark. Cox was one of his main suppliers, and over the years the two men had developed a strong working relationship. Cox understood that the success of such a deal depended on the rather small dark-haired Dane viewing the chamber, so he invited his friend to travel from Denmark to meet him at the Queensborough yard. While the two men were walking among the piles of scrap discussing the proposed purchase, Willer-Petersen asked Cox what would happen to the dock once the chamber was separated. Cox said that he was going to break it up and dispatch the metal in the same way as the two Royal Navy warships. Willer-Petersen was not convinced that was such a good idea.

'There's much more money in that thing than scrap value,' he said. 'It's got the greatest lifting power of any dock in the world.'

'What do you suppose I lift?' replied Cox.

'You've heard of the German Fleet at Scapa Flow. I don't say you could lift up the battleships, but I know there are thirty or forty destroyers lying there, none of them over a 1,000 tons – and that dock will lift 3,000 tons at a time.'

At first Cox thought the idea sheer madness and was happy to conclude the sale of the chamber and think no more about salvage. But once his friend had departed for Copenhagen, Cox's technical mind and imagination gnawed away at the problem. He had to satisfy his curiosity and at least try to figure out once and for all if he could achieve what the British Government deemed impossible. When the rest of the dock was broken up there was little chance of winning similar substantial scrap contracts, and the future of Cox & Danks would become increasingly uncertain. Still, lifting ships was beyond his engineering abilities. But Cox knew that the ships were worth hundreds of thousands of pounds and he did own one of the only docks in the world capable of at least giving him a chance.

With the same philosophy adopted during his days as a seventeen-year-old boy obsessed with electricity, Cox read all he could on the German Imperial High Seas Fleet and contemporary salvage techniques to gain a wider understanding of how ships had been salvaged before. How they were constructed was also relevant to raising them successfully, and forming a rough estimate of their market value. As Cox expected, the quality of the steel and the general structure were far superior to a merchant ship of the same size. They all had watertight compartments to enable whole sections to be sealed off if damaged. Many parts were made of aluminium for added lightness and valuable high-tensile steels were used for parts likely to be targeted when under attack, like gun turrets and engine room compartments. Cast metal was used for the sterns, stern frames and davits of the bigger ships and for similar fittings where strength and durability were not so essential. Many important internal fittings were made with gunmetal, brass or other expensive metals. Before too long he realized that each ship was a scrap metal gold mine. Many years later, Cox claimed he was such an expert that he could tell a metal simply by shutting his eyes and tapping it with a spanner.

The bigger the challenge, the more intensely his blind concentration and single-minded drive were focused on success. Either through arrogance – or clear thinking – he decided to buy part of the German fleet without even visiting Orkney. First, Cox had to visit Admiralty headquarters in London. He walked through its main entrance, found a clerk, and announced that he wanted to buy some of the scuttled German ships. Cox was directed to the appropriate department and asked if he had actually seen what he was buying. He admitted that he had never been to Orkney in his life, so his offer was refused pending his visiting the Flow and at least, as the Admiralty saw it, making a more informed decision. The Admiralty was keen to shift the cost of removing the German ships from a Government responsibility to a private one, especially after receiving complaints that some of the wrecks were becoming navigational hazards. And two private contractors trying to clear the area were better than one.

A few days later, in early January 1924, Cox was chugging around the remains of the High Seas Fleet in a small, chartered motorboat, its driver indicating where some of the larger ships had been. They entered from the north-west out of Stromness, along the Bring Deeps, and out into the main Flow. The driver pointed out to their port side where there had been a cluster of battle cruisers and battleships with names Cox knew so well: *Hindenburg*, *Kaiser*, *Von der Tann*, *Moltke*, *Seydlitz* and the *Prinzregent Luitpold* were the most advanced warships of their day. Most were heroes from the Battle of Jutland. The *Seydlitz* alone took more than twenty direct hits, and still managed to sail home, a tribute to her tough construction and obvious high steel quality and alloy content. As an imaginative man, Cox must have wondered at the irony of how these giants had taken some of the heaviest artillery the Royal Navy could muster and survived, only to be sunk at the hands of their own men.

A little further on he motored over Gutter Sound, where more than fifty destroyers with nothing but numbers for identification were slowly disappearing into the silt. All that was left of the once impressive German fleet were a few shadows just beneath the surface. Here and there he saw the odd rusting funnel, bridge or conning tower just above water, or the occasional smaller ship the Royal Navy had managed to beach before it sank. The rest had gone down in up to 100ft or more of icy water. As he slowly absorbed the magnitude of what lay on the seabed, he smiled as his logical mind began making rapid calculations of warship type, class and tonnage. 'To what extent were the ships damaged before scuttling?' 'How could any holes be plugged?' 'What kind of cutting gear or explosives would be required?' 'How many men would he need?' 'How could he bring up capsized ships, those on their side or those interlocked with others because they were lashed to the same pontoons as they went down?' 'How could divers work at depths in excess of 100ft submerged in freezing water?' The more problematic salvaging the fleet looked, the more eager his search for answers. Many years later, Cox recalled:

> The sight at Scapa Flow was one of the most fascinating I have ever seen, and could not fail to stimulate the imagination of any man who was fond of engineering problems. As one travelled round Scapa Flow, the sunken battleships could be seen, some of them projecting out of the water and others just beneath the surface so only the tops of their masts were visible. After thinking the matter over carefully I decided to undertake the work of salvaging the fleet and returned to the Admiralty with that proposal. They agreed as a start to sell me twenty-six destroyers and two battleships.

The Admiralty thought he was some kind of eccentric millionaire who was bound to fail. At least Robertson had a sound knowledge of salvage procedure. After all, when Cox was offered copies of the official salvage reports he dismissed them without even turning the first page, so how could he know what he was up against? But where they had seen only resting, rusting hulks back in 1919, Cox saw tens of thousands of tons of ferrous metals, like cast iron, wrought iron and steel – and lucrative non-ferrous metals like brass, copper, lead, bronze, gunmetal and manganese, as well as armoured cable, turbine blades, steel rope, resistance wire, anchors, and chains, which were still intact and would find a lucrative postwar market. After dismissing the professional criticism without a second thought, all Cox had to do was solve the technical and logistical nightmare he had just bought into and the biggest salvage operation in history could begin. Part of his Admiralty contract insisted that the sale price remain confidential. Even under Parliamentary pressure the price would not be disclosed for another fifteen years.

Cox must have known that Robertson was already planning to raise his first destroyer, and that he was a far better qualified salvage engineer. But Cox was totally unfazed by the competition – or their salvage methods. He threw all his energy into recruiting the most experienced staff he could find, knowing that to find men of knowledge far greater than his own was crucial to the success of the project. One of the two most important men Cox would hire was a young, tough ex-submariner named Ernest McKeown. He was ideal for Cox's team, however, McKeown had recently married and was reluctant to move to the remote Scapa Flow with his new bride. But 1924 saw many engineers unemployed with no chance of finding work, so having recently left the Royal Navy, McKeown agreed to work with Cox and advise him on salvage practice. Much of the equipment Cox needed was already on the floating dock, built into the hollow wall sections, but a great deal of structural and integral conversion was still needed to make the dock into an efficient salvage vessel. The rest of the equipment was purchased from the Admiralty as they sold off their salvage plant at the end of the First World War. Compressors, generators and extra cranes were also added.

Once the submarine pressure chamber was removed, Cox was left with one large flat platform with two 40ft high steel walls on either side. But he needed two platforms to successfully lift a destroyer. His Queensborough yard carried out part of the most dramatic conversion, which involved cutting one of the 40ft walls clean off down to the platform base. Twenty hand-operated 10-ton winches, each capable of lifting 100 tons, were mounted at equal intervals along the bottom edge of the new capital L-shaped floating dock. The extra leverage was created by attaching each winch to a six-sheaved pulley block secured to a strong diagonal facing post mounted below the main deck level. The end result was a very long, single floating dock, which could lift considerably more than all the destroyer classes lying on the seabed. However, a few more alterations were still needed. Workshops, including a fully operational carpenter's shop managed by John Scolley and William Tait were also added. Tait was a particularly popular member of the Scapa team whom Cox admired for his hard work and sense of humour.

Cox purchased two ex-Admiralty tugs called the *Ferrodanks* and the *Sidonian* to tow the dock on its 700-mile journey from Queensborough to Scapa Flow, and to assist the floating dock once there. Old Naval quarters in Lyness on the island of Hoy provided accommodation for his workers throughout the salvage project. A small tug called the *Lyness* was later purchased to assist salvage operations. The area was so remote that Cox had a cinema installed as well as radios, a small bar, billiard tables and many other leisure-time facilities to make the worker's off-duty hours as entertaining as possible. Lyness was a perfect base. Being an ex-Royal Navy depot, the small harbour offered ready-made military-style accommodation, and was only a few miles from where the bulk of the sunken destroyers lay out in Gutter Sound.

Eight days after leaving Queensborough, the two tugs steamed into Scapa Flow and the dock was beached at Mill Bay in Lyness. To work as efficiently as possible the floating dock then had to be cut in half across its centre line to form two capital 'L's', which would then face each other on either side above a sunken wreck. Once safely in Mill Bay the work began. A bulkhead already existed in the centre position within its structure, meaning that when the dock was cut in two, one section would float clear while the other would naturally sink. To overcome the problem Cox had another bulkhead fitted 18in away from the existing one, which extended right across the internal structure. At low tide men using oxy-acetylene torches cut a neat line between the two bulkheads. Then at high tide the two halves slowly and neatly floated apart and Cox had his two floating docks. The decision to cut the dock in half at Lyness was purely down to costs. Two tugs towing one dock north, albeit much larger, was much cheaper than towing two smaller ones.

His total dedication excluded all possibility of failure, which often offended those around him. Some said Cox was arrogant or pig-headed, or a ruthless bully. Others called him gifted. Whatever people thought, Cox was a mechanical genius who won the respect of his workers by showing them what could be achieved without any formal training – regardless of what the so-called experts said. Sandy Thomson was an electrician's mate on the Scapa project. 'A lot of Mr Cox never grew up,' he said. He continued:

He could never admit he was wrong until something busted. It made you wild. You knew that he knew he was doing something silly, but he was like a kid, hoping some magic would bring it right and knowing all the time it would not. Well, if he hadn't been a mixture of genius and mule he would never have started a job that size.

As the refitting of the floating dock continued to schedule, Cox had to look more closely at the practical application of salvage – which in the early 1920s was still an embryonic science with no defined boundaries between fantasy and reality.

Chapter 4

Quacks and Facts

On 2 December 1932, eighteen months after Cox had finished working at Scapa Flow, he was invited by the Institution of Mechanical Engineers to give a lecture to its members on how he managed to conceive and execute his unique salvage operation. This was the very same Institution whose more respected fellows were some of the so-called 'experts' who had once scoffed at Cox's salvage ideas. The temperature had been unusually mild for December. Rain had drizzled over a grey London all day and became much worse as night fell. As the Institution members and their guests sat down, an odour of stale, damp clothing soon filled the room. With a few rough notes for reference and a large number of lantern slides to support the success of his unorthodox salvage ideas, he now stood like a victor at the front of their auditorium.

A little before 8.00 pm, all the members were seated and hushed. As the lights dimmed, the first lantern slide projected a grainy black and white image of a cold, drab place where the land, sea and sky merged into only slightly varying shades of grey. The view recreated an atmosphere not unlike the London weather the members and guests had just experienced. But in the middle of the grainy image they could all see two massive, black, floating docks. Cox began his lecture:

> Eight years ago I was finishing the breaking up of two battleships, which I had purchased from the British Government, when the suggestion was made to me that I might make an attempt at lifting the German fleet which had been sunk in Scapa Flow. As I would shortly be without work to do, I turned over the idea in my mind, but, considering I had never lifted ships before in my life, the project was somewhat ambitious.

The full impact of 'somewhat ambitious' never really came across in Cox's dry, almost clinical account of how he went from amateur boat lifter to salvage expert during his eight years in the Flow. His previous experience of selling Western Front debris and breaking up two decommissioned warships had taught him enough about bringing scrap metal to a ready market at a good profit. All he needed now was to learn the salvage profession, which at that time counted very few experts, and for which the technical guiding rules had not yet been laid down. The only information available came from a few ships that had been raised under similar conditions, but as Cox was soon to learn, applying precedents too firmly would only lead to disaster. He had to take what he could from others and tailor-make his salvage operation to suit the constant unknown quantities which dogged him until the day he left the Flow.

Early twentieth-century salvage was similar to sixteenth-century medicine; quackery and bad techniques dominated the business. By the end of the First World War so much high-quality metal lay scattered around the seabeds of Europe that shortages began to affect postwar progress. As European economies began to recover, the demand for raw materials grew dramatically and the cost of replacing the millions of tons of steel forged into the war effort was weighed against salvaging ex-war metal. Talk of raising the Cunarder, *Lusitania*, spurred on some of the more imaginative ideas.

At about 2.00 pm on 7 May 1915, the *Lusitania* was approaching the end of her transatlantic cruise from New York to Liverpool. She was sighted by the submarine *U-20* about 14 miles off Cobh in Southern Ireland. Unfortunately for Cunard, the *Lusitania*'s silhouette was listed in *Jane's Fighting Ships* and was also designated a Royal Naval Reserve merchant cruiser in *Brassey's Naval Annual*. Both British publications were standard issue for all German U-boats. *Kapitanleutnant* Walther Schwieger ordered one torpedo to be fired at the target. It travelled 700yds at about 9ft below the surface, well out of sight of the *Lusitania*'s bridge watch. A few minutes later the torpedo hit her starboard side just behind her foremast, but two explosions were heard. The second explosion is thought to have been 5,600 cases of American ammunition recorded in her manifest, and destined for the Western Front. Aboard the *Lusitania*, Captain William Turner tried to make for the nearby Irish coast, but eighteen minutes later she sank 310ft to the bottom of the Atlantic, taking more than 1,200 men, women and children with her. By 2.30 pm that same afternoon, the prestigious Cunarder was nothing more than 31,550 gross tons of high-grade scrap metal.

The *Lusitania* was no ordinary liner. Her construction had been a joint venture between Cunard and the Admiralty in case her Royal Naval Reserve status should ever be called upon. Above her water-line she was built like a luxury liner. Below, she was built like a pre-dreadnought warship and instead of the usual mild steel used in liner construction, she was almost entirely built out of high-tensile steel. Seven years later the quacks were devising many ways to exhume her rusting remains for sale on the open scrap metal market. The Reno system was one of the more eccentric methods. In 1922 *The Illustrated London News* published detailed drawings of a Mr Jesse W. Reno's salvage designs. They showed a perfectly intact *Lusitania* sitting upright on the seabed.

Reno envisaged a 'tractor' with a watertight working chamber in place of the normal seating and engine area. The chamber, which was to be fed by an air line from the surface, would sit where the four wheels would normally be positioned and the whole contraption would ride on chain-driven caterpillar tracks clanking along the seabed up to the *Lusitania*'s side. Holes would then be drilled along her hull at close intervals. Hooks, attached to giant vertical pontoons would be guided into the drilled holes and the pontoons hooked on. The process was to be repeated until the vertical pontoons, which ran from the bottom of the *Lusitania* to her main deck, ranged fore and aft down both sides of her 800-foot length. With a few token pontoons under her keel as she rose, the process would need to be repeated some ninety times on a rocky seabed strewn with debris. All this work was to be carried out in virtual if not complete darkness and at pressures of around $140lb/in^2$. The pontoons would then be pumped full of compressed air to refloat her, and she would simply be towed to the shore.

Mr Carl Lindquist of New York had similar ideas. He envisaged wires passed under her embedded keel with both ends attached to pontoons, but above the ship's superstructure. They would then be pumped with compressed air like giant steel balloons. Lindquist, however, thought that it would be better to keep the *Lusitania* just below the surface. As she was towed towards the shore and the sea became shallower, the idea was simply to add more compressed air until she rode over the rising seabed far enough to be beached. He claimed that about three such lifts should do the trick.

27

Contrary to her imagined upright position depicted in these salvage plans, the *Lusitania* settled on her starboard side, covering the massive hole which sent her to the bottom, where she is still lying today, about 11 miles off the Irish coast. Cox needed reliable facts regarding proven rather than quack salvage methods.

Thomas McKenzie was a thirty-one-year-old, energetic and skilful marine engineer whose clean good looks were marred by a sharp scar across his left cheek. He was also Scotland's most experienced salvage diver. McKenzie was a shipbuilder by trade and worked for the Clyde Navigation Trust as a diver until war broke out in 1914, at which time he went to work for the Marine Salvage Department of the Admiralty for the duration of the First World War. When the department was disbanded in 1919 he worked for a salvage syndicate, trying to locate a Spanish ship from the Armada. The ship sank in Tobermory Bay on the Scottish island of Mull. The syndicate spent two years searching for the wreck and for all his efforts McKenzie found only a few gold coins, each of which would fetch no more than about 16 guineas. Cox had little trouble persuading McKenzie to work with him on the Scapa Flow project. For all Cox's drive and brilliant engineering qualities, his understanding of salvage technique was based on theory only. He still lacked a genuine understanding of the practical problems involved in raising and refloating sunken ships and McKenzie's experience placed him in an ideal position to make Scapa Flow work.

Like many early enthusiastic medical amateurs learning how the human body works, the salvage quacks did apply some basic understanding of how ships might be raised. Adding compressed air – either directly into a wreck or by some outside means – is today the most widespread method adopted to refloat ships. But this alone is not enough to guarantee success. When all the calculations are applied and the preparations made, the process is still based on the subtle minute-by-minute changes as events unfold. McKenzie discussed with Cox two methods of raising ships, which had been used with some success, but never on vessels of the size and condition Cox intended to attempt. The potential use of compressed air was just being recognized, but McKenzie suggested it should be used only for the larger ships and applied inside the hold rather than outside.

For the smaller destroyers, McKenzie advised Cox to adopt the tidal lift method that Robertson was about to attempt. The technique was developed in Italy more than 400 years ago to raise boats that

28

had sunk in Venice's many canals. The first known attempt of a tidal lift in England was applied to the *Mary Rose* only months after she sank off Portsmouth in 1545. After meeting the Venetian salvers the Governor of Portsmouth, Charles, Duke of Suffolk, later wrote enthusiastically to the Secretary of State, Sir William Paget:

> Concerning the *Mary Rose*. We have consulted and spoke together with them who desireth to have, for the saving of her, such necessaries as is mentioned in the Schedule herein enclosed. Not doubting, God willing, but that they shall have all things ready accordingly, so that shortly she shall be saved.

The Duke's schedule included:

> two of the greatest hulks that may be gotten, four of the greatest hoys within haven, five of the greatest cables that may be had, ten great hawsers, ten capstans with twenty pulleys, fifty pulleys bound with iron, five dozen ballast baslets, forty pounds of tallow. Thirty Venetian mariners, one Venetian carpenter, sixty English mariners and a great quantity of cordage of all sorts. I trust by Monday or Tuesday at the farthest, the *Mary Rose* shall be weighed up and saved.

Their plan was to form a cradle around the *Mary Rose* at low tide by wrapping ropes around every available point on her hull, running the ropes above the sea and securing them to beams fixed across the two 'greatest hulks'. Theoretically, this was a classic tidal lift. But although they had the right equipment, and a sound theoretical understanding, for all the Venetian efforts the *Mary Rose* was just too heavy.

Cox accepted McKenzie's use of the tidal lift method, for the destroyers, but he already saw several flaws in its tried and trusted application. First because the known format was too restrictive and time-consuming and, if he was going to lift many ships, speed meant profit.

The torpedoboat *V.70* had sunk on an even keel in 50ft of water only half a mile from Lyness where Cox's staff now occupied the old Navy barracks and air station. She was considered an easy lift and a good model on which to break his men in. Their plan was as follows. Underwater preparation was to be carried out in a conventional way.

Four divers would position themselves in pairs on each side of the *V.70*. They would then push 'prickers' (long steel rods) under the hull through the soft, slightly dug out silt to the pair waiting on the other side. Wires would then be attached to the pricker, pulled through, passed back up to the floating dock on the other side of the warship and winched tight.

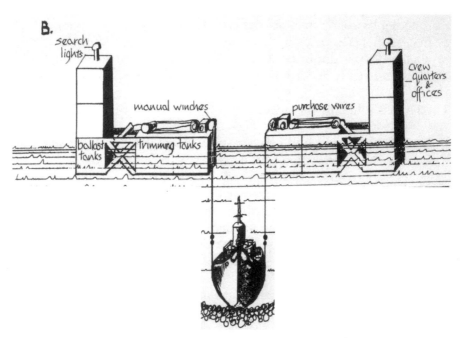

The diagram above shows how the dock looked after conversion from an ex-submarine pressure-testing facility. Many men were employed to hand-winch a vessel off the seabed, which was the biggest advance in the tidal lift method since the Middle Ages.

The procedure would be repeated ten times along the *V.70*'s hull, to form a steel cradle. But against McKenzie's strong advice, Cox refused to use steel wire because of its high cost. Instead he wanted to use old anchor chain left over from the sale of the scrapped HMS *Orion*. Cox was concerned that the cost of the salvage operation might be far greater than he had expected and he had yet to show a return. McKenzie's wire would eat another £2,000 (or £80,000 today) into his dwindling funds. The anchor chain had an impressive 3in diameter and Cox was adamant that it would be enough to complete the successive lifts needed to bring the *V.70* to the surface. The preparation took ten days and once the *V.70* was placed in her cradle, Cox's ingenuity began to rewrite marine salvage technique.

Fixing a sunken ship in a steel cradle attached to two floating docks, and waiting for the optimum tide to raise her, was not enough for Cox. For salvaging single wrecks the method was fine, but when raising many ships he knew that the restrictions of a spring tide would severely affect his profits. Speed was everything. He had to find a way to beat the tide and radically alter the 500-year-old technique or the project was doomed. Cox developed a method similar to that used for elevators in large buildings. In an elevator, the load (basically a small room full of people) is propelled up or down on a system of wires and braking pulleys under human control. 'Why can't a system be developed to raise and lower a ship and either use, or beat, the tide flow to bring a vessel to the surface quickly?' he thought. His plan was that simple. On paper his elevator method also allowed for complete vertical and horizontal control while a wreck was in ascent. This control had never been achieved before and would later allow him to raise even more complicated wreck formations.

Early in March 1924 the *V.70* was ready for lifting. The floating docks were lined up with marker buoys placed above her on either side by divers. All hands were at their places aboard the two floating platforms. Before the main lift, Cox wanted the *V.70* raised slightly off the seabed and suspended there to avoid too much sudden suction as she broke out of the silt. She weighed a little more than 750 tons and any additional strain on the chains had to be avoided. Twenty-four gangs of four men manned each winch. These winches were attached to chains that flowed over grooved wheels, then down around the *V.70*. It was essential that all winch gangs turned the same amount of revolutions at exactly the same time to ensure the weight was equally balanced.

When the tide reached its lowest point Cox gave the order, 'Six turns.' The twenty gangs slowly turned in unison. The chains began to groan, but there was no outward sign that the *V.70* was moving. 'Another six turns,' Cox yelled through his megaphone. As the men slowly pulled, Cox could see the two giant floating docks lean inwards, meaning they were starting to take up the *V.70*'s full weight. All was well and going according to theory. The tide had turned. Cox gave the order for the third time and six more turns were applied. As she rose higher the floating docks began to dip at sharper angles. Suddenly, a loud crack like a gunshot echoed across the Flow. A chain link weighing nearly half a hundred weight exploded on the first bow chain supporting the *V.70*, sending shards of metal flying around the men as they dived for cover. Cox stood by helplessly, knowing what would happen next. Seconds later a link on the second chain exploded. Then the third, fourth, fifth, right up to the eighth, when the *V.70* slipped free of the last two chains and nose-dived back to the seabed. Shattered equipment flew down in her wake. McKenzie recalled:

> Men scrambled wildly for shelter, some lay down flat on the decks, others jumped about as one thing after another hurtled towards them. The noise was terrific! I was in the middle of it all, trying to look after myself and shouting warnings to various points. I doubt very much if my voice was heard above the noise, but when, after what seemed hours, but in reality was less than two minutes, everything calmed down. I was almost afraid to look around. I shouted, 'Is anyone hurt?' several times and was amazed to receive the reply from different directions, 'All right sir!' With the exception of a few bruises and barked shins everyone had miraculously escaped injury.

Cox looked around at his workers' frightened faces and was deeply relieved that his stubbornness had not hurt anyone. For all his obstinacy, Cox was strong enough to admit when he was proved wrong. In his attempt to save £2,000 he had lost valuable time and he still had to pay his men. Cox's first salvage operation ended in disaster. Each week he was paying more than £500 in wages, which amounts to about £17,000 today. Now his men would have to sit idle until the wire arrived and then further time would be lost re-rigging the floating pontoons for another attempt. Another small fortune had to be hurled at a business enterprise that had yet to show any return. 'I'll get the wire as soon as I can,' he said. It was no doubt Cox's ability to accept failure and take full responsibility for his actions that earned him the respect of his men. Before long he learnt that they referred to him as 'Father' behind his back, and they continued to do so until he left the Flow.

The steel wire lifting gear had to be specially designed to raise the smaller ships. Each wire was made into a hawser composed of six strands, which were 1in thick. The middle section of each wire was flattened like a belt to 16in wide to form a solid bearing against the destroyer's hull. This arrangement also lessened greatly the risk of the wires 'stranding' or unravelling under the intense load they were going to have to bear. The winches were so finely geared that as the men wound in unison the destroyer's upward movement was hardly perceptible. After twenty turns, which became known as 'heaving twenties', the men were genuinely tired and needed the short break Cox gave them between winding sessions.

Watchers were posted to ensure that every man did his twenty turns and did not try to get away with seventeen or eighteen. Apart from not doing their job, several turns missed on each session would begin to put too much strain on a wire, causing it to part, and the critically balanced weight to become uneven. As more ships were winched up, some men were found to be 'swinging the lead' and if caught they were made to do double winding duties, a physical punishment far worse than skimping a few turns on a shift.

After three months passed, which saw the removing of the old chains and the re-threading of the new wires, there were new problems. The V.70's rapid nose-dive had driven her farther into the silt and the pricker rods failed to go under the hull as originally planned. At 9in in circumference, the thickness and weight of the new wires also hampered their passage.

To overcome the problem, Cox devised a simple method whereby a wire was placed around the V.70's propeller 'A' frame and secured tight to the two floating platforms at low tide. As the tide rose, she crept far enough off the seabed to easily run the wires through to the other side. This new technique would later help him raise all the smaller ships much faster than through conventional methods. Normally, passing a wire under a ship took commercial salvors a day for each line. Cox's new method cut the time to as little as forty minutes. On 31 July 1924 the V.70 was firmly fixed in her new wire cradle and ready to raise. Cox wanted to begin just before the spring tide two days later – just in case he encountered further problems and another month was lost before his next chance. At about 3.00 am on the following morning, Cox had ninety-six men ready to winch up the V.70. The tide was at its lowest mark and about to start rising.

He stood high above his men to get a good view of the operation and to pre-empt what might go wrong. 'Ten turns!' he shouted. The wires creaked and became taut as the men silently and slowly bobbed up and down while turning their winch handles. Nothing happened. Cox scrutinized every inch of the two flood-lit docks. The only noises came from the humming generators and the odd cough from a worker. The men shuffled to and fro. Cox knew that if the wires could not take the weight they would part as quickly as the chains. Unlike shards of metal flying through the air, the wires would give no warning (or at best a distinct singing which precedes a break) before sending the fractured parts flailing across the floating docks like 9in steel whips with enough power to cut a man in two. 'Twenty more turns.' The men bent to their task and to turning their winch handles. On the twentieth turn the floating docks were dipping down their centre line.

Before 9.00 am the *V.70* was 5ft off the seabed. The *Ferrodanks* and the *Sidonian* were ordered to make fast to the floating docks and steam the mile-long journey to Mill Bay on the rising tide. A full seven hours after winding had commenced, the floating docks were 300yds off the beach and the *V.70* was a few feet from the surface when the order was given to 'knock off' as the tide was now falling. The second attempt had gone like clockwork and the first ship to be raised was settling nicely on the sand at the bottom of Mill Bay. Once the tide rose the *V.70* was carried slowly between the two floating docks towards the beach until her after deck was well above the low tide mark. Five years under water had turned her hull and superstructure into a pile of twisted metal, encrusted with marine growth. Barnacles, soft corals, anemones and thick seaweed covered every inch, making her look more like a small reef rather than a once deadly warship. The fusion of vivid colours was striking. But, once the marine growth began to decay, the stench was so vile that it could be smelt right across Lyness harbour. Surprisingly, after so long under water, the *V.70*'s wheel still turned and, once cleaned of all their marine growths, the electric light switches worked perfectly.

Amid all the filth and rotting matter Cox boarded the *V.70*, immaculately dressed as always. His white shirt was spotless and a trilby was pushed firmly on his head to avoid it flying off in the Scapa Flow wind. Whether he was working in dirt or meeting people, Cox always ensured his leather brogues had a deep shine and his matching Harris Tweed waistcoat, plus-fours and jacket were pristine. He had a propensity to wear stiff collars long before a man of his age was expected to wear them. But his dress code fitted perfectly into the mindset of a man for whom precision was everything, and was practical as well as aesthetic. Because his trousers only came to his knees there was no material flapping around his ankles to be caught and ripped. Harris Tweed also kept out the wind, and to a large degree the rain. Looking as if he was about to go out for dinner, instead of having spent all night raising a sunken vessel, Cox walked up to the tip of the *V.70*'s bow and began to fix a Red Ensign on to her Jack staff. All his men clustered on her superstructure behind him and cheered while Cox laughed and the Red Ensign unfurled in the wind above *his* German warship.

A full survey was made before she could be broken up and before Cox could expect to recover some of the vast fortune he had poured into the project. By the time the *V.70* was high and dry, he had spent £40,000 from the £75,000 of available funds. Still, although her break-up and sale would have made £1,500 of much needed revenue (in 1924 this represented more than £52,000 at today's value), to everyone's surprise he decided not to have her scrapped.

Cox's lecture before the Institution of Mechanical Engineers, which began at 8.00 pm on that wet December evening, was over by 8.10 pm. He had condensed his explanation of the *V.70* lift down to half a dozen sentences and three lantern slides. The *V.70* had taught him the first hard lessons in the reality of marine salvage, and to accept the need to listen and take advice.

That learning curve had really only just started. Electrical apprentice Sandy Thomson remembered:

Apart from McKeown and McKenzie there was not one of us who knew the first thing about salvage and they did not know much at the start. We all just learned as we went along, from the boss down. He [Cox] would never listen to experts. If he had he would never have tried the crazy things he did, and pulled them off. He only ever listened to the two Macs and even with them, the rows!

The rest of his lecture to the august Institution members carried on in much the same clinical, matter-of-fact way, implying that raising the ships (that many had thought was impossible), was relatively easy. Nothing could have been further from the truth.

Chapter 5

Ships on Ships

After all the problems Cox had overcome in raising the *V.70*, he had yet to face his biggest obstacle. The value of scrap metal had dropped from £5 a ton to only 35 shillings around the same time the *V.70* was raised. Another shattering blow followed, which did more to dent Cox's pride than his ability to raise ships. Seeing her right out of the water gave everyone the first full view of the *V.70* since she slipped beneath the Flow in 1919. McKenzie, the fair-haired, stocky diver Bill Peterson and many others, including Cox, could see that much of her precious scrap content was already gone.

Her torpedo tubes alone, which were made out of the highly prized non-ferrous phosphor bronze, were worth more than £100 each. Every torpedoboat in the 1913 class like the *V.70* had six. Unlike those on a submarine, torpedo tubes on torpedoboats, and later destroyers, were deck-mounted. There was usually one on the port fore end, one amidships and one a little aft. The configuration was duplicated down the starboard side, and each tube could swivel to increase flexibility, aiming and firing. Their location and fixing also allowed for their easy removal. On closer observation everything moveable had already been taken. Cox flew into one of his famous blind rages. He cursed the air around him and verbally lashed out at any quaking worker within his range. He screamed at McKenzie, 'What the Devil … have your damned divers snarled up the cables and wrenched the tubes off?'

'Ask the fish,' cut in Peterson, who was not about to have his workmanship or that of his men blamed for the missing metal. 'Or,' he continued, 'ask some of the quiet boys ashore.'

'They've been pinched,' screamed Cox as it suddenly dawned on him that the Orcadians had beaten him to the best the *V.70* had to offer. 'I'll get the police, I'll ... I'll ... .' But he could do nothing. The cream of the *V.70*'s metal was long gone and no local inhabitant was going to help a stranger from 'down south' trace its whereabouts – or the men who took it. Until Cox purchased the wrecks, taking the metal was still theft from the Admiralty. The word around the Flow was that the valuable metal had been stripped off her long ago and smuggled back to the Scottish mainland disguised in herring barrels. Ever the practical engineer, Cox decided to remove the *V.70*'s superstructure, seal her hull and have his chief carpenter, John Scolley, fit her out as a salvage vessel to aid his two floating docks. A large crane was also added. He renamed her *Salvage Unit No. 3* and, in spite of the sudden fall in scrap value, he turned immediately to the next vessel.

The ships' approximate positions were known to every Orcadian, who could not have failed to notice them bobbing at anchor. Cox used a chart to make an educated guess as to the location of a wreck. Once a ship was selected, his smaller tug, the *Lyness*, steamed over the wreck site. A shot-rope was dropped to the bottom to help a diver guide his descent. His job was to locate the wreck and then signal his colleagues on the *Lyness* to lower down a 4in steel wire, which was fixed to the ship's gun pedestals on the fore and aft of the ship. Two different coloured floats or 'marker buoys' were then attached, one to each wire, white for forward and red for aft. The two floating dock sections were then towed out to the new wreck site, fixed in position above a sunken vessel and the whole lifting process would start again. Although Robertson began his salvage operation in 1923 he still had not raised his first ship. Cox was about to lift his second.

The next torpedoboat Cox chose was the *S.53*. Like the *V.70* she was from the 1913 torpedoboat class, which was the workhorse of the Imperial High Seas Fleet. With seventy vessels of this type built and launched, the 1913 class had the most ships commissioned out of the fourteen classes operated between 1885 and 1918. The *S.53*'s position in deeper water meant she was well out of the Orkney scavengers' range, but she lay fully on her side and no ship had yet been raised and righted from a capsized position. This was essential for bringing her to the scrap metal market at a good price. The more upright a wreck was, the further up a beach she could be dropped for breaking.

Cox's mechanical lifting method also allowed for ships to be raised enough to clear the seabed, even if completely capsized. This diagram shows the position of the floating docks as a fully capsized vessel was lifted clear before being turned.

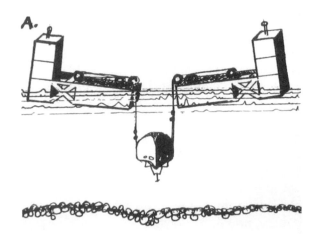

Cox's revolutionary winching method with its complex gearing and complete vertical and horizontal flexibility stood every chance of again proving the experts wrong. Most ships are built with a sharp bow section, widening amidships and tapering off again towards the stern. Lying fully on her port side meant that the S.53 had her fore and aft sections well above the seabed, so passing enough wires under her proved a much easier exercise than with the V.70. First, six wires were passed underneath her from one floating dock, up to the next, and made fast. Cox's men once again bent to 'heaving twenties' until the S.53's amidships' section had cleared the seabed enough to pass another six wires under her widest point with ease. The twelve wires, all evenly taking the 750-ton load between them, were more than enough to hold the capsized vessel securely. The next stage was to right the S.53 before winding her up for the short tow to Mill Bay where Cox could finally hope to make a return on his investment.

The men slowly wound her up until she was well clear of the seabed. He then gave the order to cease winding while she was still at a considerable distance from the surface. The *Ferrodanks* and the *Sidonian* were ordered to tow the floating docks while the men were given a well-earned rest. Some stripped off to the waist and enjoyed the mid-August sunshine. The summer of 1924 had been the hottest in Orkney for ten years. Others stood around smoking cigarettes. The rhythm of their low mutterings and occasional bursts of raucous laughter echoed with a tinny resonance across the floating docks as the two tugs towed them into deeper water. Once in position, the men put their working shirts and vests back on, flicked their unfinished cigarettes away and made for the winches. When everyone had shuffled back into place they took the winch handles in their hands and waited for the order. Cox scrutinized the two lines of poised men all looking up at him, waiting for the moment his megaphone would go to his mouth and the order, 'wind twenty', would echo around the floating docks like a verbal whiplash.

Finally the order came. But only the port-side men were instructed to wind up, while the starboard-side men were instructed to wind down. Wires and men heaved and groaned their way through their twenty turns before the long-awaited 'rest' order came. The winding up and paying out continued all morning as the deck of the *S.53* slowly levelled. Because of her sheer weight she bit into the steel cables enough to prevent her from slipping – or worse still – jumping in her cradle. Cox simultaneously ensured that every man turned in time to distribute the weight evenly and prevent another *V.70*-type accident from taking its toll on his machinery again. The hot summer day and stifling air were made worse as the climbing sun's baking heat was sucked into the black floating dock sections, raising the working temperature at deck level for the winch men. By the end of the morning of 23 August 1924, the *S.53* was successfully righted and moved into Mill Bay, using the same tidal procedure as for the *V.70*. This time, instead of the six weeks it took to raise the *V.70*, the *S.53* was turned, raised and towed to Mill Bay within twelve days. Another torpedoboat from the same 1913 class was the *S.55*. She was raised less than two weeks later.

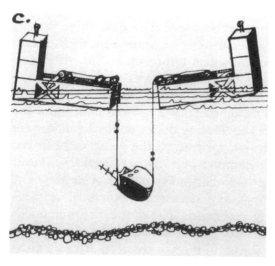

The position of Cox's floating docks relative to a wreck as one team slowly paid out their wires while the other winched them up. The turning process allowed Cox to lift ships once deemed by his contemporary salvage experts to be lost forever.

Robertson started lifting small parts of vessels later in 1923 and planned to have all his machinery and men in place for summer 1924, when the real lifting would begin. Should Robertson succeed, he could legitimately apply to buy the rest of the fleet from the Admiralty. On 29 August, Robertson was ready to lift his first ship, the 1898 class *S.131*. She was considerably smaller than the ships Cox was raising and ships in her class ranged in weight from only 400 to 690 tons. Robertson spent two months preparing to raise his first ship. Poor weather and the discovery that the wires he planned to run under the *S.131* were too short, had greatly hampered his progress.

Once his lifting system was in place, two camels, or large inflatable pontoons covered with wooden slats, were sunk under her bow below sea level and slowly inflated and then two under her stern. Camels had been in use in one form or another since the nineteenth century. Robertson patented his own camel design whereby the wooden slats were replaced with twelve layers of canvas, firmly bonded together with rubber solution. Altogether he made four of his own camels.

The weather conditions on 29 August had been ideal for both Cox and Robertson to chance a lift. The wires on the *S.131* were tightened at low water and Robertson waited for the rising tide to lift her higher for the more conventional tidal lift. As she left the seabed Robertson's camels were inflated, lifting her to the surface. The lift was a complete success and the *S.131* was towed towards the shore and lowered in Ore Bay on the other side of Lyness Pier from Mill Bay where Cox was already lowering the *S.55* next to his two other torpedoboats. By mid-September Cox had set the floating docks over his fourth torpedoboat, the 1913 class *G.91*, for what was by now a routine operation, when the first diving accident happened.

In the early 1920s, professional diving to depths of up to 100ft carried greater risks than today, mainly because of the cumbersome suits men had to wear. Another twenty years would pass before Lieutenant Jacques-Yves Cousteau would co-invent the self-contained underwater breathing apparatus (Scuba) with Emile Gagnan. Cousteau's first test dives in June 1943 reached 130ft – well below that of Cox's divers – and showed that a diver could finally achieve underwater freedom. After Cousteau had proved that his aqualung worked, he commented:

I thought of the helmet diver arriving on his ponderous boots at such a depth as this. Struggling to walk a few yards, obsessed with his umbilici and his head imprisoned in copper. On 'skin dives' I had seen him leaning dangerously forward to make a step. Clamped in heavier pressure at the ankles than the head, a cripple in an alien land.

Had Cox the luxury of Scuba equipment, his job would have been much easier as his men could have moved as fluidly as the water around them.

The professional 1920s diver was permanently bound to his diving boat by a life line and a breathing hose, which ran the constant risk of being fouled, severed or all too frequently trapped by debris. His underwater life support system was the classic deep-sea diving suit, which made him look and move more like an astronaut rather than a man under the sea. His air supply was fed from a hand-winched compressor aboard the diving boat, down through a rubber hose, and his overall safety depended solely on linesmen like Sandy Robertson reading all his signals and checking that his air supply was constantly correct. The air he breathed within the suit was finely regulated to equal the pressure of the surrounding water he was working in. A diver normally worked two three-hour shifts each day, often in near-freezing darkness.

Today, all divers in Scapa Flow wear a dry suit to keep out the piercing cold. In 1924 the average diver wore an all-in-one part woollen and part cotton underwear suit next to his skin. Over this he had a suit of pure cotton underwear, then two pairs of woollen socks underneath a pair of fleece-lined moccasins. A shirt, trousers and jersey then covered the underwear. A coat as well as a scarf and thick woollen hat completed the outfit. Sometimes another pair of trousers, and coat were added before the actual diving suit was finally fitted.

The outer diver's suit was made of rubberized twill, which covered the whole body from foot to neck except the hands. The sleeves had vulcanized rubber cuffs to provide a watertight joint at the wrists. However cold the water was, the diver always worked with his bare hands, which often became swollen and numb. The flexible rubber air-pipe was passed under the left arm from behind, over the front of his left shoulder and lashed to his helmet frame. Although the hose was made of very tough rubber, it could still easily be severed by

42

sharp metal or become trapped by falling wreckage. Then, however much his pump men tried to pass air down to him, he would eventually suffocate if help did not arrive in time. As well as the air line, the diver had a lifeline, which was his only contact with the world above and often carried a telephone wire for communication with the surface. The lifeline was passed around his waist, then between his legs, up under his right arm and lashed in a similar manner as the air line. With a breaking strain of 1,300lb, this rigging method allowed the stand-by staff to pull a stranded diver up to the surface as quickly and painlessly as possible.

Lead boots weighing up to 16lb each were not only used to keep the diver under water, but also upright. A 40lb weight on his chest and another on his back looked more like two large lead padlocks slung across his shoulders with chains. These had to be secured by a small rope running around his upper waist. The diver's heavy copper helmet had the classic three small apertures from which to view the outside world, one on each side and one facing front.

An outlet valve fitted to the helmet allowed the diver to control the air volume into his suit and so adjust his buoyancy on the seabed. By closing his outlet valve a diver's suit would inflate and help his ascent. Because the diver freely breathed the air within his helmet instead of that provided through a demand valve, quite often condensation would form on the glass plate he looked through. To clear this he had to open a small tap and gulp a mouthful of sea water to literally spit on the glass plate, giving the tap its name of 'spitcock'. This small amount of water was often enough to short-out the early diving telephone systems. A small knife completed the outfit to help a diver should he become trapped, but more often than not, getting free without assistance was impossible. A fully equipped reserve diver was always ready to go into the water at a moment's notice, should anything go wrong.

So far the torpedoboats had posed no real problems for the divers, but as the salvage operations progressed, so their work became both more challenging and, as some were to discover, also more dangerous. After the *S.55* another of the 1913 class, the *G.91*, began to be processed through Cox's salvaging and breaking factory. McKenzie was on the diving boat above the *G.91* when he was told the diver below wanted to speak to him urgently.

'Hello! You wish to speak to me?' said McKenzie reaching across to answer the call.

'Yes sir! There's a funnel or something fallen down, and I can't get out.'

'Where are you working?' replied McKenzie.

'I went down between two ships to try to reeve a wire through,' said the trapped diver in a rather jovial tone.

'Are your pipe and line clear?'

'No sir, and I can't move either.'

'Now, don't worry,' snapped McKenzie, feeling that the diver might start to panic very soon. He immediately ordered two divers to descend and free their colleague from beneath the collapsed funnel. McKenzie then grabbed the telephone to tell the diver that help was on its way and was shocked to hear a crackling and strained version of 'Home Sweet Home' echoing up through the wire. McKenzie waited patiently for him to finish the first verse and said, 'Hello, how are you?'

'Fine, sir. What do you think of my voice?'

'Pretty awful,' replied McKenzie who was just relieved to know his colleague was still alive and well, albeit an appalling singer, 'but we can stand another verse.' The diver kept calm throughout his ordeal and was finally released by his two dive partners without any problems.

The divers' ability to avoid panic in the most mentally, physically and emotionally demanding situations was to become legendary as the job of salvaging ships grew in size and complexity. Some of the divers' most skilful work at this stage was unravelling all the chaos left from warship 'pile ups'. Several German vessels had been moored to the same buoy and as they sank, ships landed on ships. Their combined weight often dragged down the massive floating buoy, which became buried among the mass of funnels, masts, aerials, ventilator cowls, wire reels, railings and boat davits, crushed together in a twisted, rusting mass. Underwater flame cutters were not good enough to use below about 15ft so divers had to use hacksaws to cut their way through the wreckage. This was a slow, cold and laborious job, which was often fraught with danger.

Another diver was nearly killed when a partly severed wire gave way, allowing a mooring buoy to rocket upwards like a seaborne ballistic missile. On its ascent the buoy pulled up a mass of twisted steel and other assorted debris in its wake, causing silt and marine life to blot out much of the light. Afterwards Cox ordered that gelignite must be used for cutting all mooring wires below the surface. Gelignite was made from guncotton, nitroglycerine and potassium nitrate. It was a very cheap and effective explosive, used mainly for demolition. Using the explosive was largely a matter of experience. As time passed, McKenzie was able to judge a blast so accurately that some metal breaks resembled a knife cut.

Sometimes danger did not always come from the ships they were trying to salvage. Seals playing in the wrecks often startled a diver, which could lead to panic. McKenzie was almost killed when the water above him went black, just before he was snatched off the seabed and dragged a good way through the water. When the light reappeared he surmised the wreck must have collapsed; that is until the light blacked out again and he was snatched off the seabed for the second time before landing back on the bottom. After being hauled back to the surface he was told that a large school of 40ft whales had just passed over the wreck site. Congers lurked deep within the wrecks, usually in pairs. One diver, Harry Grosset, was caught off guard when a conger bit his hand. 'When you cut yourself below the surface you do not bleed much,' he said. 'As soon as I came up, the blood began to gush out and I had to have the wound dressed. I still have the scar.'

Ex-Royal Navy diver Morrison Gunn was guiding wires under a ship, using his telephone to give instructions to men on the floating docks above. Without any warning his colleagues on the surface lost contact. Repeated calls down the telephone brought no answer. Harry Grosset was the reserve diver. He immediately went into the water, tracing Gunn's lines to the bottom. Gunn had not been paying proper attention to his job. A big wire reel had been torn away from her deck by one of the floating docks' lifting wires. Gunn had been too close and was now pinned down. All shouts through his telephone line brought no response. His lines were also jammed under her wreckage, breaking all his communications to the surface only a short distance from where he was trapped. Gunn was isolated and hopelessly trapped.

Grosset reached the bottom and soon found Gunn by tracing his lines as best he could. 'We touched helmets, and Gunn told me he was all right,' said Grosset. Communication between two divers on the seabed was simply a matter of touching helmets, their metal walls thus acting like transmitter diaphragms, allowing divers full and clear conversations. This was very simple and extremely effective way to discuss work in progress or to ensure a fellow diver was feeling fine. Grosset then set to work freeing Gunn as quickly as possible, in case his nerve gave out. Eventually Grosset managed to free him and they both made it safely back to the surface. Once aboard the diving boat, Gunn implored Grosset to lie to McKenzie so that he would not get into trouble for a mistake that could possibly have cost him his job, or his life. Grosset was reluctant, but agreed.

> He [Gunn] called everybody 'Sir', and if he made a mistake his first thought was to try to cover it up. He was always on the defensive. He did not know Tom McKenzie as well as I did, and simply wanted to avoid a reprimand. I agreed, and we made up a yarn about a big shackle getting foul of a torpedo tube. We also had to say that somehow Gunn's telephone had got out of order. The story was pretty thin, but no one bothered about details when they saw Gunn was safe. That was all Tom McKenzie was concerned about, although Gunn could not understand that.

Within a few weeks Gunn had another minor accident and was given a week's leave in his hometown of Kirkwall on the other side of Scapa Flow. The following Saturday evening he returned to Lyness in the *Ferrodanks* with many other workers who had been enjoying a weekend night out in the Orkney capital. The next morning Gunn was missing and later that day his body was found floating just off Lyness Pier.

He was a sober man, a very good swimmer, and only forty-five years old. The inquest concluded that Gunn died probably after tripping over a wire and falling off the pier into the water. Grosset said, 'I was one of the eight pallbearers who carried him to his grave at Kirkwall. It was a sad blow at such an early stage. We had got to like Gunn, and in a way we were glad he wasn't replaced.' Gunn's death was the first since Cox began salvage operations, but by the time he left, the death toll would climb higher.

Every diver's fear was a fall under water. Lumbering around a slippery, unstable ship in full diving gear and in poor light conditions made this a constant risk. On another ship, Grosset tripped over and fell off her bridge. He closed his outlet valve to try to maintain some pressure within his suit and at least have some air should his air line get ripped off. 'I fell about 20ft and got a nasty squeeze.' The danger of a fall was that the pressure inside the suit suddenly became radically different to that outside the suit. 'If the fall is a big one, the weight of water will squeeze the diver's whole body up into his helmet and pulp it into jelly,' said Grosset. The phenomenon is called a 'helmet squeeze'. In France another variation on the helmet squeeze is called *coup de ventouse*, a blow of the cupping glass. Jacques-Yves Cousteau crystallized its effects on the human body.

A helmet diver whose air pipe has failed is usually killed by *coup de ventouse*. If the non-return valve in his air pipe does not hold, his fate is horrible. The helmet becomes a monstrous *ventouse*, the old fashioned doctor's cupping glass, which was applied to the chest of a coughing person. By the suction of the air pipe, his flesh is stripped away in rags, which stream up the pipe, leaving a skeleton in a rubber shroud to be raised to the tender.

Although Cox and McKenzie are credited with the ingenuity to actually salvage the ships, the divers played the single most vital and dangerous role in actually putting the plans into effect. Throughout the rest of 1924, two more of the smaller 1913 class torpedoboats were recovered, but the unusually balmy summer was slipping away and the normal Orkney weather was beginning to grip the Flow. When the *G.91* was fully recovered on 12 September, the pressure of the strong early autumn wind blew up and drove the floating docks in on the shore of the small island of Rysa, between Cava and Hoy, grounding the torpedoboat. On the following tide she was lifted clear and towed the several hundred feet up into Mill Bay for processing.

By 27 September the *G.38* was up, but her raising was delayed by a lack of manpower. Most of the workers employed to man the winches were casual labourers taken from within Orkney. They were crofters, fisherman, boatmen and farm labourers. When the work first arrived it came at the best possible time for the Orkney men. The previous year the weather had been appalling, even by Orkney standards, and both the harvest and the fishing season had been a disaster. Cox paid them ten shillings a tide each. Many were keen to earn the extra money on a casual basis, which went a long way towards preventing widespread local poverty. But by the end of

September it was harvest time once again and the longest hot summer for a decade ensured a good crop. As much as the men wanted Cox's money, the crops had to come first.

Eventually he did gather enough men, including the crew of the local Longhope lifeboat. The *G.38* was successfully raised and beached in Mill Bay alongside her four sister ships. Cox would get anyone he could to man the winches. A Pathé news film crew had come to shoot a torpedoboat being wound up. While Cox and his men were busily rushing around making all the final preparations, the film crew were lounging about on the floating dock, smoking, chatting and generally relaxing until the warship was ready to be filmed. Cox had watched them for some time and as the moment came to wind the wreck up he shouted to them, 'Get on those winches.'

They looked surprised and a little uneasy, trying to treat Cox's order as some kind of joke. After all, they were a news crew there to cover an event, not part of his organized workforce. 'On the winches, or off the dock,' Cox barked. They must have thought twice about the joke, and what if they returned to London without the clip? What would their editor say if he learnt that they had lost the shot through laziness? The camera crew wisely got up, stubbed out their cigarettes and bent to the winches.

Chapter 6

Oil and Ash

As the scrap metal piled up, Cox had to order a new crane to load the wreckage into steamers to feed the southern furnaces. The brand new crane had a safe working load of between 7½ to 10 tons, a jib of 100ft and a swing more than adequate to reach from the weighbridge around to a waiting steamer. John Mowat operated the crane. He was a tall, slim man with high cheekbones, who always wore his slick, black hair with a neat, left parting.

At 9.00 am on 8 October the floating docks were placed over the *S.52*, which had sunk on the north shore of the island of Pharay. By the end of the day, two wires had already been secured around her. On the following Monday the *S.52* was on her way to Mill Bay. In less than four months Cox had cut the time needed to raise a ship from six weeks to just five days. Shortly afterwards Cox suspended lifting operations and concentrated on developing his shore facilities.

John Robertson was preparing to lift his fourth vessel, which began in December 1924 and was successfully raised in January 1925. She was to be his last. The previous year Robertson had said, 'You know, if I and Mr Cox combined, we would be a powerful combination, for we would own a fleet.' Towards the end of January a violent storm blew up and severely damaged both of his barges when their anchors dragged. They were both washed up on the shore. Robertson's salvage techniques failed to compete with the speed and efficiency of Cox's operation. By February 1925 Robertson was gone and Scapa Flow was Cox's for the taking – subject of course to expected profits and luck.

Mill Bay was rapidly filling up with recovered warships. With many logistical salvage problems resolved, and now a matter of routine, the next stage was to deliver the metal to market as quickly and efficiently as possible. Breaking up a ship profitably carried as much skill as the salvaging process itself. Logical and common sense approaches were required to prevent wasting many thousands of pounds in labour and materials that could cut heavily into an otherwise respectable profit margin. The first and most essential factor affecting the successful break up of a ship was how close to shore it could be brought on a high tide. Obviously speed was important, for the quicker Cox got the metal to the market place, the faster he would begin to recover his costs, let alone see a profit. All the ships that ended up in Mill Bay followed the same breaking up pattern.

Once a ship broke the surface and was secured between the two floating docks, divers went aboard in waders to place pumps in key positions to remove as much of the trapped water as possible, in order to raise her even higher. The vessel was then towed alongside the breaking pier at Lyness and stripped. The naked hull could then be broken-up back in Mill Bay and beached as high as possible on a high tide, maximizing the amount of the ship above water before starting the main breaking process. Then all the lifting wires were removed and the floating dock was freed to begin the next lifting operation. Once the tide dropped, stripping started at the bow and stern both above and sometimes below sea level, back to the next watertight compartment. Once the tide came up, being somewhat lighter, a ship floated even farther up the beach. Depending on the ship's design, Cox's men would also start on the side bulkheads, gradually making the vessel smaller and smaller – thus getting higher and higher up the beach on each new tide. When there was only a central box-like structure left, blocks were placed underneath it at high tide and as the water receded, the ship's remains could be dealt with well out of the water.

Lyness Pier is a large jetty for the island it is supposed to serve. Looking out across the Flow, it has two big berths, one to the right and the other along its front. Mill Bay is to the left. There were ex-Admiralty sheds already in place about 600yds from the pier with railway lines leading straight to the berths. But the time-consuming exercise of craning the metal ashore into railway trucks, transferring it by train to the sheds, then back to the pier to be shipped out was too much time wasted for Cox. It was cheaper and faster to build new sheds. More often than not the scrap lay in heaps all over Lyness Pier, rusting away until it was loaded into steamers. Eventually the armour plate from the larger ships was cut to the exact size needed to fit a furnace. The shore-side breaking operation could also keep his men employed throughout the winter months when bad weather would hamper the salvage work.

By autumn 1924, between Mill Bay and Lyness Pier, Cox had in place the means to raise, strip and deliver to market all the scrap he could recover. He sold the *G.91* to a Sheffield firm to be broken up in Rosyth near Edinburgh to save space in Mill Bay. The remaining vessels in the small sheltered inlet were then broken up at a rate of about one a month to give his men enough work throughout the winter until salvaging could resume in early March 1925.

All the torpedoboats Cox had raised in 1924 belonged to the same 1913 class. The first vessel selected for salvaging the following year was the *H.145*. She was a more modern torpedoboat of the 1916 class – the first true class of German destroyers. These ships were better armed with heavier guns and so were worth more as scrap. But above all they were, on average, more than two hundred tons heavier, meaning a considerably higher profit for the same amount of work. On 13 March the *H.145* was raised and bound for Mill Bay followed by one of her sister ships the *S.136* on 3 April. Some of the 1916 class destroyers, including the *H.145* and *S.136* were less than two years old when they were scuttled and had never had the chance to see action. Many others of this class were still in the process of being built in Germany when the war ended and were scrapped where they lay in the shipyards.

In mid-April, work began on the older 1913 class *S.36*. She was another Jutland veteran, but had only suffered minor damage throughout the whole battle. However, she was to wreak one last defiant act, which nearly caused the end of Cox's dreams of salvaging any more ships from the Flow. The *S.36* was one of those found on her side. Levelling her took four hours of strenuous hand-cranked labour. Sandy Robertson recalled:

> I was there from the end of the destroyers and the start of the big ships ... When lifting the destroyers it was brute strength and stupidity. He [Cox] would say, 'heave twenty' and we all hove twenty. There were six men on a ten-ton winch and when you got to twenty, you could do no more, and that would only bring her up about 2in. There was about a ten-minute rest, while a foreman ran around checking to see if every man had wound the full amount, before you started again.

The *S.36* was raised the final few feet, to be fixed between the two floating docks by 6.00 pm on the still, mild evening of 18 April. By the time she was secured it was too late to tow her into Mill Bay, so she was left fixed between the two salvage docks for the night. To give extra support should the wind increase during the night, most of the equipment, such as a submersible pump used to empty the tanks on the floating dock and various wires and chains, was left connected.

All but the essential workers left the floating docks for the shore. Those who remained on board secured the area and made ready for the *S.36* to begin her final journey as a complete ship. Unlike the bigger German warships, which were mostly coal fired, most of the smaller vessels ran on oil. Righting her before lifting her to the surface disturbed a great deal of the oil, which leaked out of the wreck and floated to the surface in a thick, black slick. Normally the wind and ripples on the sea would have dispersed the sticky, black sludge, but the Flow was relatively calm leaving the oil to cast fluid rainbows across the water as it caught the early evening light.

McKenzie and a diver called Malcolm Carmichael along with a few other men were among those who stayed aboard the floating dock. Before the night shift took over it was customary for the fireman to bank up his furnace ready for the evening, in order to keep all essential machinery running and offer a little warmth for the night crew. The normal procedure was to rake out the red-hot coals on to the floating dock's deck then through a small specially designed aperture where they would be extinguished immediately in cold sea water in a hissing and spitting cloud of steam.

While McKenzie and the others busied themselves, the day shift's fireman aboard *Salvage Dock A* raked out the hot coals and shovelled them into the aperture. The discarded hot ashes hit the water as normal, but did not hiss and spit as expected. Instead, a thunderous roar erupted up and around the dock with explosive force. The fireman turned to see what had happened and was faced with an instant roaring inferno as the oil lake ignited, engulfing the *S.36*, part of *Salvage Dock A* and the water immediately around them. All he could do was turn to the men still aboard and helplessly shout out, 'Look the sea is on fire!'

Within seconds the main powerhouse on *Salvage Dock A* was burning fiercely along with the floating dock's wooden decking, which had been impregnated with creosote over many years.

Unfortunately this dock contained all the explosives and detonators used to blast the wrecks, and the fire was getting dangerously close to the secure room in which they were stored. No amount of safe stowage allowed for protection against the rapidly rising temperature of the surrounding steel.

As the day shift workers approached Lyness Pier they could not fail to see that the docks were now engulfed in a towering plume of black smoke with bright orange flames flicking around and across *Salvage Dock A*. It would take several minutes for the tug to turn around, and longer to get back to the dock, rig up fire-fighting equipment and put out the fire. There was also the possibility that if the explosives got too hot, the dock would explode, taking the *S.36*, the two dock halves and the few men still aboard with it. McKenzie first ordered that all the explosives be removed immediately. He later remarked, 'Had the fire reached the store, there was enough explosive to have blown the whole dock into the air.

While men risked themselves to remove the boxes, McKenzie turned to the suction pump. Within minutes the pump was turned towards the fire and started up. The icy water from within the Flow was sucked up and then forced out of the pump like a horizontal white pillar. The water hit the flames, engulfing the fire and all the boiling deck area surrounding it like a liquid blanket. It took just over three minutes to get the fire under control. In those brief 180 seconds, part of *Salvage Dock A* was reduced to a saturated, smouldering, heat-blistered wreck, which stank of burnt wood, oil and paint.

The rope cores from two of the 9in wires were badly damaged, which meant they had to be replaced before another ship could be raised. Many of the deck planks were badly charred as the impregnated creosote sucked in the flames. Some workshop bulkheads were buckled from the intense heat and the machinery inside them had been badly damaged. The carpenters' workshop was virtually gone and had to be rebuilt by John Scolley and the popular William Tait. The day shift arrived back at the dock and everyone set to work cleaning up the mess. A full assessment of the damage was also needed. Had the few men still aboard the floating dock either not been there or not acted so promptly, Cox's salvage operation would have ended in a ball of fire, only eight months after commencing salvage operations.

Once the *S.36* was dropped as far up the beach in Mill Bay as possible, a full routine survey was made to assess her overall state and financial worth. When the divers reported their findings back to Cox, the reason for the oil leak soon became clear. At the time the *S.36* was scuttled, she was tethered like so many other torpedoboats and destroyers. She was subjected to immense structural stress beyond her construction limits as she capsized and hit the seabed. By the time she had settled, two gaping holes had opened in her hull, one of 11ft and one of 9ft, allowing the oil to pour out once she was disturbed. After the damage to the dock was repaired the business of production-line salvage resumed. Roughly every two weeks, between April and September, a vessel from either the 1913 class or the heavier 1914 class was raised. This amounted to eleven warships.

The two floating docks and the converted *V.70* were working very well as salvage platforms to bring up the smaller ships. But these smaller ships would soon run out, leaving the bigger destroyers, and later on the much larger battleships and battle cruisers. These would need a great deal more support than that represented by the plant machinery Cox already had. To date he had successfully raised and sold eighteen vessels, bringing him about £36,000. After taking out his running costs he still had a handsome sum in hand, which he decided to plough straight back into the business. The move put Cox right back on the bankruptcy line, but he felt absolutely confident he would succeed. Although his smaller docks could lift the bigger destroyers easily, they were on average 70ft shorter than the destroyers they were raising, making towage and stability of the ships very difficult indeed.

Cox's submarine pressure-testing dock, handed over by Germany as war reparations for the scuttled fleet, made up only a fraction of the harbour plant, tugboats and other assorted machinery the Allies were demanding. By the mid-1920s another floating dock was anchored off Sheerness in Kent to add to the Allied reparations for von Reuter's scuttling of the German fleet. Where the previous dock was the biggest in the world for testing submarines, this new one was its equal for lifting whole ships up to 40,000 tons out of the water for maintenance or repair. Being such a colossal size and weight, it was bigger than any vessel Germany then owned, and was ten times more powerful than his first dock.

The new dock was 700ft long and had two 40ft high walls on either side, giving the dock the appearance of a large capital 'U' shape if viewed from the front or back. The dock could be sunk to the seabed by flooding her tanks, which formed her base. Once submerged, a tug could tow a ship over the dock before it was made fast to mooring bollards along the 40ft upper sides. The giant tank spaces were then vented by the dock's powerful pumps before both dock and ship were raised until the bottom platform was above sea level and the ship was completely out of the water. The dock could then be towed easily to anywhere necessary for the ship to be repaired.

'Why,' Cox thought, 'with a little innovation and adaptation, could this bigger dock not be used for lifting sunken ships and bringing them safely and quickly to the scrap metal market?' Most of the larger destroyers were bound for the breaker's yard at Rosyth. Mill Bay was again becoming choked with rusting hulks, but they still had to be dropped somewhere above the high tide mark to be patched and made seaworthy for the journey south. Another application of the larger dock would be to use it as a platform on which to walk around the wreck when she was clear of the water, spot the openings and seal them without having to drop the ship back into the water and work at the mercy of the tides. Thus a ship could be raised and patched in record time at less cost. Just like his theory for righting capsized ships, Cox believed he had another simple, revolutionary idea and, if all went according to plan, he could quickly recoup his second capital outlay.

The dock was made up of six removable sections. The number of sections used at any one time was dependent on the size of the ship that needed to be dry-docked. Each part was so big that they had to be towed to England separately. Cox only needed the main section, which housed all the pumping equipment. The new dock was towed up the River Medway to his Queensborough yard where the main section was refitted for salvage work along similar lines to the first, smaller, floating dock. The remaining five sections were broken up at Queensborough, giving his men there ample work for many months. Once the fitting out was finished the dock was towed out of Queensborough on a high tide in late August 1925 for the ten-day journey to Lyness.

The new dock did need a little customizing in order to turn her into a viable salvage unit. One of the 40ft high walls had a central chunk 30ft wide and 36ft high cut out and removed. This allowed the bow of a raised destroyer to sit neatly on the base of the floating dock with her bow poking through the hole, being supported on all sides. Eight pumps were added, each having a 6in diameter. A 220-volt generator, to supply enough power for lights, smaller plant and other day-to-day running, finished the major alterations. On 27 August 1925 the new dock was towed out of Queensborough by two tugs for the journey to Scapa Flow. The plan for the bigger destroyers was now fully formed.

The letter that prefixes the identification number of each torpedoboat and destroyer, refers to the shipyard that built her. For instance, the 'V' in the *V.70* denotes that she was built by the A. G. Vulcan yard. The bigger destroyers were prefixed with an 'H', referring to Howaldtswerke, Kiel and a 'B' for the Blohm and Voss of Hamburg. The 'S' in the *S.53*, refers to Shickau, Elbing and the 'G' in the *G.103*, stands for Germaniawerft, Kiel.

The *G.103* was the next and bigger destroyer class Cox aimed to raise in the near future. This destroyer type was the second largest built by Germany between 1885 and 1918. The *G.103* had four deck guns instead of the normal three and her six deck-mounted torpedo tubes had a diameter of almost 20in. But best of all she was nearly twice the weight of the smaller 1913 class torpedoboats, so hopefully she would bring in nearly double the revenue for half the work.

Cox's theory for lifting her was as follows: once she was wound up fast within her steel cradle, both the *G.103* and the submarine platforms could be towed by tugs into the submerged dry dock. As the dock was raised, the *G.103* would then become slack in her cradle and the smaller submarine docks could easily be removed, leaving the destroyer on the bottom of the floating dock before being raised high and dry. The dock could then be towed into shallower water where the *G.103* would be quickly pumped and patched before being dropped off, removed and dispatched to Rosyth. The rest of the larger destroyers could then follow the same path.

Meanwhile the men took the opportunity to pack in the overtime during the long summer days, and work double and sometimes even treble shifts to make the money while they could. One chance arose during the lifting of the 1913 class torpedoboat *S.32*, which was delayed for two days by a gale that blew continuously throughout the whole lifting operation. The *S.32* was the thirteenth ship to be salvaged and brought more than just bad luck to the men. Too much metal had piled up on Lyness Pier and had to be cleared to make way for the incoming wrecks. Men and machinery were pushed to

their limits to keep ahead of the mounting workload, which led
to devastating consequences.

Chapter 7

Bigger Ships, Bigger Problems

At 4.00 pm on 20 June 1925, Lyness Pier was abuzz with frantic activity. The tugboat *Sidonian* had arrived from Cox's scrapyard at Queensborough with replacement machinery parts on the previous Tuesday. A steamer was already alongside to load much of the scrap cluttering the pier. The two-day delay in bringing in the *S.32* meant that she docked, ready for processing, late on the Friday evening. Everything was now happening at once and all available men capitalized on the unlimited overtime Cox offered.

One of the busiest operations that hot summer day was around the new crane as it worked incessantly to fill skips on the weighbridge with scrap metal before tipping them into the waiting steamer's hold. Crane driver John Mowat, labourer Donald Henderson, foreman Ernest McKeown and eighteen-year-old Sam Smith had worked eighteen-hour days since the cargo steamer arrived five days earlier. On top of this workload they had all just worked a straight thirty-six-hour shift, without sleep, but planned shortly to have a meal break.

Donald Henderson hooked a skip on to the crane while Sam Smith guided John Mowat with simple hand signals to manoeuvre the 100ft jib from the pier, up, across to the steamer and over its hold. One of the last loads before their break was only 25cwt. Donald Henderson hooked the skip on to the crane and stepped away from the swinging load, Sam Smith was standing on a nearby railway truck watching Henderson closely as he completed the task. When Smith was satisfied that the skip was safely attached, he put his arm in the air and gave a rapid winding motion with his hand, meaning Mowat could now safely lift the skip. As the skip left the ground the crane wire became taut. Mowat turned the jib to face the steamer. Henderson stepped a couple of feet the opposite way from the load as the jib passed over his head.

McKeown was working by the scrap metal dump when he heard a worker shout, 'Oh, it's going!' He turned and saw the 100ft jib falling through the air. At the same moment Sam Smith was watching the jib turning when, without any warning, he saw it snap off its central 'king' post. Smith had to dive off the railway truck as the jib plunged to the ground with an almighty clatter, bouncing and vibrating as it crashed into the granite pier and the railway line running along it. Mowat was also able to jump clear and his first thought was to check the other men who had been with him. He came around the side of the king post and saw Henderson, who had been unable to respond as fast. He was now pinned under the jib with his leg doubled up underneath him and his head pinched between the collapsed crane jib and the railway line.

George Doherty was a cashier for Cox & Danks and had been working in the site office when the crane collapsed; he was also the official first-aid officer. Upon being told of the accident, Doherty ran to the spot to help Henderson. The sight he saw did not give him much hope that the poor labourer was still alive – but after checking Henderson's wrist he did find a weak pulse, which gave all the men much needed encouragement. Within two minutes of the collapse, McKeown had the jib carefully removed by another crane and the local doctor was called. By the time the doctor was found and he arrived at Lyness Pier it was 6.00 pm. An hour had now passed since the accident. Henderson died ten minutes before the doctor reached him, having never regained consciousness. He was twenty-three years old.

The accident stunned everyone. The crane was only eight months old. It had been well maintained and was only lifting a small load, well within its safe operating limit of up to 10 tons. But more tragically, why was Henderson under the jib at the time? A full public inquiry was ordered to find out how such an accident could have happened. If Cox was found to be negligent in some way in causing Henderson's death, he was unlikely to be allowed to continue operating in the Flow. Some of his workers could be at fault – at best they could lose their jobs; at worst they could face a manslaughter charge.

Everyone who was working around the crane that day was called to give evidence. The inquiry opened a fortnight after the accident and was heard in Kirkwall's tiny court on the first floor of the Sheriff's Courthouse with Orkney Sheriff-Substitute, Alfred Martin

Laing, presiding. Kirkwall's Sheriff's Court looks more like a small chapel than a seat of law. A tiny vaulted ceiling hangs over a handful of pine pews where the public is allowed to sit. Pine panelling runs from the floor to a few feet up its walls. Six large elongated clear glass windows allow daylight to stream in and illuminate the court.

McKeown was called first to explain why Henderson was standing clear of the rising skip, but directly under the jib when it collapsed. He stood in the witness box looking up at the Sheriff and the jury who, in Kirkwall's Sheriff's Court to this day, sit elevated above the witnesses and the public. The Sheriff looked down and asked him bluntly, 'Is it not perfectly easy for the man, even if he had to stand there, to stand to the side opposite to that to which the jib is going to swing?'

'It would have been wiser to do so,' replied McKeown looking up in the direction of the question, 'if he had done that he would not have been in the line of the falling jib. One movement a few feet to the right or to the left would have cleared him.' A full investigation showed that although the crane was new, the central bearing holding the jib to the king post had split in half. The pin had in fact been worn down in a matter of months to within only half its safe working diameter of 1in. John Mowat was responsible for oiling the crane and he was now on the stand trying to defend his actions, keep his job and if possible not allow the court to bring a verdict of negligence against himself or Cox & Danks.

Mowat was next to give evidence. Looking and feeling uneasy, he had already explained to the dismayed court how the men had worked a total of about eighty hours out of eighty-six prior to the accident. The Sheriff asked, 'Is it all a matter of money?'

'Yes', Mowat replied without any hesitation, 'we try to make as much as possible.' Mowat had to give a full account of his procedures for oiling the crane. He oiled all the wires daily and lubricated the centre bearing by pouring oil into either side, allowing it to flow through of its own accord. Upon further official inspection it became clear that the oil had not seeped in far enough, causing the spindle to dry out and eventually wear down. The mechanism was shown to the court, including the aperture for pumping grease straight into the spindle. Its grease cup was indeed missing, rendering it useless, but a hole was there for the missing part. Mowat stood in the dock, a little stunned as his fellow colleagues watched him from the church-like pews. Henderson's father, Henry, was among them.

Without a moment's hesitation the Sheriff rammed the point home. 'Did you seriously think,' he shouted at Mowat, 'that pouring oil into the space between the retaining arms and the side of the pulley would be sufficient lubrication?'

'I could see no other way.' Mowat replied uneasily.

The Sheriff then opened up with a barrage of questions fired at Mowat, one after the other, barely giving him time enough to answer. 'Do you seriously consider it's the case that lubrication of that nature is sufficient for a moving article, for an article taking a heavy strain?'

Mowat managed to say, 'No sir, I would not.'

'Did you, when you oiled the bearing, test it to see if there was any weakness?'

'No, sir.'

'Did it not strike you when you found that a method for oiling the bearing wasn't in the place where you looked for it, on the side of the pulley, that there had to be a means of lubricating the spindle somewhere else?'

Mowat snapped back, 'It struck me that it might possibly have been omitted to be drilled. I never noticed the hole at the end of the spindle, until the pulley came down. I know now it's for a pressure grease cup.'

Mowat was asked to stand down. He looked set to take the blame for his friend's death. Factory Inspector John Savage Young on behalf of the Home Office, was next called to the stand. Solicitor Henry Scarth, representing the British General Insurance Company, wanted to know why Henderson was standing under the crane jib at such a potentially dangerous moment. Once Savage Young had taken his place in the dock, Scarth wasted no time. 'Can you give any reason why Henderson should have been standing on the side of the jib in the direction in which it was to be moved instead of on the other side.'

Savage Young confidently replied, 'I don't think there's anything in that. The men instinctively avoid the load – but they don't avoid the derrick because they don't expect the derrick to come down.'

Scarth was not satisfied. 'At the same time there's a chance that the jib might come down on them!'

'Yes, but it's remote. If the crane has been loaded to its full capacity, everyone would have been standing clear. There's nothing in the actual side the man was standing on.'

Scarth backed off. Sheriff-Substitute Laing then rounded on Savage Young to back up his own pet theory that Mowat was to blame for the death. 'Do you not think it was rather inexcusable on the part of a practical man not to see that this was manifestly a grease-lubricated moving part?'

'Perhaps,' Savage Young replied.

'Taking the fact that this was a new crane from a reliable firm it's likely it was pretty close fitting?' suggested Laing.

'Yes. Consequently there would not be much play,' agreed Savage Young.

'Doesn't that irresistibly raise the question in one's mind – there must be some means of lubricating it, and there being no orifice giving direct access through the bush, he would look about for the means of lubrication?' continued Laing.

'Yes,' Savage Young answered.

'Do you not think, taking the material as it has been worn here,' Laing said, pointing at the worn spindle, 'that there must have been some little time at any rate when there was audible and reasonable warning that something was wrong.' He was sure that if he could prove the spindle became noisy and was ignored, especially by Mowat, he would get his man.

'I would have expected that,' replied Savage Young, 'but evidently it hasn't been so. The spindle has been reduced by more than half its thickness. The material of which the spindle is made is rough.'

The Sheriff saw his opening. 'Would that not point to screeching?

Savage Young was unfazed. 'It has been done so well – as if in a turning lathe – that there might have been no noise. All the witnesses say there was no noise.'

Laing had no more questions. All the verbal evidence had been given and the physical evidence presented to the court. The jury of five men and two women retired to deliberate. The verdict could go either way for Mowat, the crane manufacturers or possibly Cox & Danks. Before long the jury reached their decision, which by today's blame-culture standards was a surprise. They concluded, 'So far as the evidence shows, there's no person to whose fault or negligence the accident is attributable.'

On the day the public inquiry took place Cox raised his fourteenth vessel, the 1913 class torpedoboat G.39. She was lying on her side on top of the G.86, which was also on her side, forming a massive steel 'X' on the seabed. Although the impressive wreck formation would have looked complex and dangerous to an outsider, Cox managed with ease to extricate the *G.39* and bring her up to Mill Bay. On the next torpedoboat, the 1913 class *G.36*, he again beat his own record and showed the world and his critics what foresight and experience could achieve. Almost exactly a year before it took about forty-two days to raise the *V.70* from an upright position. The capsized *G.36* was turned, raised and beached in just over seventy-two hours.

Casual manpower continued to be a problem. Unemployed men, including ex-seamen, were attracted to Scapa Flow and its promise of regular well-paid work, from as far away as Devon and Portsmouth. But although well paid, some of the work was too strenuous for some men. Sandy Robertson saw many come and go while he worked for Cox.

> There was no work at the end of the First World War and there was no dole. Men came from all over to work for him [Cox]. Twenty new men started on the first of each month. Most left within two weeks. If you survived two or three months, you were an old hand.

The men who remained each week after the inevitable 'wastage' had given up and gone home, settled into an effective salvage team that was being worked much like a ship's crew. Cox was like their Captain, McKenzie their First Officer and McKeown the Second Mate. The carpenters, divers, electricians and burners were the equivalent of petty officers and the labourers and linesmen were the able seamen equivalent. Most of their living accommodation ashore at Lyness was also divided up according to their equivalent rank or rating, and a similar marine discipline existed, but not as strict as aboard a Royal Navy vessel. However, as with any ship, 'Everyone carried on and you kept your head down,' recalled Sandy Robertson. With time the men gained more experience and some ventured to put their ideas to Cox when he was considering another engineering problem. He had the same reply for every suggestion, 'Quite a good idea, Sonny, but we'll try it my way first'. Sandy spent most of his working life in Scapa Flow, spending five years as a linesman for Cox & Danks before going on to be a diver during the Second World War. Altogether he spent thirty years salvaging wrecks.

Cox and his men had recovered eighteen warships by the time the new dock arrived, amounting to more than 12,000 tons of high-grade scrap. The last of the smaller torpedoboats of the 1913 class was

V.78. She capsized completely before hitting the seabed and came to rest with all her superstructures, funnels and masts crushed into the mud. Divers had to blow channels underneath her with compressed air lines to allow the wires to pass through. Then the usual procedure of towing her out into deeper water was followed, and after six tidal movements she was high and dry and ready for breaking. Everything was now in place to put Cox's theoretical plan into action to lift the first of the bigger destroyers, the *G.103*.

Once again, sound common sense and previous experience told Cox and his men that the bigger ships could be raised to the same formula as the smaller ones. And even the same righting techniques would work. If he was lucky, raising the larger destroyers would clear his remaining debt and he would be in a position to tackle the bigger battleships and battle cruisers where the real money was to be made. The *G.103* was located, prepared and winched up between the two submarine floating docks just like the smaller vessels. The massive new floating dock section was then sunk to the bed of the Flow to allow the tugs to tow the smaller docks – with the destroyer inside – into it, as Cox had planned. He calculated that there was just enough clearance to fit one dock inside the other. Then, just as the tugs got the smaller dock part way over the sunken platform, all the theoretical calculations became useless. The tugs just did not have enough control in such a tight working space.

In its present form the new floating dock proved useless, but Cox hoped that drastic modification might still save the day. He was still convinced that to sink the platform to the bottom and raise the *G.103* out above the water was the answer. If space was the only obstacle, then simply create more by loading the destroyer on to the platform sideways, secure it there by wires and then lift as normal. The big dock was towed back to Mill Bay where the end wall was cut off and made watertight. The new L-shaped dock was again towed out to the *G.103* site for the sideways lift and sunk to the seabed. After all, although one wall was now missing, the massive lifting tanks were still very much in place. The destroyer was lifted on to the platform without a problem. Nine-inch wires were used to secure it to the lifting platform by running them from its base plates, around the vessel, and firmly securing them to the dock's mooring bollards along its one remaining wall. The modified dock, with the *G.103* secured to her side, was vented and both ship and dock left the seabed as planned. The L-shaped platform continued to rise steadily as she brought up the *G.103* – for a short while at least.

The plan to increase the overall buoyancy did little to maintain the dock's overall stability. It began tilting just enough for the *G.103* to slip slightly and again throw out all Cox's calculations for a smooth ascent. The sliding action caused the dock to lurch a little more. Cox knew what would happen next. He ordered the dock to be sunk fast before the *G.103* could slip off altogether and cause untold destruction. Before the order could be carried out, the destroyer slid further. The dock was only a short way from the seabed and the sliding action drove it down so sharply that its underside struck some submerged rocks, ripping open several buoyancy tanks and rendering them and the dock instantly useless. The new dock and the *G.103* went to the bottom like two stones in a rock pool, amid a mass of bubbling water and fine, white spray.

Cox's reason for using a bigger platform was because he did not believe his original submarine floating docks had the power to support the bigger ships for towing across the Flow. The new dock now lay useless on the seabed. He could not afford an alternative so he was forced to use what he already had or face defeat. But the bigger destroyers were 312ft long and the old submarine docks were only 240ft long. What of the unknown and untested quantities of instability, cost and danger of working the docks way beyond their design capabilities? Perhaps they, too, would end up wrecked on the seabed. With no more money to invest in new ideas, none of which he had anyway, Cox would just have to have a go and find out what the submarine docks could take.

For the third time he set out to capture the *G.103*. Cox moored the two submarine platforms above the destroyer, resetting the wires between the two platforms and running them under the sunken vessel in a standard cradle format. As the docks were towed down Gutter Sound, Cox realized that his previous fears were groundless. The smaller docks were more than capable of maintaining stability with their much larger charge. On 30 September 1925 she was dropped high up on the beach next to the other ships and was patched up ready for delivery to Rosyth. However, a few months later an event took place that nullified all the hard work and ingenuity ploughed into the *G.103*, and Cox never saw a penny from all the cost and labour he had invested in her recovery.

Just before midday on 25 November 1925 the small tugboat *Audax II* was towing the *G.103* on the long journey to Rosyth. Captain Angus Hulse aboard made good time at a steady 8kts for the rest of the day. But as night fell the weather changed. At first the wind increased before gradually turning into a horizontal blizzard. The wind kept shifting direction and Hulse tried repeatedly to alter his course in order to head into the storm and lessen the wave impact against the destroyer. During these many course changes, and with waves breaking over the *G.103*, the storm knocked out the tugboat's navigation lights. In the dark there was nothing to see except the two towing lines groaning and straining as they tried to hold on to her. Just after midnight the wind shifted again and as Hulse tried to turn into the new position, both steel lines parted with explosive force and the *G.103* disappeared into the darkness.

Hulse cruised around in the storm hoping to find her again, but due to the wind, snow and absence of navigation lights, all his attempts were futile and he made for the shelter of nearby Aberdeen. Just after daybreak the residents of the tiny Scottish town of Rosehearty in Aberdeenshire woke to see the rusting hulk dashed on the rocks about a mile from their town. But the power of the storm had taken its toll and even though the *G.103* was a solidly-built warship designed to take direct shell hits, the violent seas had torn her in half. Once in two pieces, the storm threw one end alongside the other, giving the impression from the sea that two vessels rather than one had foundered. Recovery was impossible and Cox had to write off more than £2,000 of revenue, let alone the salvage costs he had worked so hard to earn.

The last five remaining destroyers were the heaviest and longest of the many classes the German navy operated. These were the experimental *Torpedobootzerstörer* (torpedoboat destroyer) class. One, the *V.100* had even been converted to carry a seaplane. They were 321ft long, more than 230 tons heavier than the *G.103*, and more than 50ft longer than the two ex-submarine floating docks. With no other alternative available, Cox had to use these two smaller docks. The *B.112* was also lying on her side and was the first to be attempted. On 11 February 1926, 150 men wound her up on the half ebb tide. Many years later when worker Jim Southerland was raising bigger ships in Scapa Flow, he fondly recalled what life was like lifting the destroyers with brute force:

One thing I should say about those days was that it did not matter if you got the heavy end of the ship, you had to do your twenty all the same. The same thing happens now. Some men have an easy job and some have a hard one, but still all have to carry on. You get no sympathy.

To make the most of the rising tide, the operation had to be carried out at night under floodlights and powerful searchlights, which lit up the outward breath of the 150 men like a small fog. Over the next three days the *B.112* was edged closer and closer to the beach until she finally arrived. She was then prepared for the journey to Rosyth. The remaining four *Torpedobootzerstörers* were also raised without any difficulties. The last destroyer was the *G.103*'s sister ship, the *G.104*, which like so many other destroyers was lying on her side. She was the twenty-sixth and last destroyer Cox raised in Scapa Flow, all having been salvaged in less than two years. Altogether sixteen were broken up in Mill Bay and ten were shipped to Rosyth. Cox finally had the money he needed to invest in bringing up the bigger ships, and the salvage experience he thought necessary to achieve it, when another obstacle was put in his way.

The day after Cox raised the *G.104* the Trades Union Congress called the notorious 1926 General Strike of all transport and railway workers, dockers, steel and iron workers, printers, and of course coal miners. Their joint action effectively paralyzed the country. However, the General Strike lasted only nine days before the TUC gave in, fearing militant factions in these industries might gain too much power. The coal miners fought on for many more months. The price of coal increased dramatically – a swift action that would bite deep into Cox's hard-earned profits. He needed 200 tons of coal a week to run all his plant and coal soared from £1 to £4.15d per ton, more than trebling his fuel bill to a price he simply could not afford. As the miners' revolt dragged on, Prime Minister Stanley Baldwin's Conservative Government instituted coal rationing under the Board of Trade's Emergency Regulations 1926. This specified that a commercial business could only have 50 per cent of the average weekly quantity consumed over a four-week period. Now, even if Cox could afford the coal, he would only be allowed half the amount he needed.

Without coal, all the ingenuity and manpower in the world would be useless. He had overcome every obstacle and would not be beaten by lack of fuel. It is a credit to Cox that throughout the General Strike not one of his men walked out, although they were facing far more hardship than many other manual labourers involved in the strike. Cox pondered the fuel problem like so many others he had encountered since entering the Flow, and formed a plan.

The 25,000-ton battle cruiser *Seydlitz* was lying on her port side in about 70ft of water, however, she was more than 100ft wide, meaning some 30ft still lay well above the high-water line. From previous surveys, he knew exactly where her coalbunkers were located and hopefully, he reasoned, she should have been carrying enough coal for her day-to-day running before being scuttled. If he was lucky, the coal would be dry as well. He ordered a section of the armour plating in her side to be cut open with an oxy-acetylene burner at the exact point at which the coal was supposed to be located. Her bunkers were full and the coal was dry. Grabs were soon above the hole. Cox was able to feed all his tugs and machinery with free German coal and thereby continue to raise German ships until long after the General Strike ended in October 1926, when personal hardship forced the strikers back to work. Cox & Danks was one of the only coal-reliant businesses to keep working at full capacity during those dark days.

There was now nothing to stop him going after the biggest and most lucrative warship of the Imperial High Seas Fleet, the *Hindenburg*. She was the scrap metal equivalent of a gold mine. Cox knew that if it cost as much as £30,000 to bring her to the breaker's yard, he could still make a good profit on his investment. Her total scrap value was estimated at £75,000. He would be clear of debt, well in profit and in a perfect position to raise the other ships to make a scrap metal killing.

Fire, storms, death, the General Strike and competition from Robertson had all threatened to finish his salvage operation and had all had failed to stop him. Ironically the first ship Cox raised, the *V.70*, greatly helped in raising the last destroyer, the *G.104*, bringing to an end a busy couple of years. Some of his men said he only kept the *V.70* for good luck. The tugboats *Sidonian*, *Ferrodanks* and the smaller *Lyness* all worked together to bring the *G.104* into Mill Bay on 19 May 1926. As they steamed slowly towards the beach, all the tugboats were flying bunting and blowing their whistles to celebrate the twenty-sixth and final destroyer to be brought to Lyness. All hands were in high spirits and cheered her arrival with 'refreshments' from their boss. Luck had played a massive contributing part in Cox's success. Self-confidence in his abilities and those of his men were at an all-time high and the real work was about to begin. But he was a little sad to see the end of the torpedoboats and destroyers and all they had taught him. 'I'm sorry there were not more of them,' he said. 'They were just beginning to pay nicely.'

Chapter 8

Coming Alive

The *Hindenburg* was the third and last battle cruiser of the *Derfflinger* class. This class was a complete departure from the standard German warship design and superseded anything British naval architects were then building. Until the class was commissioned, all German capital ships (meaning the most important warships in a navy with the heaviest firepower and armour) had their deck guns staggered from port to starboard along the main deck. The *Hindenburg* and her two sister ships, the *Lutzow* and the *Derfflinger*, were the first modern warships of the German fleet to have their guns centralized down the amidships line. Diagonally placed gun turrets created much more difficulty when concentrating fire ahead or astern. Placing all main guns along the centre line gave a far wider arc of fire right around the ship without obstruction.

The internal subdivision and overall armour plating aboard the *Derfflinger* class were also greater than any warship then in German service, which contributed greatly to the *Hindenburg*'s salvage value. She was nearly 700ft long, 96ft wide, drew 28ft and weighed 28,000 tons. Her eight main 12in guns were racked in pairs and were the biggest of their kind in the Imperial High Seas Fleet. A further fourteen smaller secondary guns, eight light guns and four 20in submerged torpedo tubes completed her firepower. Of the three *Derfflinger* class ships, the *Hindenburg* was by far the fastest with a top speed of nearly 27kts. At a speed of 10kts she had a range of 9,000 nautical miles.

But the *Hindenburg* did not go into service until 1917, nearly a year after Jutland. Her combat career consisted of two failed minor operations in the upper and western North Sea. Her next mission was into internment at Scapa Flow. Just two years after her commission, this devastating war machine went to the bottom of the sea at the hands of her own crew, without ever firing a shot. The German Government spent more than £2m. building her. In 1917 this amount had the same buying power as nearly £75m. today, which was roughly enough to put three divisions or about 30,000 extra German troops on the Western Front.

The *Hindenburg* settled upright on the seabed in 70ft of water. She was so big that her bridge, funnels and two masts were still above water. Her armour plating alone was a foot thick amidships, ranging like a steel belt right around her, tapering down to 4in at her bow and stern. Much of her interior was a rich cocktail of brass, phosphor bronze and rare alloys, which were then all in short supply. Every porthole was open and many of the glasses were smashed. All hatches, vents, sea cocks and just about every other opening in her hull and superstructure, including lavatory wastes, were either severed or jammed open when she was scuttled. Apart from her scrap value, if Cox succeeded in raising her she would be the biggest ship ever to be salvaged.

But a closer inspection revealed a problem that would affect the *Hindenburg*'s commercial value. It was a problem Cox had seen before. Every single piece of phosphor bronze, brass, copper and alloy of value above the low-water line had been stripped by the locals long ago. Even some rivets had been taken out of her hull plating. A local reporter noted, 'Many of the islanders are descendants of the Old Norse freebooters and the old habit still seems to cling!' After the *V.70* fiasco it is unlikely Cox was surprised when his divers reported back the bad news. But she was a big ship and luckily most of her wealth still lay below the low-tide line, well beyond the freebooters' reach.

The next problem was purely one of engineering. If the technology did not yet exist to raise such a massive vessel, how was he to succeed? Any ideas that came close to solving the *Hindenburg* problem were still in the realms of theory. The fundamental difference between a warship and a merchant ship is that the former is built as many different watertight compartments while the latter is not, as this would impede cargo stowage and handling. In theory, the more watertight compartments a ship has, the greater the chance to remain afloat, keep fighting or limp back to port. Cox decided to capitalize on this design feature for the complete opposite of what it was intended to achieve. Instead of sealing flooded compartments for control and stability he would instead vent them

71

under controlled conditions and thus bring her up, hopefully in a stable attitude.

Two ideas to raise the *Hindenburg* were discussed. One was to enlarge his idea of supporting a wreck in a steel wire cradle, supplemented with camels. Another suggestion was to freeze over all the openings then pump the internal water out, forcing her to rise. Both ideas were riddled with logistical problems and Cox rejected them both.

Another consideration was that the *Hindenburg* was far too big to be broken up at Lyness. She would have to be towed to Rosyth and this would be impossible if she was strung between four pontoons, supported by a few camels, or with rapidly melting ice covering her many openings. The ice theory almost bordered on the quack methods touched on earlier, but again, the idea of using air to replace the water was realistic. McKenzie recalled:

A thorough survey was, of course, the first proceeding. This was carried out by our best divers, and I made a good many descents myself to clear up some doubtful points. A meeting was held after the divers' reports were received, and it was decided, in salvage parlance to make a 'pumping job' of her.

This literally meant that all the water now weighing her down on the seabed would be removed, which amounted to roughly the 28,000 tons she would displace if afloat, thus giving the *Hindenburg* back her original buoyancy. The salvage work was further complicated because many of the valves and openings were located on the bottom of the ship, which was now pressing into the seabed. Other openings could only be reached from inside her, which was a dark and dangerous situation for anyone to work in on a day-to-day basis, and would take special skill, nerve and emotional control to complete.

Eight hundred patches were needed to make the *Hindenburg* watertight and ready for pumping. The outer holes were mostly normal porthole size, needing a patch about 18in by 18in for safe cover. The diver would make a template of the hole. This was the best method because the working conditions and poor light precluded any chance of accurate measurements. Once the mock-up was made, usually out of thin plywood, a stronger version in metal was copied ashore in the workshops on Lyness Pier. Two holes were then drilled and tapped to make a solid thread on the right and left sides of the plate. But however smooth the fit between the *Hindenburg*'s steel hull and the metal patches, the immense pumping pressure would still force the air and water through the joint; enough to prevent her coming off the seabed.

To overcome this a 'pudding joint' was used for each fitting, which acts similarly to a modern-day gasket in a car engine. Where a gasket prevents oil being forced through joints under the extreme pressure generated when an engine is running, the pudding joint would do the same for escaping air. First, a canvas strip is tightly packed with loose fibres from old rope called oakum to a width of about $3\frac{1}{2}$in by about $2\frac{1}{2}$in. It is then secured lightly around the edges of the metal plate resembling a sausage-like pudding. The patch is then placed over the hole, and corresponding holes are pneumatically drilled or punched through the ship's hull, deep enough to secure the plate. 'We sometimes had a gun, which fired a hardened bullet-like projectile threaded on the upper end,' recalled Sandy Robertson. 'The idea was to pierce the hull plate deep enough for the bolt, but if you used too much charge, it shot right through!' The pierced hole made by the compressed air gun used a pressure of about 100lb/in^2, self-threading itself as the bolt penetrated the ship's side.

The tool was called a 'Cox submerged bolt-driving and punching gun' or 'Cox gun' for short. The name is purely coincidental and bears no connection whatsoever with Ernest Cox. The gun weighed a hefty 36lb and had to be supported on a thin steel wire from above for a diver to accurately and repeatedly fire the bolts into the steel plate. Each bolt was made from a heat-treated alloy steel; much harder than the plate it was penetrating. The bolts were then wound tight, compressing the pudding joint from 3in to about $\frac{1}{2}$in to create a watertight fixing. The joint was then smeared all over with tallow to further waterproof the fixing once it had set hard. The Cox gun had many other applications. Salvers used them to fire a bolt through a loose rivet in order to tighten it instantly or to pin eye bolts, steps, brackets or anything else that needed to be effectively pinned to a submerged ship, like a giant stapler.

Twelve divers took more than three months to complete the process, methodically working in pairs from the *Hindenburg*'s bow to her stern so as not to miss any opening – sometimes in dark, freezing water. The biggest patch was 850ft^2, weighed 11 tons and was made to cover a gaping hole where a funnel once stood.

The patch was made from wood reinforced with 12in by 6in steel 'H' beams. The structure was so big it had to be made in Lyness and brought out by tug, lowered using a crane over the massive hole and fixed in place.

Working inside the *Hindenburg* was a wholly different matter. Some of the bottom valves were too inaccessible even for these divers, so to cover them, a quick-drying cement called *'ciment fondu'* was pumped over a large area around each bottom valve to completely smother it. *Ciment fondu* was first patented in 1908 and is an extremely versatile substance. It acts like normal cement, but without the limiting effects of cold, damp or lengthy drying times. After twenty-four hours, the substance is as hard as normal cement is after twenty-eight days because it dries chemically rather than through water evaporation. It is ideally suited for marine salvage work due to its resistance to the corrosive action of sea water.

Seven years on the seabed enabled a vast quantity of silt, decaying debris, oil and coal dust to settle like a thick oily carpet throughout the ship. Sending divers blindly into such a hostile environment with no direction as to where to find anything amid the maze of pitch-black steel decks and rooms, let alone the key valve points for closure, would have been suicide. However, they were about to get their first lucky break. McKenzie said:

> We were fortunate about this time to discover some plans of the ship in the control room, including the one we wanted more than anything else at the moment, a plan showing the piping arrangement of the whole ship. This was certainly a gift from the gods.

The gift proved to be even greater when upon cleaning the plans, which were etched on to sheets of non-ferrous metal, they not only showed the ship's piping arrangement, but also the control points for each valve. The plan allowed two pairs of Cox's most experienced divers to descend into the *Hindenburg* and be directed to the exact location where a valve needed to be sealed. Stocky, fair-haired dive leader Bill Peterson and his partner Nobby Hall were chosen for the job.

Although the divers now knew exactly where the valves were located, every time they made the slightest movement, the silt was so heavily disturbed that no light from their submersible lamps could penetrate its inky blackness and they had to wait for the silt to settle back down again before moving on. If the lights did manage to give some dull foggy glow, they often shorted out, 'Just when they were most required' remembered McKenzie. Consequently one diver stayed in a section – finding each valve by touch – while his partner stayed outside the compartment in case something went wrong. The dive partner did have submersible lighting, but all too often he, too, had to work by touch and memory instead of relying on the inadequate lighting system.

Still, with all their experience, safety precautions and guiding plans, the underwater environment of a sunken warship was never to be taken for granted. Hall was the first diver Cox had employed when he began salvage operations in 1924. Peterson had entered the engine room area to seal some openings while Hall remained just outside to ensure his colleague's air and lifeline did not get snagged. Peterson began to work his way slowly down a wooden engine room ladder in complete darkness. As he stepped clear of the ladder he felt a rush of water go past him and a dull thud above his head – the diver's slow, but deliberate movements had caused the ladder's rusty fittings to snap off. In an instant the ladder regained its buoyancy and shot up through the hatchway from where he had just climbed down. The wooden ladder now separated the two divers and was jammed tightly in place by its own natural buoyancy. The result was that Peterson's air line and lifeline were trapped somewhere up above his head. He knew he only had about five minutes of air left before he slowly suffocated 70ft below the surface deep inside a rotting warship.

Hall knew what had happened, but he could not move the ladder. At the point at which most people would panic and die, screaming and fighting for rapidly depleting air, the two men's training and professionalism took over. Peterson shut his air valve, which meant he would naturally rise upwards as air was still being pumped into his suit from a compressor on the surface. As he ascended, Peterson felt above his head until he reached the ladder. Hall carefully felt for Peterson's air line, which luckily was only partially flattened and not severed. He worked it free and violently shoved the ladder from above with his heavily weighted boot, freeing it long enough for Peterson to keep rising clear before turning on his air supply and breathing freely once more. The whole incident took less than a few minutes, and both men were very lucky to escape unhurt. By the time they were ready to surface, both their air and lifelines had become inextricably tangled, meaning both men had to be brought up together. Once they were up and safely aboard the dive boat, one of their colleagues, who had no idea of the drama said, 'You two been havin' a dance down there?'

Due to the *Hindenburg*'s immense size, Cox's two submarine floating docks were used as well as the new dry dock section, which had been successfully refloated after sinking while trying to lift the *G.103*. The platforms were then towed out to the *Hindenburg* and held in place around her by no less than sixteen anchors. Access between the floating docks and the ship was gained using a length of flimsy rope and wooden footbridges, which tended to sway violently with the slightest movement. Finally, two of the previously raised destroyers were anchored at right angles in front of the *Hindenburg* to act as two massive floating breakwaters should the weather deteriorate. Once she was up, the *Hindenburg* would be secured between the sections for towing to Lyness before final preparation for Rosyth.

The sequence of pumping her out had to be carefully considered. Cox used more than half a dozen 12in centrifugal pumps and a dozen 6in submersible pumps, which were placed mostly around her fore end, to be lowered down through the bow as the water-level receded. Keeping the *Hindenburg* stable while in ascent was crucial to the success of the salvage. To ensure the stability of such a mass, Cox planned to raise the bow first, keeping the stern firmly on the seabed. The soundings around her showed that she was sitting on shingle so, as the bow rose, the stern would dig into the bottom and maintain an even ascent until enough water had been removed to lift the stern evenly to the surface.

On 13 August 1926, after pumping out 3,600 tons of water an hour, the bow came alive, meaning it was clear of the seabed and in ascent. This was the key moment in the salvage operation when the operators began to take control of a wreck. Later that same day her bow was above water while her stern sat squarely on the seabed as planned. As the water-level in the *Hindenburg*'s hull dropped, other places needed to be found for the suction pipes. The divers lashed back all doors above the water-line so the water could drain back to the stern, taking the pressure off the hull as the water began to flow aft.

Had the *Hindenburg* risen bow first with water trapped in the amidships section, too much pressure could have broken her back and thus she would have been worthless for scrap. After water was released from a central compartment, workers entered the space and found another door tightly closed. After prizing the door open, they entered a room that had been completely protected from the inrush of water when the *Hindenburg* sank seven years before. Everything was intact. Even the paint on the walls and ceiling was as fresh as the day she was scuttled. The room had frozen in time an eerie impression of those desperate men who fled their ship as she went to the bottom.

Very few people have been privileged enough to see the inside of a sunken warship. Local Orkney photographer William Hourston was commissioned by *The Times* to get inside the wreck and photograph such a rare view for its readers. He was able to descend five decks into her murky interior, and with only flashlight powder and magnesium ribbon Hourston positioned his bulky camera to take a stunning series of pictures with only a candle to light his way within the steel maze. Hourston's fascination drew him deeper into the ship, taking pictures as the icy sea water constantly dripped from the deck heads. When Hourston decided to leave, he realized his candle had burnt down to only about half an inch – not enough to light his path all the way back to the main deck. Moments later the candle flickered and went out.

As the last orange ember died on the wick and the smell of acrid smoke reached his nose, Hourston knew he was in trouble. 'Why didn't he take more candles?' he thought. As his eyes adjusted to the darkness, Hourston could just make out a dim spot of light, up in the distance. Trying to carry his heavy camera on his back, Hourston kept his nerve and felt his path back towards the light. It was a way out to safety. He was saved from being trapped inside the sunken ship, which could have flooded again at any moment. Although he had fulfilled his commission for *The Times*, they wanted more pictures. The next time he ventured into the *Hindenburg*, Hourston made sure he had a much bigger supply of candles and matches. And – should they fail – like a character in a child's story book, he took a ball of string which he tied at the deck opening and unravelled as he descended again deep into the *Hindenburg*'s dark and eerie interior.

Although the pumps were working at full capacity, the *Hindenburg* was not coming up fast enough. Something was wrong. Cox knew he had covered every aspect of her controlled ascent and according to his calculations she should be coming up faster. There was no other alternative but to lower her again and check for any missing holes. Divers were sent down to see if any patches had been missed or if anything had drastically altered since pumping began. What they found led to another innovation in salvage practice.

The divers discovered many tiny leaks in the pudding joints. Further observation showed that for no apparent reason all the tallow had gone. McKenzie said:

Small fish [called saithe from the cod family] had eaten every particle off the patches and there were small leaks everywhere. This was a bit of a problem, as I realized that if the fish had eaten the tallow once, they would certainly do it again. We solved the problem by mixing a small percentage of Portland cement with the tallow, which made it too indigestible for the fish. So we had no more tallow eaten and incidentally discovered a new compound for sealing up small leaks. Tallow mixed with cement in proportions of one part cement to ten parts tallow, sets very much harder under water than does the pure tallow.

Once the new cement compound was added and set, pumping began again. Everything was now going to plan. She was coming up by the bow and her stern was holding on the seabed to keep her trim. But when the bow was afloat she developed an alarming port list and the stern refused to come alive. The more water Cox pumped out, the more the list grew until it reached more than 37°. If she continued listing, she would capsize and recovery of the vessel would certainly be lost. Divers were sent down, hopeful of finding a simple explanation for the problem, but to no avail. Cox was under pressure to find answers.

'I've called up the divers. They say the bottom seems intact,' said Cox.

'We've got to stop pumping,' replied McKenzie. 'She'll roll over.' They were losing the fight. She was now at 40°. A few more minutes and it would be too late.

'Stop pumping', shouted Cox, 'and let her down.'

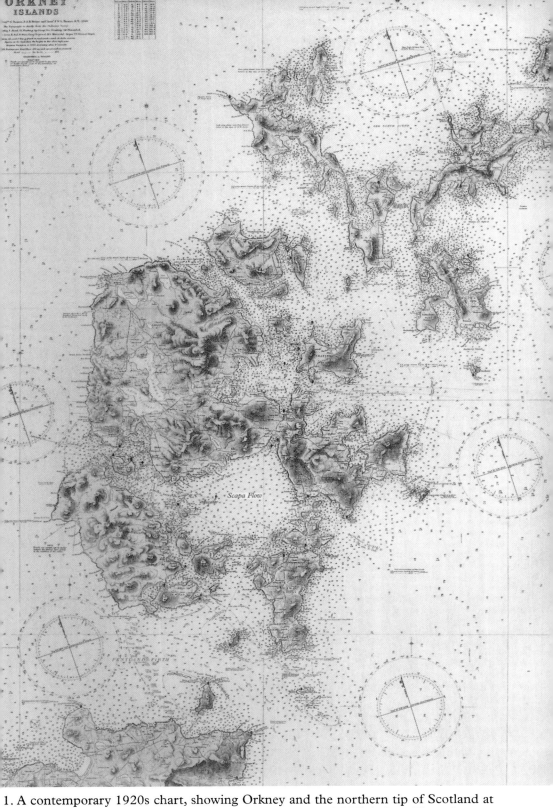

1. A contemporary 1920s chart, showing Orkney and the northern tip of Scotland at the time Cox undertook to salvage the German Imperial High Seas Fleet. Scapa Flow is in the centre of the main island group.

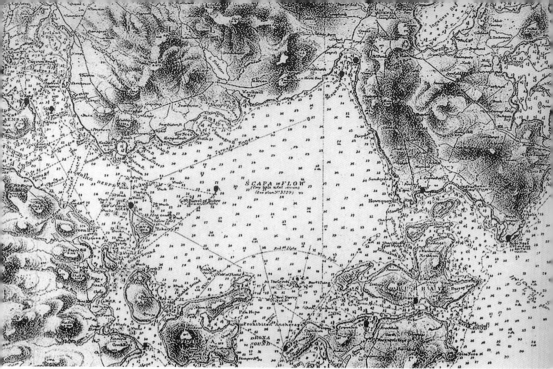

2. Detail of an Admiralty chart, showing Scapa Flow and the surrounding Orkney islands. This chart was updated in 1924 when Cox began salvage operations and shows the positions of the many wrecks he raised. Lyness, on the island of Hoy, where Cox based his salvage operations is far left.

3. The German Imperial High Seas Fleet interned in Scapa after the armistice in November 1918. Vice Admiral Ludwig von Reuter ordered their crews to scuttle all seventy-four vessels rather than hand them over to the Royal Navy. Here a Royal Navy guard threatens a destroyer captain at gunpoint to stop him from sinking his vessel. Altogether nine unarmed German sailors were killed and fourteen injured when the Royal Navy shot them, making these victims the last casualties of the First World War.

4. Ernest Cox poses for a London photographer, immaculately dressed as always, even when at work in the filth and squalor of a sunken warship. He later said, 'Without boasting, I do not think there is another man in the world who could have tackled the same job. Before I undertook this formidable task, I had never raised a ship in my life. Quite frankly, experts thought me crazy, but to me these vessels represented nothing more than so much scrap of brass, gunmetal, Bronze, steel etc., and I was determined to recover this at all costs.'

5. Looking down a line of winches aboard one of Cox's floating docks. The winches can be seen clearly in the foreground where teams of men literally heaved a sunken warship to the surface. The technique became known as 'heaving twenties' because the men could only turn their handles twenty times before needing a rest.

6. A raised destroyer between the floating docks during the 1920s, having just been dropped in Mill Bay. Smit Salvage of Rotterdam used a similar method nearly eighty years later to raise the Russian nuclear submarine, *Kursk*, in 2001.

7. Aboard Smit's barge, used to raise the *Kursk*, the cable lifting equipment is very similar to that used by Cox to raise the *V.70*, except that here the winches are mounted centrally, rather than on either side of a sunken vessel.

8. Two beached destroyers waiting to be broken up in Mill Bay. It took about one month to reduce them to scrap metal. Each ship was methodically stripped down to allow the vessel to float further up the beach on the next high tide to be further broken up until nothing was left.

9. Lyness Pier as it was in the 1920s when the salvage operations were well under way. Mill Bay, where the vessels were broken up, is on the right and Ore Bay is to the left. The large crane that killed Donald Henderson is in the centre.

10. All the German warships salvaged in Scapa Flow met the same fate. Sometimes their armour plate was as much as 12in thick and was a great source of revenue. Here a burner cuts the armour plate into convenient chunks to fit into a furnace. Behind him are propeller blades, which were also a highly prized commodity from the wrecks.

11. 'Lyness Pier 24/6/25.' This picture is dated four days after Henderson was killed when a 100ft jib collapsed on top of him. The crowds of men on the pier are preparing to attend his funeral. Loose wires can still be seen hanging down from where the jib once stood. Cox's white pinnace is moored alongside. She was named *Bunts*, after his daughter, and no doubt conveyed him to Lyness Pier for the funeral.

12. Sandy Robertson (*right*) working as a diver's assistant to Sinclair (Sinc) Mackenzie, standing on the ladder. Sandy helped save Sinc's life after an accident on the *Von de Tann* as well as that of Thomas McKenzie. Sinc Mackenzie was the last diver to detect life aboard the doomed submarine HMS *Thetis* in 1939.

13. Sandy Robertson in January 2004 at the age of ninety-four. He worked for Ernest Cox for five years and still lives in his home overlooking Lyness Pier where he has been since 1927.

14. Cox's Senior Salvage Officer, Thomas McKenzie, talking to a diver by telephone. McKenzie was a fully trained diver himself and had some salvage experience before working in Scapa Flow.

15. Local Orkney photographer William Hourston was commissioned by *The Times* to take a series of photographs inside the sunken *Hindenburg*. He went into her murky interior by candlelight and took this picture inside one of her many casemate gun turrets with only flashlight powder and a magnesium ribbon. Hourston miscalculated how long his candlelight would last and barely made it back to safety.

16. The *Hindenburg* heeling over to starboard on the first attempt at raising her in
1926. Jenny Jack, Cox's wife, is standing centre, facing the camera. A storm is
beginning to blow up that eventually led to Cox losing the fight to raise her – this
time.

17. The storm that sank the *Hindenburg* on the first attempt to raise her in 1926 as the
waves lashed the men and vessels trying to keep her afloat. Cox's floating dock was
holed, his pumps had failed and his men were exhausted, but still he fought the
storm to hold on to his ship.

18. 'Cutting up *Moltke*. A burner at work.' With no Health and Safety regulations, the burner, with a cigarette in his mouth, cuts up the battle cruiser with an oxy-acetylene torch. He was breaking no rules in the 1920s as he stripped away metal to lighten her for the voyage to Rosyth.

19. The capsized *Moltke* en route to Rosyth, surrounded by tugs. Through a misunderstanding two pilots were appointed to guide her to the dry dock. An argument over who should command her led to the *Moltke* being cast off as she headed for the Forth Bridge's central pillar, completely unassisted. The temporary housing for men and machines while on the journey was built on the ship's bottom, which was now her top.

20. Ernest Cox, immaculately dressed as always, looking very pleased as he stands on the bottom of a salvaged warship.

21. A 'runner crew' of eleven to fourteen men took the salvaged vessels the 270 miles from Scapa Flow to Rosyth. In good conditions they could play cricket on board, but they also weathered some terrifying gales.

22. The *Seydlitz* weathering the storm that struck while she was being towed to Rosyth. She arrived there despite the loss of both equipment and supplies in the raging seas.

23. The *Seydlitz* in her dry dock, ready for breaking up. A sad end for a battle cruiser that survived the Battle of Jutland and got back safely to Germany in spite of damage from twenty-three direct shell hits and a torpedo strike.

24. The 24,000-ton upturned battleship *Kaiser* shortly after breaking the surface in March 1929. Men had to gain access to the sunken warships' hulls through airlocks. The four airlocks needed to enter and prepare the *Kaiser* can be clearly seen here, looking more like ships' funnels. In order to reach a sunken ship, some of Cox's crudely built airlocks were 60ft high.

25. Jim Southerland climbs down an airlock on his way to work. The hatch was closed behind him and he climbed down to the bottom hatch, knocking on it to let the men inside her know that he was there. The airlock was then pressurized to equal the air pressure inside the compartment, and Jim would climb through for his eight-hour shift.

26. The fast minelayer *Bremse* was one of the ships that the Royal Navy tried to save when the fleet was scuttled; to no avail. She ended up like this, capsized and partially beached in Swanbister Bay on the main Orkney island of Pomona.

27. After finally beating the *Hindenburg*'s stubborn attempt to be salvaged, the most powerful tug in the world at the time, *Seefalke*, leads the raised *Hindenburg* into Rosyth on a perfect summer's day in 1930.

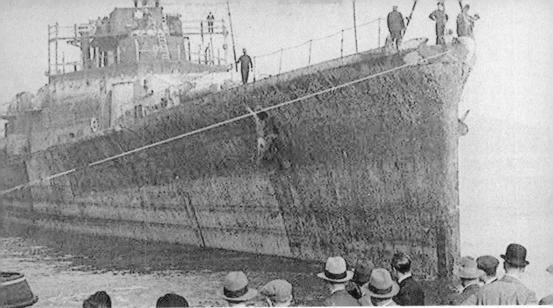

28. Filmed by a Pathé news crew, Ernest Cox stands on the *Hindenburg*'s bridge (*far right*) along with his wife Jenny Jack and daughter, Bunty. Cox had proved all the salvage experts wrong and the crowds on the quay were there to witness his triumphal docking.

29. The runner crew aboard the *Prinzregent Luitpold* pose for a picture in front of the corrugated iron kitchen named the Hotel Metropole, built on the upturned hull. Their sense of humour could be seen everywhere. The mess and bunkhouse were the Apartments de Luxe. The notice to the left reads 'Honeymoons arranged, spring mattresses fitted with speedometers. First aid equipment in all rooms. Second class rooms no spring mattresses.' The menu on the right reads, 'Boiled Luitpold with knobs on', 'Scapa salvage stew' with 'dock broth'. Reporter James Lewthwaite of the *Daily Mail* is in the centre of the back row.

30. Adolph Hitler came to power a few months before the *Von der Tann* was towed to Rosyth. The Nazi Swastika flies over the tugboat *Parnass* on the *Von der Tann*'s starboard side. Many sightseers were in Rosyth to see Cox deliver his last salvaged German warship. They were also among the first to see this Nazi emblem in British waters, which six years later would be a common symbol of evil throughout the free world.

31. Thomas McKenzie working at his desk, probably aboard the salvage vessel *Bertha*, after Cox left Scapa Flow and Metal Industries took over. In June 1939 McKenzie led a team of salvage divers to help rescue ninety-nine submariners trapped aboard the sunken submarine HMS *Thetis*, which ended in tragedy after his offer of help was accepted too late. When the Second World War began, like many of the Scapa Flow team, McKenzie worked for the Admiralty Salvage Department, which distinguished itself during the Battle of the Atlantic and from D-Day onwards in Northern Europe. He was eventually awarded the CBE and CB for his work.

Cox gave the order to transfer several pumps to the stern, believing that perhaps the shingle was too soft thus causing her port list. A few days later, pumps were relocated at the stern and pumping continued to bring up both ends simultaneously in a bid to cancel the list. Over the next few days Cox raised her by bow and stern, separately and together, many times, as he tried in vain to find a sound engineering reason for the list. McKenzie thought that perhaps a watertight bulkhead had collapsed in the ship due to the immense weight of the water mass.

'The damned ship is heavier on the port side,' Cox snapped in his usual gruff manner, 'and that's all there's to it.' Cox began to wonder if the stern might actually be resting on rock in just that one place, so each time she came up, all 28,000 tons of her would be balancing on only a 3ft wide keel. Trying to support a ship nearly 100ft across at its widest point, instead of digging into the seabed, might be causing an imbalance, toppling her over every time her rising critical mass became too great. As the weather began to deteriorate another idea was tried.

The *Hindenburg* was lashed by the foremast to one of the 1,000-ton destroyers beached at Cava island about three-quarters of a mile away towards the *Hindenburg*'s starboard side. The destroyer was partly pumped full of water and acted like a giant counterweight, exerting about 200 tons of purchase while the *Hindenburg* was in ascent. A second wire was run to another destroyer on her starboard side as an extra precaution. Cox was convinced that the increasing list fighting against the two opposing forces would now make her come up on an even keel.

Around mid-afternoon on 2 September 1926, a cry rang out on the floating dock. 'She's rising.' The *Hindenburg* was, indeed, slowly creeping up, and on an even keel. Almost an hour later the barnacle encrusted after deck was above water with her glistening marker buoy now bouncing around. Diver Harry Hall rowed out to the rising deck, jumped aboard and hoisted a Red Ensign on the *Hindenburg*'s ensign staff. Jenny Jack, and Bunty, who was now eighteen years old, both stood by Cox as he watched the *Hindenburg* rise out of the water. Bunty leaned across and kissed her father, 'For luck,' she said. Without warning, the wire leading to the sunken Cava wreck parted like a piece of cotton. In the next moment the *Hindenburg* developed another 25° port list. Cox's luck, like his ideas, was running out fast and he was now desperate not to allow the *Hindenburg's* stubborn attempt to remain on the seabed beat him again.

To make matters worse, the weather began to deteriorate further. Within fifteen minutes a strong wind began blowing down from the north-west, but the two destroyers-come-breakwaters offered some protection. Rain was now lashing horizontally across the floating docks, which started rocking in the sudden swell, and strings of lights went black as the power failed. The sky grew darker as the wind drove the rain harder. The *Hindenburg* was by now rolling so violently that one of her derricks, some 2ft in diameter and 30ft high, snapped off and crashed across her decks. Like a demented King Lear cursing the storm-ridden sky and his own ill fortune Cox refused to part with his half-raised prize and all the money she now owed him. He knew that raising her under such conditions was now impossible, but if he could just keep her up as far as she was, perhaps they could progress once the storm subsided.

Cox drove his men on in appalling conditions as he tried in vain to capture his battle cruiser. Still the storm sneered at him. During the night all the diving boats were carried away by the storm. They were replaceable, but the floating dock had also been badly damaged when one of the destroyers, the *G.38*, was no longer protecting the salvage operation from the gale. The makeshift breakwater was blown hard on to the end of *Floating Dock A*, and the constant storm-driven pounding was so severe that several plates on the dock burst open. As the water flooded into the dock, its main boiler gave out, leading to the failure of the whole pumping system. Water started rushing back into the *Hindenburg's* hull, helped considerably when one of her larger patches collapsed. Still Cox would not give up the fight.

He ordered the *Ferrodanks* to come alongside so that her generators could supply power to his pumps and keep the *Hindenburg*, at least, above water. For all the power the *Ferrodanks* could raise, it still was not enough. Cox and his men laboured all through the night, fighting against the continuing storm to secure her. His vital power supply had been knocked out. The *Ferrodanks* simply could not muster enough steam to keep up the necessary air volume. The *Hindenburg* was sinking, and *Salvage Dock A* was badly damaged. As the *Ferrodanks* squeezed every last burst of steam out of her boilers, Cox stared powerlessly through the driving rain as the black, rusty hulk slipped slowly away from him.

Cold and wet, mentally and physically exhausted, he was forced to shout the three words he dreaded having to utter, 'Let her down.' Like switching off a life support machine, the crew of the *Ferrodanks* knew it was the right choice under the circumstances, but felt considerable grief for Cox's loss. They reluctantly obeyed their boss who could be seen staring into the dim light as the *Hindenburg* disappeared into the blackness for the fourth time in seven years.

Chapter 9

Balancing Billiard Balls

One contemporary writer said that controlling the constantly shifting compressed air, steel and water to successfully raise a capsized ship carried the same odds as balancing three billiard balls on top of each other – basically impossible. Place an empty glass face down in a bowl of water. Press it to the bottom with your finger, then release it. The glass will shoot to the surface, right itself, then plummet to the bottom as the trapped air surges out and the water pours in. Cox had to metaphorically find a way to remove his finger and have the glass rise slowly, evenly and sit nicely floating on the surface without trying to self-correct through massive air loss.

As far back as 1880 the London Wrecking Company considered using compressed air to raise the 6,800-ton German warship *Grosser Kurfurst*. She had collided with another warship in the English Channel two years earlier and went down with more than 260 of her officers and men still aboard. But the London Wrecking Company went out of business before their revolutionary method could be tested.

Nearly forty years later, Royal Navy salvage officer Captain Fredrick Young used compressed air to raise the 2,600-ton British submarine *K.13*, which foundered in January 1917, instantly drowning thirty-one of her seventy-six-man crew in the Gareloch, near Greenock, Scotland. The *K.13* accidentally sank while on her last sea trial operation before Admiralty acceptance. The K boats soon developed a bad reputation throughout the Royal Navy when 'K' became synonymous with 'killer' after so many of these steam-driven submarines were lost or suffered accidental damage.

During the First World War, the 16,350-ton dreadnought HMS *Britannia* had just returned to her anchorage in the Firth of Forth after a North Sea sweep. A heavy squall soon blew up and she was thrown on to the island of Inchkieth. All normal towing methods failed to free her until Young employed compressed air and the *Britannia* was saved. But being a submarine the *K.13* was already an airtight steel tube and the *Britannia* was only towed off rocks, so the experts confidently held to their opinion that compressed air played no real part in the future of commercial salvage practice.

On a sultry August night in 1916, Tarranto Harbour in Italy became as day for a few moments when the 23,000-ton battleship *Leonardo da Vinci* exploded, capsized and sank after a concealed enemy bomb detonated in one of her ammunition magazines. The Italian Government decided that the £4m. pride of their navy must be raised and refitted. Salvage officers General Ferranti and Major Gianelli of the Italian Naval Engineering Corps led a team of men in an to attempt to raise her using compressed air. They spent many months practising with scale models to see exactly how she would react to many different scenarios. Eventually, in early 1919, the *Leonardo da Vinci* was successfully raised. Going one stage further, Gianelli completely righted her under controlled conditions for an attempted refit. This eventually failed and she was scrapped. Cox recalled:

> The Italian who had lifted this boat came to Scapa to see my own work, and as I gave him freely all the information I could, he was courteous enough to give me in return full information regarding his work. Unfortunately, however, it misled me. Not because it was inferior, but because the circumstances were essentially different.

Indeed they were. The *Leonardo da Vinci* was down in only 36ft of water with a slight 8° list. Such a small amount would, and did, automatically correct itself while in ascent. Her whole superstructure had sunk into the deep mud and was completely intact.

The next ship Cox targeted was the battle cruiser *Moltke*, which was one of the oldest warships in the Imperial High Seas Fleet. She took part in all offensives mounted by Germany and suffered four direct hits at Jutland. The *Moltke* was the only German warship to visit the United States when she steamed into New York in June 1912. Her final resting place was just off the island of Cava in an area notorious for its strong currents. Unlike the *Leonardo da Vinci*, a preliminary diving survey concluded that the *Moltke*'s masts and funnels were buckled and, due to her immense weight, the after bridge was crushed flat when she, too, capsized and hit the seabed almost upside down. They would all have to be blasted free before she could be raised. The *Moltke*'s list, combined with her bow settling much higher than her stern, made her a particularly uneven platform on which to achieve an even ascent. Still, her awkward landing position did allow the divers easy access, enabling them to blast off the buckled funnels and masts and just about anything else that might hinder her coming alive.

Straight away the problems began. Finding and covering her external vents, torpedo tubes and side valves should have proved much easier than aboard the *Hindenburg*. Aboard the *Moltke* they were nearly all facing upwards, not buried in the seabed. But six years under water had allowed a massive seaweed forest to grow. Each plant was as tall as a man and each stem was as thick as his wrist. Divers began using their knives to cut the weed away, but eventually axes were needed to hack it off and expose the open apertures.

Sealing her for raising followed the same routine as for the *Hindenburg*. The smaller openings were filled with wooden plugs, which were hammered in tightly and allowed to expand as they absorbed the sea water. Larger holes were covered with steel-coated pudding joints and smeared with McKenzie's special Portland-cement-and-tallow-mix. The larger holes were filled with *ciment fondu*, but unlike the *Hindenburg*, the *Moltke*'s sea valves were left untouched. At first there was no apparent reason for this, and without their blocking she would never come up. For Cox, this was a perfectly natural decision to make.

Somehow the compressed air had to be delivered into the ship. Cutting holes into her solid bottom plates, which now faced upwards, would have been both arduous and costly, and perhaps too ineffective for removing enough water, as their placing would have been partly based on guesswork. Cox thought to himself, 'Why should I plate over perfectly adequate holes – only to once again cut several more to do the job?' Instead, air pipes were embedded into the bottom valve openings with *ciment fondu*. Once this had hardened, the pipes were run up to the tugboat *Sidonian* and connected to three powerful compressors, which could pump 300,000ft^3 of air into her hull every twenty-four hours.

After 'getting the first pound on', which was the term for the moment when the air pressure began to force the water down, pumping continued non-stop for ten days to generate enough pressure to squeeze the water back out. By the eleventh day her bow was almost 7ft above the water-line. Suddenly a bubbling air mass escaped rapidly from under her bow sections and her port list increased to 33°. Just like the glass, the 24,000-ton mass was now shooting to the surface, trying to expel air. Cox shouted through his megaphone to cease pumping. She had to settle back down before any more of the 3m.ft³ of compressed air now inside her was lost. The *Moltke* was becoming 'common', which meant that the compressed air was freely moving between each section without any internal control. Naturally the compressed air headed for the highest and lightest part of the ship, which in most cases is the bow.

Cox was certain that parts of the ship were heavier than others, 'probably', he thought, 'due to the positioning of the internal machinery'. But how could he keep her trim while in ascent and maintain a balanced compressed airflow within the hull if certain areas weighed more than others? The common air mass had to be divided and regulated to correct the discrepancy. Returning to the glass scenario, divide the glass into sections and pump more air into some parts than others, depending on weight distribution, and it should float to the top without the entire air mass fighting to escape.

The only answer was for men to work inside the *Moltke*'s hull in a compressed air environment, but first he had to find the bulkheads. With no copy of the ship's plans available, Cox used a pre-war edition of *Jane's Fighting Ships* to locate roughly where the main bulkheads were. Three were chosen for sealing up. Once this approach was agreed upon two more problems arose; how to pump in enough air to lower the water without raising the *Moltke*'s bow, and then how to physically get the men inside her to seal each bulkhead section.

To solve the first of these problems Cox's men would have to find every single aperture in the chosen bulkheads and seal them to allow different air pressures in different sections. It was a massive undertaking and the work was far too intricate and dangerous for divers to carry out. To use an electric kettle as an example, once the pressure reaches a set point it will release that pressure through its whistle. Cox decided to use a similar method. A control valve (similar to the valve on a diver's helmet) was fitted to the *Moltke*'s bow. A man was posted near the valve throughout the working day to release the pressure as and when necessary. The method allowed for more air to be pumped in, but as the increased air was about to raise the bow, the valve was vented in a controlled manner to prevent it from leaving the seabed. The result was that more air, but not enough to raise her, could reach the stern. A quantity of water was then removed, but not enough to make her go into ascent. This process is called 'negative buoyancy' because the ship is emptied of enough water to work in, but not enough to come alive or achieve positive buoyancy and trigger an ascent. The system was repeatedly tested and was found to be very efficient indeed. Once a breathable atmosphere was created, it was time to deal with the second problem; how to get the men inside.

The only way for the men to get in was through an airlock, and the most suitable place for it to be located was on the fore end, which was just high enough above the water to test the method. The airlock was made in Lyness, taken out to the *Moltke* on the *Sidonian* and lowered into place by the tug's outriggers and chains. Cox recalled:

> The airlock, which we fastened to the *Moltke* was the first with which I had anything to do, although the device is quite simple and has been in use for seventy or eighty years. It was very crude, but worked quite satisfactorily.

Cox's airlocks were crude. They were made out of old boilers with the ends cut off, 6ft in diameter and 12ft long. The sections were bolted together and then bolted to the ship's bottom.

To protect the flimsy structure from wind and tide the airlock was secured with dozens of stays like a tall, thin radio mast. A worker entered, shut the upper hatch, then turned a valve allowing compressed air to rush into the sealed tube equal to the environment he was about to enter. He then climbed down a ladder, opened the inner hatch and moved freely within. The process was reversed upon leaving to return to a normal atmospheric environment and an outside ladder allowed for easy access to a waiting boat.

The most difficult operation was to breach the hull. The men were not sure about having to cut into her bottom plating in such a confined space. McKenzie took part in the first airlock operation:

> As soon as the torch pierced the hull, dense volumes of evil-smelling acrid smoke came up into the airlock and became denser, and the atmosphere more foul every moment, in spite of

the fact that compressors were continually pumping in fresh air. To give the men confidence, I went into the airlock with a burner while one of them cut the first hole. I shall never forget the experience! By the time he had cut the first hole we could scarcely see each other, and by the time we had climbed out of the airlock, we were nearly suffocated.

From then until the last airlock was placed on the last ship Cox raised, smoke helmets were always worn.

Finally, after the acrid smoke had cleared, the first men to board the *Moltke* for almost six years climbed gingerly into her dark and stinking hull. Their initial job was to survey the interior and string lights along every main passageway the workers would use. The lights also acted as a warning signal to get out, should they be seen to flash rapidly. The first problem they encountered was the placing of the airlock. It was 50ft away from its proposed location. Walking such a short distance above ground is nothing for most healthy people, but in an upside-down warship sitting on the seabed, this oversight meant a long walk in a hostile environment.

Cox decided to fix another airlock. This second one was assembled at his works in Queensborough, but had to be longer as its base would be below the water-line. The airlock was lowered into place in the same way as before, but the divers had to secure angle plates on the ship's bottom for it to slot into. This was no easy job because the airlock had to be lowered from a crane in the October winds. Once secured, and the trapped water blown out, divers wearing smoke helmets were able to breach the hull without the risk of suffocation.

When the men finally got to the engine room, they found little to show that the *Moltke* had once been a cutting-edge warship. Most of the internal damage they saw occurred when the *Moltke* capsized. Heavy machinery had torn away and plunged to the ceiling, which now rested on the seabed. Her heavily laden coal boilers had also broken free and split open, spilling their contents all over the engine room compartment. Her bilge oil had escaped from her bottom plates, which were now her ceiling (or deck head), and mixed with the coal dust to form a thick, stinking slime. The filthy sludge had coated everything as the water level receded. In the crew accommodation personal effects still lay scattered amid the debris. Clothing, photographs, books and even money were still in drawers and lockers, showing that the German seamen really did leave in a hurry. Many bottles of good quality wine were also found. In an officer's cabin, his spring mattress had fallen off his bunk and was lying on the ceiling in the upturned world and a bed blanket was hanging out of a drawer, still in very good condition. Many German chocolate bars were found and even after four years, at a time before sell-by dates, they were still perfectly edible. Several cat-o'-nine tails were also recovered and have often been attributed to barbaric punishment. They were, in fact, used only to beat officers' uniforms clean.

Working within a sunken ship was dangerous and as McKenzie once said:

> If a man is unwilling to try or if he is nervous, he is not dismissed. There's no medical examination, but there was a doctor at Longhope, and the men can be examined at the firm's expense if they wish it.

Once the lights were put in place, each burning an equivalent of 100-candle power, they threw out eerie shadows and patterns in the upside-down world.

Work was well underway by mid-February 1927, clearing as much metal as possible and sealing the three chosen bulkheads. They were easily identified by a double row of rivets running from side to side on both sides of the bulkhead. All the holes were plugged and stopped. Every pipe that ran between the bulkheads had to be cut on either side and a wooden plug smeared with red lead putty and hammered in. Some areas were more than 300ft^2 and had to be shuttered and pumped with *ciment fondu*. Some of the rubber door seals had also perished after six years in salt water. Other doors had buckled as the water poured in and had to be removed, then shuttered, and concrete used to fill the gap. Sandy Robertson recalled:

> The main thing was the cables going through the bulkhead. The Germans were economical and all the cables went through at one point. They were sheared off flush with the bulkhead, punched back and a cement box was placed over the hole.

The box acted like shuttering and was filled with *ciment fondu* to permanently seal the opening.

Foul air was a constant problem. Fumes built up as the oxy-acetylene flame consumed much of the available fresh air in order to maintain its more than 3,000° heat. One worker became badly gassed and another was slightly affected. Lighting a match solved the problem. When a new compartment was entered, if a match burnt brightly they would carry on working. If the match immediately died, they knew they had to leave and request fresh air to be pumped back in. McKenzie was deep inside the *Moltke* with twenty other men who were busily filling and plugging gaps. He and a few others were right aft at the furthest point from an airlock preparing the engine room bulkhead. They all noticed that the lights were beginning to look hazy, as if a fog was forming in the compartment. McKenzie knew the fog-like effect meant the compressed air was starting to expand and vaporize. Before they could act, the bow shot upwards as the air at the stern rushed to the fore end, causing an instant 20° list. Pressure was being lost somewhere and this meant the ship was sinking slowly with all hands trapped below decks.

He instructed everyone to down tools and make for the nearest airlocks just as the internal lights began to flicker rapidly, signalling abandon ship! Then the lights went out, instantly plunging the men into total darkness. McKenzie remembered:

> We shouted to the men to make for the airlock and as soon as all had been warned, made for it ourselves. The angle of the ship began to alter quickly, and the air rushed forward. To reach the airlock, we had to pass through doors little bigger than manholes, which we had cut in each of the bulkheads between us, and the airlock. The air was rushing through these holes with the force of a hurricane. Our hats were blown off. Our jackets were blown over our heads and flapped wildly around us. Pieces of rust and coal stung our faces as we forced our way forward. The men scrambled wildly along from one compartment to another towards the airlock. My first impression was that something had gone wrong with the airlock and we were as good as lost.

It looked as though they were about to drown like trapped oil-coated seabirds in the rising black sludge. McKenzie slipped. Another man fell on top of him in the rush to get out. Then the lights spluttered back on and although they were all still trapped, seeing their way gave the men monumental relief. As they ran for the hatch, McKenzie noticed that the air was rushing past them away from the airlock instead of towards it. He realized the airlock could not have failed. If it had, the air would have been rushing towards them – not away from them. The men entered the airlock and climbed like madmen being chased by wild animals. McKenzie continued:

> We went up and arrived safely on top, a rather grimy and scared crowd. The little incidents which happened on the wild scramble to the airlock have caused many a smile once they were all safe, but it was very far from being a laughing matter at the time.

Human error had been responsible for the near death of twenty men. The worker attending the bow release valve had misunderstood an order and shut it by mistake, preventing the free flow of air that was keeping the *Moltke* level. By shutting the valve the worker prevented any form of release, so the air forced the bow upwards violently in a bid to escape its prison and vent back into the vast expanse of Scapa Flow.

In the unpredictable salvage business, problems tended to come from completely unexpected directions. An influenza outbreak developed among Cox's men, inevitably spread by their having to work in such close confines. Some of the cases were serious, but even with many workers laid off, the remaining workforce still managed to work steadily towards raising the *Moltke*. By the end of March 1927 all compartments were watertight and plans were made to lift her by the bow and stern independently before the main lift was scheduled to begin. Cox had certainly mastered control over the airflow, but every time she was raised at either end the 33° port list came back, and doggedly refused to leave. She had to be sunk again. He sifted his ideas with his usual pragmatic approach and eventually hit on one he felt would certainly work. Why not utilize the *Moltke*'s own ballast tanks? They were built to trim her while afloat. Although she was now submerged and upside-down, there was no scientific reason why they could not still do their job.

Air was pumped into the starboard side as before, but this time water was allowed to rush into the port side tanks and bunker areas to counter the list. As an added precaution, Cox had nearly two-dozen 9in cables shackled to gun turrets and other strong points aboard the *Moltke*'s bow section and pinned aboard the floating docks. They were used to steady her ascent rather than take any significant load. The combined pontoon, wires and flooded starboard ballast tanks, as well as a little control from the bow release valve, should be more than enough to keep the *Moltke* trim as she came up. In early June 1927 she again came alive and began to rise. Cox and his men relentlessly checked every piece of equipment to ensure no strain was too great on any given part. Everything was going to plan. As the *Moltke* rose yet higher the men felt proud that all their work over the past nine months was now finally paying off. She was alive, trim and coming up well.

The slow, rhythmic harmony of generators and compressors doing their job was suddenly interrupted by a dull thud somewhere under the water. At the same time a new vibration rumbled through the floating dock as one of the steel support wires went limp. She was listing again. A second wire went limp. If Cox did not act fast, too many of the wires would part and she would be lost. Being far bigger and heavier than a torpedoboat or destroyer, she would drop like a stone and possibly come to rest in a completely irrecoverable position. He immediately ordered the remaining cables to be slackened off and for her to be re-sunk while he still had control. All his instincts said that the combined wires, pontoons and on-board ballast trimming should have been enough. But something must have been missed. The wires parting just did not make sense. Divers were sent down to investigate and they found that the wires were straining right where the *Moltke*'s deck met her hull. This was by no means a sharp point, but under a 24,000-ton load the normal blunt right angle acted like a wire cutter, snipping the 9in steel wires like fine thread. It was then simply a matter of protecting each wire at the point of contact with a flat steel plate. Two new wires were re-threaded and a final survey was carried out before lifting was resumed.

On 10 June 1927 air had been pumped into the *Moltke* for many hours, but there was still no sign of her breaking the surface. By lunch-time some men had knocked off for the day while others sat eating their lunch. While the pumping continued, a few workers carried out their duties around the floating docks. Without any warning there was a sudden rush of water and the stern reared up out of the sea, groaning like a sea monster with long tendrils of seaweed flailing in the summer breeze. 'She's up!' someone shouted.

Every man stopped what he was doing and rushed out to see the spectacle as the stern settled about 20ft above the swirling white water. By 3.00 pm she was resting with her bow still below the surface.

There was never any way to control the speed of ascent once a ship, under the influence of compressed air, went from negative to positive buoyancy. The wrecks would always start rising slowly and gradually gain speed as the compressed air fought to expand, only to find it could not. Sometimes it was only a matter of minutes from leaving the seabed to breaking the surface.

To give some indication of where a wreck was below the surface, a thin wire was fixed to the ship's bottom with a marker buoy located roughly every 10ft up from the hull. When the first buoy broke the surface, someone would shout, 'Ship's coming.' The next buoy would break the surface, then the next, until the hulk was up followed by a great deal of air bubbling out from underneath as the internal compressed air rushed to match the surrounding ambient air pressure. The speed of the ascending *Moltke* took everyone by surprise.

The Orkney ferry, SS *Countess of Cadogan* steamed close to the *Moltke* to give her passengers a closer look at the upturned hulk. Ever the opportunist, Cox hailed the ferry to approach and allowed its passengers to walk around the upturned hulk and ask questions. The publicity stunt worked well. A few days later, the spontaneous visit received comprehensive coverage including photographs in the local newspaper *The Orcadian*.

Some patches still had to be made before the bow could be brought up. The following Saturday she was well above water with only a slight 2° list. The *Moltke* was captured and secured. She then had to be towed inshore to the tiny island of Cava. The plan was to extract enough metal to lighten the hulk for towing alongside Lyness Pier where she would be further stripped before her final voyage to Rosyth.

Another improvisation in the process was to gut the *G.38*, which had previously been used as a breakwater for the failed *Hindenburg* attempt. She was used as a small freighter to carry the stripped metal from the *Moltke* site across to Lyness Pier for processing. The *Moltke* was then towed the short distance to Lyness Pier where sixteen openings, 6ft by 7½ft wide were cut into her hull at key points. More than 3,000 tons of her non-ferrous metal was removed before she was finally sold to the Alloa Shipbreaking Company. In preparation for her towing to Rosyth the following spring, the open hatches were plated over when Cox could not profitably extract any more scrap and towing bollards were added. A machine room was also built on the bottom of the vessel to house and protect the three compressors needed to maintain a constant internal air pressure for the journey.

Finally, at midday on 8 May 1928 the *Moltke* began her last journey, stern first and completely upside down. Ironically, three German tugs, the *Seefalke*, the *Simson* and the *Posen* assisted by Cox's own vessel the *Sidonian*, towed the *Moltke* out of Scapa Flow, through Cantic Sound, into the Pentland Firth, and eventually out into the open North Sea with her 'runner crew' aboard. At first the tidal conditions in the Firth meant the *Moltke* 'walloped' violently until the tide turned, but the men found a mascot to give them hope. No sooner had they left Lyness than a rat appeared in the crew cabin on her upturned hull.

'No rat stays on a sinking craft,' said one worker. For the rest of the voyage the rat frequently appeared at meal times for its ration and became a much-loved rodent. Four days later the *Moltke* entered the Firth of Forth near Edinburgh. Cox radioed ahead for an Admiralty pilot to board with him so he would not miss his triumphant arrival. As they drew alongside, Cox was amazed to see another pilot already commanding the *Seefalke*'s bridge. The German captain had naturally accepted the first pilot who hailed him as he entered the Firth of Forth, which happened to be a Firth pilot. Once appointed he could not be removed until the job was done. However, Cox had already contracted an Admiralty pilot to do the job, but failed to tell his German tug master. A ridiculous situation occurred where neither pilot could leave the bridge nor share command.

During the heated discussion that ensued, a sudden chorus of whistles and horns went up from the other tugs. The *Moltke* was being dragged by the ebb tide towards the Forth Bridge's central pillar. Both pilots forgot their petty grievance and ordered all tug lines to be released. Moments later the *Moltke* went broadside, just missing the pillar as the tugs steamed past the other side. The 24,000-ton hulk continued its journey – unassisted, in a busy shipping lane and completely out of control. It took the tugs more than half an hour to regain control. By then she was near enough to the Admiralty dock for Cox to sign off the German tugs, thus solving his pilot problem, leaving the *Ferrodanks* to manoeuvre the *Moltke* into the dry dock.

Nine gruelling months were spent raising the *Moltke*. Thirty men were needed, working eight hours a day inside the ship in pressures of between 15lb and 22lb/in^2 patching her up. Six divers worked six hours a day in pressures of 35lb/in^2 securing her from the outside. She had repeatedly tried to escape, but Cox had countered her every attempt and now she was just outside the Admiralty dry dock. No one had ever lifted such a ship before or towed it so far upside down, lost it en route and got it back. But there were still five more tense hours left trying to secure her without damaging the Admiralty dry dock.

Most of the time was spent shouting strained orders through his megaphone as the *Moltke* continued to defy him to the bitter end. Through a slow, patient technique called 'inching', she was literally coaxed inch by inch to her final resting place while Cox raced against a falling tide and the wind's constantly changing direction, her lower superstructure about to dig into the bottom of the dock with only 6in of clearance. Cox had proved that perhaps it was possible to balance three billiard balls on top of one another after all. He had gambled and won his first major prize in the Flow. Once he was sure the *Moltke* was secure, Cox yelled with relief and flung his megaphone high into the air.

Chapter 10

Seydlitz

The 26,000-ton battle cruiser *Seydlitz* was the flagship of Rear Admiral Franz von Hipper's First Reconnaissance Group. She is notorious for having led an eight-ship group, including the *Moltke*, to attack British east coast defences. By 8.25 am, on the quiet morning of 16 December 1914, the battle group was less than 4,000yds off the coast. In a little more than one hour they had rained shells down on Hartlepool, Scarborough and Whitby in one fell swoop. Unfortunately a number of the armour-piercing shells had time delay fuses. They bounced off the batteries only to explode in the towns, killing, maiming and separating children from their parents.

Within forty-five minutes 1,150 shells pounded the British coast, killing 112 people and wounding 200 more. Not since 1667 had British residents been killed on home soil by enemy naval gunfire when the Dutch navyentered the Medway, blazing a trail of destruction in its wake to within 20 miles of London. Nearly 300 years later, the German naval attack greatly embarrassed the British Government. Whitehall fought back with the only weapon they had left – propaganda. The attacks were called the 'baby killer raids' or the attack of the 'Scarborough bandits'. The Germans' battle approach was labelled, 'butcher and bolt' tactics. As they were fortified towns, Berlin called the raids a legitimate act of war, especially as the shore-side guns retaliated. When the dust had settled over the north-east coast, and in Whitehall, the British victory of words far outweighed the strategic gain made by the German navy.

The *Seydlitz* has the most distinguished combat history of any German warship of the time. In January 1915, during the Battle of Dogger Bank, an armour-piercing shell tore through her stern gun turret, igniting sixty-two complete charges. More than 160 of her officers and crew were killed. Her surviving complement managed to save their ship and after months of repair she was ready to fight again. During another German coastal attack on Yarmouth the following year, the *Seydlitz* hit a mine and was again badly damaged. At Jutland she survived twenty-three direct shell hits and one torpedo fired from a British destroyer, the most any German ship sustained during the campaign. During this onslaught the *Seydlitz* still managed to hit the British battle cruiser HMS *Queen Mary*, which was bigger and heavier than her German adversary. The 27,000-ton *Queen Mary* eventually disintegrated under fire and only nine personnel survived out of a full complement of 1,285 men. By then many of the *Seydlitz*'s crew were already dead or injured and her decks were ablaze, but she still managed to steam back home to Germany – backwards, due to severe damage in her bow section. When she arrived home, the *Seydlitz* had taken on more than 5,000 tons of water and was very close to going down. Apart from brilliant seamanship, her stubborn refusal to sink was directly due to her internal and external structure, which made her the toughest warship in the Imperial High Seas Fleet.

The *Seydlitz* was an improved version of the *Moltke*. She was 46ft longer and 3½ft narrower, making her much faster. But her greatest asset was an enhanced hull design, especially in her internal subdivisions, which were much stronger than on previous German warships. Capital ships of any nation are a fine balance between speed, armoured protection and firepower. At the turn of the twentieth century, German shipbuilding philosophy centred on sacrificing some armament and speed to make their ships tougher, their argument being that it was easier to repair a damaged warship rather than build a new one. The *Seydlitz* was the epitome of this ideal. Some Royal Navy capital ships exploded after only four hits.

As Hipper's flagship, the *Seydlitz*'s last mission was to lead the German fleet into internment at Scapa Flow. Seven years after her humiliating and ignominious end at the hands of her own crew, she was the property of Messrs Cox & Danks Limited, who were about to capitalize on German shipbuilding philosophy and plunder her for their own commercial ends. By the late 1920s the embodiment of German naval architecture was nothing more than a giant rusting hulk, often mistaken for an island, and was a notorious shipping hazard. With part of her hull above water it was inevitable that the locals would steal her valuable scrap offering right down to the water-line. There was so much to remove that the thieves rowed out to the wreck, temporarily sank their boat, and lived aboard her for many days while they selected the most valuable pieces for exporting back down south.

The large volume of scrap metal already piling up on Lyness Pier was also attracting attention. Cox's own workers were told they could buy, at a reasonable price, anything they wanted from the wrecks, but still the temptation to just take things was too strong for some. One labourer helped himself to a vice, claiming that his employers 'could charge for this vice between two shillings and sixpence and five shillings, whereas if it went for scrap they might only get a few pence'. The court was not impressed. The labourer lost his job and was fined 20 shillings or ten days in prison. Captain Angus Hulse's tugboat crew were caught trying to sell scrap brass in Aberdeen, including two ship's whistles that they stole in Lyness. After being arrested and held in custody, six out of his eight-man crew were 'escorted north' and tried at Kirkwall Sheriff's Court. Some were fined while others received a twenty-five day prison sentence. After these two trials no more scrap metal was known to have gone missing.

Raising the *Seydlitz* presented some of the more unusual engineering problems to face Cox and his men. If a vessel was upright they would adopt the pumping-out method. If she were nearly or completely capsized they would opt for a compressed air lift. Although she was still resting 70ft below the surface, with part of her hull above the water, it was not possible to either turn her to an upright position or completely upside down to effect a normal salvage procedure. The usual process of elimination and enhancement took over like a reflex action as Cox formulated a sound engineering plan. Should it work, he would achieve another great salvage first – he would lift the *Seydlitz* sideways. Once she was up, he would go one stage further and tow her in that position through the North Sea to Rosyth.

Some men said that the plan was madness and fraught with danger. A few of his workers confronted him. 'Safe as houses, Sonny, safe as houses,' Cox jauntily replied. 'We won't touch anything while you're down there.' Some were still genuinely afraid. Sandy Robertson remembers working inside the *Seydlitz* a little differently, 'We were scared for our bloody lives working inside her.' McKenzie also had his doubts, but the plan did have some sound engineering merits. And Cox had an uncanny ability to achieve the impossible. The men nicknamed her 'Seidlitz Powder'; the 'morning after powder' as it was more fondly known was a 1920s equivalent of Epsom Salts or Andrews.

Preparations to seal the *Seydlitz* began in June 1927. To ensure she stayed on her side once she broke the surface, and to make a quick sale, all the armour plating down her high port side was stripped off. This impact-resistant metal was bolted to the ship's side in slabs 14ft long and 1ft thick. The bolts were also extremely valuable as scrap metal. Altogether, 1,800 tons of armour plate was shipped to the United States at a good price. Once the metal was removed, the low starboard side, now being considerably heavier, would act like a keel and help her to maintain a sideways position once afloat.

Patching the *Seydlitz* was much harder than aboard the *Hindenburg* and the *Moltke*. Having opted for a sideways lift, Cox had to cover every uptake, stokehold, engine room ventilator, gun turret, shell hoist, hatch, skylight, bunker, porthole, and a great many other openings that were above her new water-line. Sealing all the openings was executed in the usual way, but some ventilator patches were 450ft². Her two funnels were also gone, leaving gaping holes of more than 1,300ft². Instead of three internal compartments used for the *Moltke*, the *Seydlitz* was divided into eight sections, with six airlocks, to provide more control over each part should she become unstable. A small generator room for lighting was later built on her exposed port quarter. Most of this work was carried out during an unusually stormy season. Although the bad weather affected work outside, deep inside her hull the only indication of the stormy weather was the wave rhythm pounding against her steel hull. In early April 1928 the storms were particularly bad.

During one particular lull, four men had opted to stay behind and finish a concrete patch on the outside. The *Sidonian* was set to come back later to pick them up. While the four men were finishing off the patch, the storm blew up again like a tempest, preventing the tug from leaving the safety of Lyness Pier. The men were marooned and exposed to the spray now pouring over the ship's side. Shelter became the first concern. Among the diving gear left on board they found four diving suits, which kept them relatively dry as the driving spray rained down on them all through the night. The following morning, after a night with no food and water, the storm was showing no sign of abating. The *Sidonian* crew managed to throw some food to the men who were by now very cold. It was not until later that same day that they could be lifted off and taken to the safety and warmth of the barracks in Lyness. Had they not found the diving suits to give them at least a little protection, it is unlikely they would have survived the night wearing normal clothing and exposed to the full force of an Orkney gale.

As the months passed, many more holes were covered over. By the time the job was finished, the workload had been more than both the *Hindenburg* and the *Moltke* put together. Cox decided it was time to re-enter the record books. On 12 June 1928 the sea conditions were perfect to attempt a lift – calm and with a good flood tide. Her bow and stern had been raised separately to test their integrity and all other equipment had been checked and rechecked. The floating docks were now in position around the wreck and compressors aboard them were forcing air into the hull. Due to her sideways position the bottom valves could not be used to press in the air as they could aboard the *Moltke*. Instead it was pumped in through thick rubber hoses fed down into the airlocks and was allowed to fill each compartment.

More than a year's work and more than £30,000 of investment had gone into this moment. By early afternoon the vessel was teetering on the edge of negative/positive buoyancy. Some workers nervously shuffled their feet or were hunched over with hands in their pockets, self-consciously aware that they were doing nothing while their boss looked on. The machines whined under the burden that they were called upon to bear. By 3.00 pm, amid the din of hissing air and oily exhaust odour, her bow was slowly but surely creeping up. The *Seydlitz* was sideways, in ascent, with only a slight list. Sighs of relief were audible among the workers. It was yet another engineering triumph. Cox was now the first man to raise a ship sideways.

Suddenly, amid the rhythmic hum of machinery some men thought they felt a dull thud emanate up through the water and into the surrounding steel. Cox also felt the rumble and immediately ordered her vented and sunk again, should further damage occur. No sooner had the words left his mouth than another longer and louder rumble was felt. Before the order was executed the *Seydlitz*'s bow shot up out of the water. Despite her toughened internal bulkheads, two compartments had collapsed into one. A massive displacement in the finely regulated pressurized sections put the *Seydlitz* out of control. Her 26,000-ton bulk thrashed about as if in great pain, violently pitching, rolling and screaming as steel twisted and ripped while the pressurized sections fought to equalize.

After what seemed like hours, but was barely seconds, she had vented all her rage and finally calmed down. She settled in much deeper water and was only prevented from completely capsizing because her guns and upper structure bit into the seabed. A full year's work was wiped out in a few moments. The airlocks were now submerged or crushed beyond use. All the deck tools were gone and the port quarter generating house was somewhere, useless, under the water. The financial and professional losses Cox sustained were huge.

For Cox it was always a case of whether his cup was half empty or half full. Viewed as half empty, many of the patches were blown off, some costing thousands of pounds; the airlocks and powerhouse were gone; a small fortune in tools was also gone; and she now had a 48° list with a great deal of superstructure jamming her firmly at that angle. But if viewed as a cup half full, the *Seydlitz* now resembled the position of the *Moltke*. There would be no need to remake all the expensive patches as all her funnel openings, engine room vents and skylights were now under water. Her list was much greater than the *Moltke*'s 17½° angle, so why not blast off every obstruction pinning her into the bottom silt, forcing her to continue capsizing and becoming far more receptive to a standard compressed air lift? In less than twenty-four hours Cox was back at the *Seydlitz*'s new resting site and it was business as usual.

A great deal of intensive labour was needed to hacksaw, cut or blast the *Seydlitz* out of the seabed and restore some patches, but Cox still considered the effort worth the gain. New and taller airlocks had to be fitted. Inside her hull, her divisions had to be changed to allow for being fully capsized. Three separate compartments covered the massive boiler room space alone. Just like the *Moltke*, her longitudinal bulkheads were also made tight just in case they needed to be either pumped with compressed air or water for lateral stability.

Four months later, at the beginning of October 1928, all the patching was finished and the internal sections were ready to be pressurized. Each section was tested and the *Seydlitz* was brought to negative buoyancy throughout. The side tanks were pressurized on the low starboard side and flooded on the high port side to level her as she broke out of her superstructure debris. Cox gave the order to start the compressors. The *Seydlitz* should now come up trim. The compressors again hissed and spat as they pumped in the air. Gradually she came alive by the bow perfectly trim. But, before the congratulations and back patting could begin, she continued going over and eventually settled at 50° the other way. Cox immediately ordered her to be lowered again before any further disaster could strike. There was no sound engineering reason why this should have happened. Throughout the rest of October, Cox raised the *Seydlitz* by bow or by stern many times, trying to understand why she would not ascend evenly. 'Twenty times she was nearly right, and twenty times we had to begin all over again,' Cox remembered.

Amid the remaining scrap pile at his breaking yard there were still quite a few boilers waiting to be cut up and moved south. He ordered the ends removed. Each one was then filled with 50 tons of concrete. Like aboard the *Moltke*, nearly two-dozen 10in steel cables were fixed at key strong-points aboard the *Seydlitz,* running across to the floating dock to support her and keep her level until she had regained her own buoyancy. All her compartments were pressurized again to lift her about 7ft off the seabed, which was still low enough to prevent an alarming list. The remodelled boilers were lowered by floating dock directly under her port quarter. The *Seydlitz* was slowly lowered on to the cement blocks in a bid to correct the list from outside rather than within. If the *Seydlitz* ascended with her remaining internal water mass level, she might well stay that way until enough of her own buoyancy was gained. Much later, and after a great deal more experience of raising ships, McKenzie explained just what they were up against in trying to lift a badly listing ship.

> The critical period in the handling of these ships was always when the buoyancy was just on the borderline between positive and negative. One degree list at the critical period may cause hundreds, or even thousands, of tons of loose water to rush over to the low side, and in a very few moments you will be unable to control the trim of the ship.

For many months leading up to the lifting day, men worked in shifts around the clock, sometimes in appalling weather, to make the final lifting preparations. But the last week of operations was the hardest. The men worked in freezing conditions under floodlights, trying to get the job done in a biting wind, which in Scapa Flow stings any bare flesh and feels more like a burn than a chill. On the afternoon of 2 November 1928, pressure was building up nicely in all compartments and she was coming up level. Then she began to rise too much at the bow. The pumping volume was eased off forward and increased aft. She maintained a trim position, inching upwards until her great rusting underbelly broke the surface. Up she rose, level fore and aft, trim port and starboard. Cox's men began to relax. Some looked at him and could see that his face, too, was beginning to soften. Then without warning she dipped by the bow as more air was pumped into the heavier stern section. A sound like a canon echoed about the floating docks; the first cable had parted.

The strain on the remaining twenty-one finely regulated cables was now out of balance. Another parted. Then, like a line of discharging Howitzers, the sound of one explosion after another rang out as the wires parted. In a matter of seconds ten wires had gone and no explanation was needed for what was about to happen next; but the fears were not realized. When the cables started parting, she had gained enough of her own buoyancy to recover naturally and was fully afloat. As the water ran off her underside a blue-white light glinted off thousands of mussels encrusted all over her hull. Cox's men had to shovel them off into the Flow, which attracted hundreds of fish and birds, who quarrelled over the sudden and abundant feast. Judgement and luck had worked together and the toughest salvage operation to date had been accomplished. But only seconds had separated victory from defeat, and Cox had won.

The *Seydlitz* was immediately towed by three tugs down Gutter Sound towards Lyness and anchored for the night while waiting to be moored alongside the following morning. Although the excitement and relief were plainly felt, everyone was too exhausted to show joy. But the storms persisted and it was more than two weeks before the *Seydlitz* could be towed the last few hundred yards alongside Lyness Pier, allowing enough time for the men to recover fully and their celebrations to begin as if she had just been raised. When she was 20yds from the south side of Lyness Pier, amid the flying of flags and the blowing of sirens, she was secured alongside.

As much removable metal as possible was stripped from inside her, gaining another 7ft of freeboard. Cox's attempt to strip off the armour plating the previous year for a quick profit came back to haunt him. Before the *Seydlitz* was towed to Rosyth, every ton had to be replaced by hand with bags of gravel. For a sideways tow its

102

removal might have been fine, but in a capsized state she would be far too unstable for the open sea. By May 1929 all available metal had been stripped away and all necessary accommodation (namely engineering crew housing), was in place on her upturned hull. McKenzie led eleven men to crew the upturned *Seydlitz* for the four-day trip to Rosyth.

The three German tugs, *Seefalke*, *Simson* and *Posen* were chartered again. At about 5.00 am on the morning of 29 May, the bizarre procession set out in fine weather. As they headed through Cantic Sound, into the Pentland Firth and out into the North Sea, the wind freshened from the south-east. By midnight a fairly heavy sea was running and a crosswind was forcing waves to lumber against her, causing an 8° port-to-starboard roll. Thousands of tons of water smashed against her and sprayed in high white columns all along her side. Still she maintained good stability and speed, and the compressors in the pump room were more than able to keep the required pressure for maximum buoyancy.

The wind had increased to gale force by dawn the next morning. The dramatic white spray, which hit her the previous day, was now fully green sea slopping over the narrower bow and stern sections. McKenzie ordered the tugs to tow her into the wind. Although this action took her some considerable distance off course, heading directly into the weather rather than meeting it side on limited its rapidly swelling impact. Should she roll too much, too quickly, then millions of cubic feet of compressed air could escape and if the compressors could not keep up, the *Seydlitz* was doomed. The course change helped, but as the sea conditions worsened, so did the conditions for the crew. McKenzie later wrote:

> Our compressors were now going at full power, but the freeboard was noticeably decreasing – which meant that we were losing air faster than the compressors could pump it in. In short, things were beginning to look distinctly uncomfortable.

A little before 8.00 am the sea was so bad that the tug masters lost sight of the *Seydlitz* when she fell into the troughs between the ever-increasing waves. White foam was now streaming down the green mountainous sea. There was little Cox's men could do except stay in the steel accommodation, try to eat their breakfast and wait for the weather to turn. McKenzie continued:

103

At eight o'clock in the morning we took two very heavy seas on board, which swept the full length of the ship. Lashings of various things were carried away. Our life-saving raft swept along the ship and burst the main pumping line, which fed the fore end of the ship. Barrels of paraffin, petrol and oil clattered wildly along with the sea. Some went overboard and some were caught in various corners.

Among the flying debris was a pump box holding about 2 tons of spares. The box was torn out of its lashings, lifted up by the sea like a piece of matchwood and pummelled into the crew accommodation. The impact caused the steel housing to rip open like a Japanese paper house, allowing the North Sea to pour in. The *Seydlitz* was now sinking and her new course put her a great deal further out to effect a rescue. One of the crew said to McKenzie, 'How do we get off Mac?'

'We don't!' came the curt reply. McKenzie knew that if the *Seydlitz* went down, there would be no time to be saved in such a wintry North Sea storm. Although their only shelter was split open, the most urgent repair was the air line to the bow. The men had to grab what they could amid the debris and fix the breach. In freezing conditions on a pitching and rolling platform they went out to save their ship – and their lives. The only respite McKenzie could offer them was to order the tugs to reduce their speed by half. The move went a long way towards reducing the volatile pitching and rolling movements, but she was still far from stable.

Nearly five hours passed before the repairs were satisfactory and power was restored. McKenzie recalled:

> The engines and compressors were able to give out every ounce of power possible, but we were only just holding our own and unable to increase the buoyancy. It was now noon and all were soaked to the skin and feeling utterly miserable.

The atrocious weather conditions ground on for the remainder of the day until late that evening. Twenty-four hours later, enough air had been forced in, but the *Seydlitz* was still no higher. Although the storm was easing, she was still rolling and pitching enough to lose much of the air the compressors were straining to replace. Three days later the utterly exhausted men were still trying to save their ship when the *Seydlitz* developed a port list. The obvious procedure was to flood the starboard tanks to counter the balance, which McKenzie was forced to do. But the action made her sit even lower in the water, exposing the men to greater danger from the storm-force seas.

Another two days passed before they sighted May Isle, a few hours from the Firth of Forth. Very shortly thereafter, cold, exhausted, hungry and very tired from their ordeal, McKenzie was able to order the tugs to finish with engines and anchor. They were too late to catch the tide that would carry them into the Firth, so they stopped for the night. Cox was well aware of the strain his men had endured and was relieved when McKenzie radioed him to say they had finally arrived. To their great credit and professionalism, not one man was even slightly injured.

A big food hamper was sent out to the *Seydlitz*, containing cigarettes and dry clothes. Once they were safe aboard one of the dry, warm tugs, the men fell into the usual masculine banter of how, under such great stress, things were never really that bad. During their first hot meal for nearly a week, some made fun of others for the way they responded to such dangerous conditions; others nervously joked that they knew all along everyone would make it. But all the over-emphasized laughter ringing out from the tug's smoky mess room was clearly fuelled by relief to still be alive. As they bobbed up and down, anchored safely in the mouth of the Firth, McKenzie summed up what they all really felt. 'After a hearty meal, we all turned in and enjoyed our first real sleep for six days.'

Chapter 11

Kaiser and *Bremse*

The 25,000-ton *Kaiser* had the reputation for being one of the luckiest warships in the High Seas Fleet because, for all the firepower she unleashed at Jutland, she took only two direct hits with one crewman injured. The *Kaiser* had a distinguished combat record. She fired more than 220 shells at Jutland, the second highest shot count of any German ship that fought in the battle. Along with four other warships, she relentlessly pounded the British armoured cruiser HMS *Defence* until she exploded, killing every single one of the 893 officers and ratings aboard. The *Kaiser* also scored a direct hit on the armoured cruiser HMS *Warrior*, which was scuttled the next day, and damaged HMS *Warspite*'s rudder, forcing her to steam in two complete circles under unrelenting enemy shell fire.

The *Kaiser* class ships were the cutting edge in German maritime propulsion technology. They were the first warships to be driven by turbines rather than piston engines. Five years before the *Kaiser* was built the Royal Navy first used steam turbines, in the revolutionary HMS *Dreadnought*. Cunard had already adopted the technology for RMS *Mauritania* and *Lusitania*, both Blue Riband winners. Still some conservative German naval architects considered the new technology a waste of valuable resources because turbine engines were considered cost-prohibitive, but what they lost in production costs, they certainly gained in speed and performance.

The *Kaiser* managed 24kts on her trials and was able to cruise as far as South America, which was considered a staggering feat for a battleship at that time. Steam turbine engines were small and light. They were totally enclosed and rarely needed maintenance. Steam pressure, and thus power, could be raised far beyond that of standard piston engines. The pressures and temperatures needed to create steam propulsion relied on steel alloys used to construct the boilers and turbine blades. The *Kaiser* needed sixteen coal-fired boilers to turn three turbines – a massive source of extremely rare and valuable scrap metal for postwar Europe.

She saw only six years as a working warship before coming to rest at the bottom of Scapa Flow, capsized and submerged in about 80ft of water with an 8° port list. The *Kaiser* looked like a textbook compressed air raise. To cope with any possible shift in air pressure Cox decided to create thirteen airtight compartments throughout her hull, accessed by three airlocks. Although her port list was only 8°, and all engineering theory and practice dictated that this should self-correct, he still had two 30-ton cement-filled boiler sections built up like pillars along her port side similar to those he had made for the *Seydlitz*. In theory, should she develop a greater list, the pillars would again act as a giant concrete shoulder that the *Kaiser* could lean on and counter any possible roll from the moment she came alive. Cox also ordered the construction of a large cement-filled boiler section to be placed at about the ship's length aft from her current position. The structure appeared to have no part in the following salvage attempt.

All external sealing followed the same procedure as with the other wrecks, but the divers were only able to work during the brief slack tides due to the strong currents whipping around the sunken hulk. Some air compressors were lowered into her interior to force the water-level down. Very soon they had built up a pressure of 9lb/in², forcing the water-level down by 18ft. Workers entered at once to begin the internal preparations. The work was always the same except that conditions were far worse on the *Kaiser* than on any other ship. Another of her engineering innovations was an oil-fired system used to supplement the coal-fired boiler arrangement. As she heeled over, a great deal more oil poured out and mixed with the dust that slopped around her bottom areas. The danger of flash fires was too great to allow any internal heating, so the men had to work their daily eight-hour shifts in a very cold, damp and filthy environment.

Their misery was increased during February and March. Storms were so prevalent that the floating dock sections offering all their warm, dry conditions, could not be moored nearby. Also, the compressed air being forced into the hull was already cold and damp from whatever storm was blowing over the Flow that day. Freezing, wet through to the skin and covered in glutinous oil and coal dust, which had seeped into their waterproof clothing during the day, they had to finish their shift by climbing up an airlock, often emerging into night conditions. The workers then had to chance jumping off a ladder on to a launch as it rose on an upward wave.

Cox's first understanding of compressed air technology came from the 1924 book *Wonders of Salvage*, by David Masters. He read the book with great interest, especially with its detailed account of the *Leonardo da Vinci* salvage operation. A friendship developed between the two men. Cox often invited Masters to visit him at Scapa Flow and on one occasion he allowed the author to venture inside the *Kaiser* under compressed air conditions. Towards the end of the Second World War, Masters told his story. It is probably the only record of what it was really like to enter an upturned sunken ship and helps readers to grasp the miserable and dangerous conditions that these men had to endure on a day-to-day basis. Master's began:

The tender brought me to the tugs, which were ceaselessly pumping air into the upturned battleship.

'Would you care to go inside her,' Cox asked me, 'it will be all right if your heart is sound.'

Where other men went to work, I would go to watch. I climbed the iron ladder up the side of the airlock, with the sea washing the lower rungs, and stood on the top. Mr Cox struck four heavy blows to tell those within to close the inner door of the lock so that we might enter. A couple of minutes later air began to shriek from a valve as it escaped, and lowered the pressure inside the lock until it was equal to the pressure in the outer atmosphere.

The heavy iron door on top of the lock opened inwards and I went down the ladder. A man swung the door upwards into place. A valve was turned, and it seemed that all the locomotives in the world were letting off steam at once, as the compressed air began to shriek its way through the tap into the airlock.

'Let me know if you feel unwell, and we will go out,' said Cox.

I swallowed and swallowed to adjust the pressure inside my eardrums with the increasing pressure of the air in the lock. I swallowed until I had no saliva left. I held my nostrils tightly and blew down them to force open the tubes and adjust the pressure on my eardrums. Once or twice it felt as though my head were about to burst, but at the psychological moment I managed to click open the tubes leading to my ears and adjust the pressures, and all was well again.

I watched the needle on the dial showing the air-pressure swing round until the whistling and shrieking died away, and I knew that the pressure in the lock had been raised to the same pressure as that in the ship.

The door at the centre of the lock dropped down, to disclose a hole leading into the murky depths of the overturned monster. Lit by electricity was a fluid black as ink, moving with an oily motion far below. For a moment I wondered if I would have to shin down a rope, then a little iron ladder tucked out of sight beneath the metal floor was pointed out and I swung on to it and between the inner bottoms of the ship. Everywhere was red dust and oil and coal dust. The mess was appalling. All you touched smothered you with filth.

Cox's men laboured in these gruelling conditions for more than six months, sometimes working up to their armpits in freezing oil and water. Eventually the task was finished. Extra compressors were run from the deck of the *Ferrodanks*, their rubber air lines twisting like cracking whips as the air pressure was fed down the lines and through the airlocks to bring the *Kaiser* to negative buoyancy. Once this was achieved, the bow would be lifted first. Because the *Kaiser* was so exposed to bad weather the men needed shelter to finish the job, and without the floating docks there was no other alternative but to shelter them within the ship. Once the bow sections were sealed, the *Kaiser* would be re-sunk to negative buoyancy and the stern sections treated in a similar way. On 7 February 1929 the weather was unusually fine for winter and the sea was smooth. Shortly after midday, with no fuss, shouting or open display of excitement, the air pressure was forced up to 14lb/in^2 and the bow came alive. As the afternoon wore on, the huge steel point broke the surface and carried on rising until it was a good 20ft above the sea.

Three weeks later all the fore end sections were airtight and the bow was lowered to just above the surface while more air was pumped into the stern section. It rose well above the surface and the final preparations were made to secure the stern bulkheads. By 21 March all compartments were airtight and the compressors were again run at 14lb/in². The bow rose to just below the surface and the stern crept up slowly. As she climbed higher the 8° list levelled out, thus rendering the two concrete pillars useless.

She rose evenly, slowly at first, but as the compressed air tried to expand she accelerated rapidly. By early evening she broke the surface amid sprays of escaping compressed air, which turned the surrounding sea into a dirty white-brown colour as air, oil and agitated sea water mixed. Finally she settled down on the surface, floating evenly fore and aft with only a slight starboard list. The tugs started towing the *Kaiser*, but not towards Lyness.

An immediate underwater survey showed that although she was clear of the seabed, the *Kaiser*'s superstructure, particularly her bridge and gun turrets, were hanging down too low to allow a secure mooring at Lyness Pier, or to get over the lip on the dry dock in Rosyth. Much of the twisted and buckled debris was blasted or cut off, including two of her 400-ton gun turrets, which fell to the seabed and were recovered later. But the bridge section was too big. Cox instructed a team of men to re-enter her hull and, with oxy-acetylene burners, to cut around her bridge structure at the main deck level. They then cut through every other deck following the same pattern, from the top of the upturned ship to her bottom – just enough to greatly weaken the bridge structure.

The *Kaiser* was then towed aft from her original position so that the bridge area was directly above the sunken cement-filled boiler Cox had prepared earlier. He then gave the order for all the compressed air to be released at once. As the air screamed out, the *Kaiser* plummeted downwards, her bridge section striking the concrete impregnated boiler with the full force of 25,000 tons above it. Every deck collapsed into the next with a muffled sound like distant thunder as the *Kaiser*'s bridge was rammed back up into her hull. The method worked well – at least for a while. When she was alongside at Lyness Pier the whole bridge section began to slide back out. Wires had to be run across the vast opening to underpin the steel mass. Meanwhile, inside her hull, work continued to seal up the final few openings before the long voyage south.

On 27 May the *Kaiser* was a hive of activity. Diver's attendant Magnus Scott was taking care of the air lines and signals for Herbert (Nobby) Hall, the diver who had remained calm while trapped by a wooden ladder aboard the *Hindenburg* a few years before. They were busy working in the fore end. At about 4.00 pm the two men were instructed to move aft and seal up a breached watertight door. Although lights were strung throughout the ship, Hall still carried a submersible lamp. He had to climb down a ladder, through another door, and into a much darker compartment to complete the job. Scott remained on the deck above to maintain Hall's air line and watch for his signals. There was no lifeline to look after because Hall refused to wear one while working deep inside a ship. Although failure to do so was punishable with dismissal, Hall felt that wearing a lifeline was one more way of being snared by any number of obstacles that lurked deep inside a capsized sunken battleship.

Once Hall had climbed down the ladder and ducked through a first door, he found the water depth was only about 5$^{1}/_{2}$ft. As the bright shaft of light from his lamp bounced and danced around the confined steel space he found the breached door. He then had to clump along in his heavy lead boots for about 16ft into the compartment to reach it. Hall first tried to close the door from the front facing side, but when this failed he carefully climbed through the open space and tried again. The door was jammed fast. Suddenly all the main lights and Hall's lamp went out.

Scott signalled with four tugs for Hall to come back up. Although by now most helmets had telephones, the dive crews preferred to rely on the simple but effective method of tugs on the lifeline, or in Hall's case the air line. They often considered it quicker and safer because the phone system was subject to misunderstanding. One tug meant 'more air'; two tugs, 'less air'; four meant, 'come up' and a rapid succession of double tugs meant, 'in distress'. On this occasion Hall signalled his acknowledgement by striking a hammer on the steel plating, which was quite a common response. He began coiling up his air line as he moved back through the tiny steel compartment. Scott could clearly hear him clumping back along towards the doorway and the ladder. After a while the sound of noisy, metallic footfalls stopped. Scott lit a candle just as the lights stuttered back on. He waited and waited. When Hall did not appear, Scott leaned over the companion-way and looked down the ladder.

'He was just floating, he came through floating,' Scott said. 'I called for assistance and got him up. We took off his faceplate and slipped his leads.' Hall's head was unnaturally swollen, and he had lost blood from his mouth and both his ears.

Salvage Foreman James McAusland was working inside the *Kaiser* when he heard his name being called very loudly from a distance, echoing along the passageways. He rushed to the scene. 'Before I got him out of the water I had already sent a message all over the place for doctors and also for my chief, Mr McKenzie.'

Thomas McKenzie was working aboard the *Hindenburg* nearby. As soon as he arrived McKenzie looked for signs of life. 'I took his pulse and such like and to all intents and purposes he appeared dead. I felt no pulse and no respiration.' McKenzie then took a knife and sliced Hall's diving suit off his body 'as the quickest method of getting him out of it'. The compressed air was still being pumped into Hall's suit and it gushed out with a loud hiss as the canvas fabric parted and deflated under the blade. The only way to get a doctor was by messenger. 'I then continued artificial respiration for two hours,' said McKenzie, 'until a doctor arrived.'

All the diving equipment was working perfectly. Hall was a healthy, experienced ex-Navy diver who had already proved aboard the *Hindenburg* that he could cope with any sudden emergency in a cool and professional manner. When the doctor arrived he pronounced Hall dead. The lighting system going out was caused by a generator changeover and was a frequent occurrence. Hall's failure to use a lifeline would in no way have contributed to his death in such shallow water. The volume of air gushing out of his suit also showed he did not suffocate. Had he thought his air supply was blocked, Hall would have closed the inlet valve and given the rapid double tugs that he was coming out. The inlet valve was still three quarters open, that being the normal working position. If he had shut the valve there would still have been at least six-and-a-half minutes of breathable air left in his suit – more than enough to reach safety.

Working in depths of around 6ft was harder than, say, 30ft. Between the two 40lb lead weights on the diver's back and chest, as well as a helmet weighing more than 60lb, a diver had to carry more than 1cwt on his upper body before even starting his day's work. At about 30ft the air pressure in Hall's suit would have kept the weights away from his body and appeared much lighter. In such shallow water the weights, or 'leads' as they were commonly called, would have pressed on his shoulders and back, causing an immense but controllable strain on his chest, back and internal organs. McAusland said:

From my own actual observations at the moment I can find nothing to cause this fatality. I would think nothing of sending a learner, let alone an experienced diver of perhaps twenty years, to do the job he was doing. There was a missing link somewhere, but I cannot place it. That missing link can only be supplied by the medical people.

A post-mortem found indentations in Hall's chest and back from the leads. Two doctors concluded that these compression marks and the considerable swelling to Hall's head, together with the blood loss, showed that Hall had died of traumatic asphyxia, 'probably' as the weights pressed together like a vice against his upper body when perhaps he slipped. But McKenzie hotly contested the medical version of McAusland's 'missing link'.

The lights went out only about five minutes after Hall had entered the compartment. Once he got into difficulties it took less than two minutes for him to die, most of that time being spent in total darkness. That was the medical opinion. With more than twenty years' diving experience as both boy and man, McKenzie did not agree.

I cannot bring myself to believe that a diver of Hall's experience, even if we assume there was a shortage of air, would not be able to walk 15 ft and come to the ladder and get his helmet off. My considered opinion is that there was some natural cause that at least accelerated his death.

Whatever happened in those last minutes, after entering the stern compartment at about 4.00 pm, Herbert (Nobby) Hall was dead within half an hour. Hall was in good humour throughout his last day. Alice, his wife, buried her forty-five-year-old husband in Kingston Cemetery, Portsmouth.

The sealing process continued to prepare the *Kaiser* for the trip to Rosyth. By early July she had been stripped as much as possible, plated over and prepared for the voyage. Shortly after she left Lyness the bridge section again dropped, grounding her in the southern entrance to Longhope Bay on the edge of the Pentland Firth. She had to be taken back to Lyness on a rising tide and into deeper water, where the whole mass was finally blasted free. On 20 July she resumed what proved to be the smoothest journey south of all Cox's ships to leave the Flow so far. The *Kaiser* arrived on the evening of 23 July and was docked the following night, only six weeks after the *Seydlitz*.

The 4,200-ton *Bremse* (meaning a small insect) and her sister ship the *Brummer* were the only two fast mine-laying ships in the Imperial High Seas Fleet. Like the *Kaiser* they were turbine-driven, but were fuelled entirely by oil instead of coal. They could steam at an impressive 28kts and could deliver 400 mines each. The *Brummer* and the *Bremse* developed villainous reputations throughout Britain's Grand Fleet for their devious approach to naval combat. The very nature of laying mines meant that the ships had to operate dangerously close to the enemy coastline. To avoid detection they were designed to look like British naval cruisers of the *Arethusa* class. Allowing the *Bremse* and the *Brummer* to drop their masts further augmented the deception. The attempt at subterfuge worked well.

On 17 October 1917 a convoy of twelve merchant ships escorted by the destroyers HMS *Mary Rose* and HMS *Strongbow* and two armed trawlers were en route from Bergen in Norway to Lerwick in the Shetland Islands. The *Bremse* and the *Brummer* got to within 3,000yds of the convoy before firing. In the surprise attack, both destroyers were sunk along with ten merchant ships. In the fire, death, oil and chaos that followed, many men went into the freezing sea. One of the armed trawlers, the *Elise*, went back for survivors when the *Bremse* opened fire on her – men were again in the water. It was a massacre that resulted in the Admiralty adding more and bigger warships to protect convoys.

Both the *Brummer* and the *Bremse* were interned at Scapa Flow. The *Bremse* was one of the few sinking warships the Royal Navy tried to save when von Reuter gave his order to scuttle the fleet. On the afternoon of 21 June 1919 she was in an advanced state of sinking. A fully armed Royal Navy party tried to get aboard, reach the bottom valves and prevent her from settling any deeper. It was too late. The bottom valves were well below the rapidly rising water-line as it poured up through the ship. The only chance to save her was to blast off her anchor chains, take her in tow and race for Swanbister Bay on Pomona, the main Orkney island, which is also known as Mainland.

The waters around Swanbister Bay drop off sharply from the beach. This allowed the Royal Navy to get the *Bremse* very near the shore. The destroyer HMS *Venetia*, supported by a tug, did manage to tow her the quarter-mile distance to the beach. But just as the *Venetia*'s crew had managed to manoeuvre the *Bremse*'s bow to hit the beach, a problem arose. Being 460ft long her fore end dug into the beach and her stern was precariously balanced on a rock shelf about 75ft down, with a shear drop into even deeper water. The steep angle made her turn on her starboard side with her razor-sharp bow jutting out diagonally at about 116°, like a giant striking axe blade. The *Bremse*'s position made her an obvious straight compressed air lift. She was divided into five separate compartments with airlocks. The only major problem was her oil-fired engines. On all the previous wrecks, workers had contended with a sticky cocktail of lubrication oil and coal, which could have been flammable. But the many tons of refined fuel oil that had spilt throughout the *Bremse* made her a particularly dangerous working environment.

Bulk fuel oil is unlikely to ignite easily, but if vaporized, or if fumes build up, the hazard becomes much worse. While the divisions were being sealed and made airtight, an oxy-acetylene burner accidentally triggered a flash fire, which luckily caused no serious injuries. But McKenzie said, 'On more than one occasion we had to run for our lives with the flames chasing us as far as the airlock, owing to the fuel oil having become ignited.' From then on, closed areas were regularly vented to lessen the chances of an explosion. Work started on bringing up the *Bremse* in late July 1929. Two floating dock sections were towed out and both, unusually, were anchored on the *Bremse*'s port – shore side. Several 9in wires were then pinned from the docks down the same side. As compressed air was forced into the hull, the wires were gradually tightened to correct her list and so prepare the *Bremse* for a trim ascent.

In late September, for no apparent reason, she toppled to starboard and a great deal of fuel oil poured out on to the surrounding water. At first it was thought she had slid off the rock ledge, but a survey found she was still safely perched on the outcrop. Too much remaining superstructure was thought to be the cause. The quickest and most expedient way of removing the spilt oil was to set it alight. The flames took immediately and engulfed the *Bremse*'s forward section and the surrounding water in seconds. The brisk westerly breeze blowing off the land carried the choking, black smoke out low across much of Scapa Flow as the flames crackled through every porthole and even though some joints in her steel plated hull.

Having been patched up and put under pressure without any major problems, she eventually broke the surface, smooth and trim, on 29 November 1929. Any remaining underwater obstructions were blasted away. Once she was secure in a moderate sea and with the wind on her beam, the tugs towed the *Bremse* stern first across Scapa Flow and alongside Lyness Pier. The fire had caused more damage than was first realized and Cox decided that she was too unsafe to tow to Rosyth. Instead she was broken up at Lyness and in Mill Bay according to the same gradual and methodical stripping process as the torpedoboats and destroyers. The work took much longer than planned and she became a spare-time job for when the men were short of work. Her sister ship, the *Brummer*, is one of only eight Imperial High Seas' warships that to this day are still at the bottom of Scapa Flow.

Cox now had more than enough experience to tackle the *Hindenburg*. Four years earlier as he watched her slip under the storm-driven seas, he already knew what he was doing wrong. Now was the time to risk everything to get back the £40,000 he had already invested in her recovery, and reclaim the valuable scrap metal still lying just beyond his reach.

Chapter 12

Heavy Metal

During a thick fog in the early hours of 10 December 1928, the 21,000-ton White Star liner, *Celtic* was steaming towards Cork Harbour in Southern Ireland when she grounded on Roches Point near the harbour entrance. Her captain ordered the engines full astern and was able to slip off the rocks with relative ease – only to ground on the nearby Calf Rocks. She was now firmly jammed. The *Celtic* was carrying 500 passengers and a considerable cargo of maize and fruit for the approaching Christmas festivities. The following morning all 500 passengers and her crew were transferred to the shore without injury.

Cox's old friend Otto Willer-Petersen of Petersen & Albeck was awarded the contract to salvage her. He soon found the job more than his expertise and equipment could handle and approached Cox to see if he was interested in offering assistance. Since the *Bremse* was not going to Rosyth, McKeown was charged with towing her to Lyness for breaking. With no need to stay in Scapa Flow for the foreseeable future, Cox decided to help his old friend. After all, he had never tried to raise a merchant ship and, like the *Hindenburg*, the *Celtic* had come to rest fully upright and needed to be pumped out and floated off the Calf Rocks on a high tide. Diver William Peterson, carpenter Robert Mowat and charge hand Malcolm Carmichael, who had helped McKenzie extinguish the fire aboard Cox's floating dock in 1925, joined Cox for the operation, along with more than fifty men from the nearby town of Cobh.

Part of the operation meant pumping surplus water out of her holds. The work was frustrated constantly by her cargo of maize endlessly jamming the pump suction inlet. On 30 November 1929 the pump in Number Three Hold jammed again. Carmichael asked for a volunteer to go down and free the blockage. A local fisherman, twenty-eight-year-old Jeremiah Burke, climbed down the steel ladder into the hold's gloomy and stinking interior where sea water and rotting maize had been mixing together for more than a year. As he climbed down a few steps, Burke fell backwards off the ladder and splashed heavily somewhere in the darkness at the bottom of the hold. His friend, twenty-four-year-old John Wilmot dashed into the hold after him. Wilmot, like Burke, got a few steps down the ladder when he, too, fell backwards and plunged into the inky darkness.

Malcolm Carmichael decided to do all he could to rescue the two men and climbed down the same ladder. He also fell after only a few seconds. By now there was a great deal of concern over the fate of the men. Still others entered the hold. Another local man, naval pensioner John Findlay, fell unconscious immediately, but was pulled clear of the hold. He died in hospital early the following morning. Burke, Wilmot and Malcolm Carmichael had died instantly. Another sixteen men were poisoned. Eight became unconscious, including Robert Mowat who suffered severe side-effects such as burns to the eyes, skin irritation and vomiting. For some men the symptoms lasted many weeks.

Cox was ashore when he heard that the men were in trouble. He immediately left for the *Celtic* with a doctor and a diver, but it was soon evident that a priest was also needed. The following day a diver searched the hold. Due to the foul conditions, many hours were spent combing every inch in the pitch-black maize and sea water mush. Eventually all three men were found face upwards, suspended about 8ft below the surface and 12ft from the ladder. An inquest was held in Cork to determine the cause of death. The coroner ruled death in all four 'was due to sulphuretted hydrogen'. Today the gas is more commonly called hydrogen sulphide and is a natural by-product of decaying matter. The gas is extremely toxic and in a high enough concentration it can kill after only a few breaths. Loss of consciousness can occur after only one breath.

The four bodies were taken ashore in coffins roughly made out of wood from the *Celtic*. The tragedy had a deep impact on the local community. Friends and fellow workers carried the coffins of Burke, Wilmot and Findlay three miles to the village cemetery in nearby Ballymore. A cortege half a mile long walked behind the coffins and was made up of more than 3,000 people. Carmichael's body was carried to the local church a few days later by the Scapa Flow team. Diver William Peterson later wrote, 'Passing through the town en route to the church the cortege was met by townspeople who insisted on carrying the remains shoulder high to the church'. After a brief ceremony Carmichael's body was shipped to Glasgow where he was buried next to his mother and father. All attempts to salvage the *Celtic* were abandoned. She was eventually broken up by Petersen & Albeck on the Roches Point and shipped in pieces to Cork. Out of thirty-five ships, the *Celtic* was the only one Cox failed to salvage.

Nearly four months passed before Cox wanted to start his second attempt on the *Hindenburg*. He briefly toyed with the idea of turning the *Hindenburg* over for a compressed air lift. But such an attempt would have been too costly and take too long. Anything other than lifting her upright would have cut deeply into his greatly diminished return. If he could raise her as she was, he could recoup the £40,000 already sunk into her and still, hopefully, make a tidy profit.

'I know enough now to stop her rolling and get her up level,' Cox said just before he started his second *Hindenburg* attempt. One of the reasons she kept heeling over to port back in 1926 was the top-heavy attitude created by her upper superstructure and especially her distinctive tripod mast. Cox hoped that removing this hampering metal would help greatly towards correcting the list when she was once again in ascent. Preparations began by burning off her mast and conning tower as well as her two funnels and everything else removable above the low-water mark. The metal was taken to Lyness Pier and immediately cut into pieces for resale.

After six years of continuous use, much of the salvage machinery was worn out or in need of an overhaul. In January 1930 work began to upgrade equipment aboard the four floating docks and went on for three months. Cox was taking no chances on a possible mechanical failure compromising his now part financial need and part stubborn determination to salvage the *Hindenburg*. She was his property and had been for more than four years. Cox was not about to lose her through something as simple as a pump breaking down or a frayed wire parting at a crucial moment. From January to March the docks were fitted out with new machinery, wires were re-threaded, existing machinery was overhauled and all the floating docks were ready for the 'big push' as McKenzie called it.

On April Fool's Day 1930 the first newly overhauled dock section was towed out and placed by the sunken *Hindenburg*. Each week for the next three weeks the other dock sections were towed out one at a time and placed, like the first one, on either side of her hull to form a stable, working platform around the wreck site. The flimsy wooden bridges were again strung together with rope and threaded like a spider's web between each floating dock and the *Hindenburg*, for quick access between the platforms. Cox then set out to correct his previous mistakes and put all his ingenuity and experience into trying to raise her – trim.

> I realized when commencing the second attempt that I had made a big mistake formerly by placing the whole of the pumping equipment forward. The water ran down to the stern of the ship quickly as the bows rose out of the water, and it was necessary to get access to the remaining water in the stern without delay.

First, a full survey was carried out to see how many of the 800 patches were either torn out by the 1926 storm or lost over the intervening years. To Cox's pleasant surprise, only 300 patches were broken, decayed or completely gone. By mid-June 1930 all the new patches were in place. Constant streams of mercury-like air bubbles could be seen breaking the surface as divers busied themselves replacing porthole patches and others that could not be reached from within.

Several round steel boiler sections, each one being 7ft in diameter and 20ft long, were bolted securely to the *Hindenburg*'s after deck area. They were to be used as cofferdams, which looked like small funnels. A cofferdam is a salvage technique used in shallow water whereby a wooden or steel trunk runs from the ship below the surface to above the high-tide mark. The water within the cofferdam is then pumped or blown out, creating a water-free passage down to the ship. Once the water was pumped out, holes were cut in the main deck plating and submersible pumps were lowered in. The plan worked, but the *Hindenburg* still failed to rise fast enough. His idea needed further refinement.

> At first the water was forced through the sides of the cofferdam, but after one or two pump failures which went undetected for a long time, I decided to have all the outlets above the water so one could see that every pump was working satisfactorily.
> I now literally had pumps all over the ship and by bringing the electrical connections up to the bridge it was possible to

control the pumping operations in the whole of the ship from one point. If it was found that water was leaking into any compartment an additional pump could be brought into operation quickly to suck it out.

As the level dropped, the pumps were lowered further into the ship. Outward support also needed to be drastically rethought if this second attempt was to be a success. The problem back in 1926 was not to make her watertight, but to master stability and keep her trim.

While the docks were being overhauled, Cox cut a 40ft by 30ft engine room section out of a destroyer in Mill Bay. Like with the *Seydlitz*, he planned to help the *Hindenburg*'s stability from outside her hull as well as within. The engine room section was chosen for its better structural design. Once in place the hulk was sunk beneath the *Hindenburg* on her starboard side aft to counter the possible list. More than 600 tons of cement were then tipped into the engine room section to take the tremendous forces that were soon to be exerted upon it. The work added another £2,000 to Cox's outlay. Due to the high cost, he gambled that the *Hindenburg* would tend to list only to starboard as she had four years earlier.

On 19 June 1930, two days before the eleventh anniversary of her scuttling, Scapa Flow was calm. At 10.00 am, Cox was standing on the *Hindenburg*'s bridge like an orchestra conductor in a theatre pit. Before him were all the controls to command the pumps into action. This time two pairs of 12in pumps and twelve 6in pumps were more or less evenly distributed around the *Hindenburg*'s deck, finely tuned and ready. First the 12in pumps began, clattering and vibrating amid clouds of exhaust smoke as they came to life. Then, one after the other, the electric 6in pumps hummed gently as they started. Each unit was capable of pumping out up to 300 tons of water per hour. Altogether sixteen water jets gushed out of the pump outlets and flowed into the sea or cascaded down the deck like brilliant white columns. About five hours later the level inside her had dropped to about 30ft. To everyone's intense relief the *Hindenburg* came alive and did not list.

The process had to be interrupted to allow some of the pumps to be lowered deeper into the ship. To move the smaller pumps to a lower level, all but four had to be switched off. McKenzie expected some water to seep back into her hull, but instead the *Hindenburg* began flooding too quickly. Divers were sent down to feel along both the port and starboard sides. After about half an hour a diver working down the *Hindenburg*'s starboard amidships section signalled that he needed urgent help. As he ran his bare fingers along the steel plating, which was encrusted with seaweed, shellfish and barnacles, his arm was suddenly snatched up into an open inlet valve, slamming his body hard up against the *Hindenburg*'s side.

He was completely trapped, unable to pull his arm out or push himself away from the ship's hull. When his distress was discovered, all the remaining pumps had to be turned off to allow him to pull away from the ship with the help of his reserve diver. As the pumping stopped he was easily able to extricate his arm, without risking tearing his suit. Ripping the tough fabric would have meant he would drown slowly as the outside water seeped in. Apart from bruising there was no serious damage. 'It cost several hundred pounds to flood the ship, in order to release the man,' said McKenzie, 'and then to pump her out again; a very expensive bit of plugging.'

For two days the pumps hummed relentlessly as they transferred water back into the Flow. Men scurried around the ship and the floating docks, making adjustments to equipment or checking readings. She rose 17ft out of the water without tilting, but as the men were congratulating themselves she suddenly tilted over the other way. For no apparent reason, the *Hindenburg* now took on a port list. With no cement protection she healed over more than 17° and was in imminent danger of capsizing. She had to be lowered. On Midsummer's Day 1930, exactly eleven years since she last sank, the *Hindenburg* went back to the bottom of Scapa Flow, for the fifth time.

'I had half expected this and was sorry I hadn't provided for it.' Cox said in his usual optimistic way, 'But at any rate I was now assured that I was on the right track. We therefore let her down again and built another concrete block on the other side.' Only placing a wedge under the *Hindenburg*'s starboard quarter was done partly as a cost-cutting exercise and partly in the hope that she would again only list that way. Cox had to spend another £2,000 and wait three more weeks for the new port quarter wedge to be ready and in place. When the new wedge was finished the *Hindenburg* was sitting snugly in her cement cradle. It had to work. Cox recounted:

I knew that the next time we commenced to raise the ship would be the critical point in the whole operations. I had already spent £40,000 during the first attempt to raise the battleship and my money was going like water again. If this next attempt was unsuccessful, it would mean my complete ruination.

At 8.00 am on the morning of 15 July 1930 the pumps were ready. The *Hindenburg*'s central division was pumped out first. The after section was left full of water for the time being to press it into the concrete cradle instead of the rock bottom Cox had relied on in 1926. She ebbed up so slowly that fish became trapped in pools around her remaining superstructure and deck areas. As the pools slowly evaporated, seagulls, guillemots and shags swooped and dived, disappearing around the ascending steel mass only to reappear with stranded fish flapping madly in their beaks.

Cox was visibly tense and alert to everything happening around him. Just after 2.00 pm the bow was a good 30ft above the surface and the stern began to leave the concrete cradle, the water still trapped within her acting as ballast, having been kept level by the cradle. Workers and some visitors, including members of the national and international press, an Admiralty observer and Bunty were there to see his finest moment achieved or dashed.

The pumps had to be lowered further into the *Hindenburg*'s hull to attain more height. Once they were in place nearer the ship's bottom, the white water turned to a filthy yellow-brown as the bilge oil was sucked up and out into the open sea. Workers entered the main boiler room area and sealed any holes to prevent the water escaping back through the section when she became more level fore and aft. By 3.30 pm the stern gun turrets were breaking the surface. As she came up, the dozen or more cofferdams housing the pumps looked like tiny funnels scattered about the deck area.

Ladders criss-crossed everywhere and men were constantly running to and fro, manhandling the pumps, adding longer lengths of hose or scurrying around doing other jobs as Cox continued to bark out orders through his megaphone. As her bow rose higher the *Hindenburg* appeared to sag a little in the middle. The divers brought up worrying reports. The intense pressure from about 15,000 tons of water still slopping around in her after end, combined with the ever steeper angle she was attaining as the bow rose, was buckling some of the *Hindenburg*'s hull plates. Should they wrench too far, at best they would allow water to pour into the *Hindenburg* and she would sink again. At worst she would break her back and Cox would be finished. There was no way to overcome the problem. He could immediately quit, – or take a gamble that German shipbuilding integrity would take the strain far beyond its operational limits. He decided to trust the ship. Cox gave the order to start the aft pumps. As the stern rose up higher and cleared the cradle, her back did not break. She stayed trim.

If he was going to lose control of her, now would be the decisive moment. To pre-empt any possible list he placed a worker in a life-jacket up on the *Hindenburg*'s bridge, saying, 'He was perfectly safe since there were plenty of boats handy should she turn over.' The worker's job was to watch for any angle of tilt on a plumb line showing degree increments from port to starboard against a curved plate. As a ship rolls to one side or the other, the centre pendulum-like weighted line stays still and the plate moves with the ship, allowing the observer to read off accurately the degree at which the line stops.

The *Hindenburg* was coming up nice and trim when the worker shouted, '2$1/2$° to port'. Just when Cox thought he had won, she was starting to list again. About a minute later the observer called back, '3° to port.' Then, came the call, '3$1/2$°'. Now everyone could see that all her 28,000-ton mass was lurching as the *Hindenburg* heeled over again. The readings kept coming every few minutes: '4°', '4$1/2$°', '5°', '5$1/2$°'.

Only $1/2$° more would mean that Cox was dangerously close to losing the fight. He was in imminent danger of leaving the Flow bankrupt and, although he had achieved so much since he had arrived and smashed so many salvage records, he knew the so-called experts would only remember this one and only catastrophic failure. When the *Hindenburg* reached 5$1/2$°, Cox later said, 'I thought everything was lost again.'

The only sound to punctuate the harmonic vibrations from the pumps was the call, '6°', from the observer. Everyone waited for either Cox to gain control and sink the ship, or the next call from the bridge, which meant the end. Murmurs among the men mingled with the sound of vibrating metal. A full fifteen minutes ticked by. Everyone including Jenny Jack and Bunty were waiting for him to give the order to stop pumping and sink her again – but he just stood staring as if frozen in time.

Suddenly a voice cried, '6$1/4$°'. Cox still stood motionless as if somewhere else. In a few moments it would all be over. The next call came a little more excitedly, '6°'. A few murmurs could be heard from workers on the floating docks. The next call said, '5½°'. They changed into whistles of delight. Cox cracked a smile:

> I knew very well, although I cannot say how I knew it, that if I could once get half the ship completely out of the water, she would have enough buoyancy to remain stable. It was impossible to make the ship jump up, the water could only be pumped out gradually and additional buoyancy was gained every moment. The question was whether sufficient buoyancy could be gained by the time the stern commenced to rise.

A loud and unanimous cheer went up from the floating docks. All the tugs sounded their whistles. Cox was so excited that when her decks were just breaking the surface, he jumped on them in his waders to take possession of his prize. Another worker jumped down after him. Cox manhandled the man on to his back and proceeded to give him a piggy-back ride around the deck. The mighty *Hindenburg* was never going back to the bed of the Flow. She was now his and Cox had earned her, fair and square.

Later that night she was up fully and almost trim, with only a very slight starboard list, which melted away as her internal water level continued to drop. The following day the tugboats *Ferrodanks*, *Sidonian* and the SS *Hoy Head* towed the *Hindenburg* towards Lyness from the west side of Cava, then down between Rysa and Fara. The operation started in the afternoon and went on until early evening while a fresh northerly breeze blew across the Flow. Crowds occupied every possible vantage point on the land, wanting to witness Cox's triumph. Those farther away in Stromness watched the spectacle through telescopes and binoculars. Small motor boats of every description circled the procession as a welcoming committee would today for a round-the-world yachtsman. Cox stood on the *Hindenburg*'s prow, looking down on the spectators like a victorious army general at the head of his war booty.

The Red Ensign was hoisted above her bridge as the *Hindenburg* came down Gutter Sound towards Mill Bay stern first. By 9.30 pm the wind had dropped; she was driven into the sand amid the continuous roar of sirens and whistles from every ship and boat in and around Gutter Sound. Four weeks of extensive preparations were required before she would be seaworthy for the journey to Rosyth.

The twelve small cofferdams were cut off and seven generators were mounted in the *Hindenburg*'s wardroom below her boat deck. Their job was to supply enough electricity to the eighteen pumps scattered throughout the ship to remove any surplus water. The seventh generator was used to run compressors in the after section, which would be kept under compressed air for the journey. Two bunkhouses were built to house the twelve-man crew as well as cooking facilities and provisions.

On 25 August 1930 the weather was described as 'brilliantly fine' as the three German tugs, *Seefalke*, *Pontos* and *Ajax*, flying the German Republican flag, secured their tow-lines to the *Hindenburg* under the Red Ensign just before noon on a high tide. The *Hindenburg* was unusually high in the water, just in case another drastic air loss occurred. At 12.30 pm the order was given to commence towing. The slack came out of the tow-lines as the tugs slowly pulled forward. The steel lines creaked, becoming rock-solid as the *Hindenburg* lumbered forward on her last journey. In less than an hour the cortège cleared Cantic Head and was in the Pentland Firth. Being so high in the water, she dwarfed the three tugboats. One contemporary writer said:

> The *Hindenburg* appeared as if moving under her own steam. Mr Cox himself went away with the vessel. Such was the last of the great battle cruiser *Hindenburg* as far as Orkney is concerned.

The voyage to Rosyth was smooth all the way from Scapa Flow to the Admiralty dock and took only three days, one full day ahead of schedule. The sea was like glass. The sun was glinting off the water like arcing electricity and a thick summer haze hung over the estuary. As the procession entered the Firth of Forth, both banks were lined with many more spectators than in Scapa Flow, straining through the mist to catch a glimpse of the mighty *Hindenburg*'s last voyage. As the afternoon wore on, the haze burnt off, giving many watchers a much clearer view of the rusting hulk. Sightseeing trips were organized aboard small motor launches to allow the lucky few to get a much closer look. Hundreds of people were already waiting at the Admiralty dock.

Finally the *Hindenburg* turned slightly to port for the last few hundred yards to the dry dock and was made fast. Cox's radical techniques were now being copied by other salvers around the world as the news of his successes spread. He was well and truly at the pinnacle of his salvage career. He had nothing more to prove to the experts who once laughed at the jumped-up scrap dealer from Wolverhampton with an insane plan to achieve what they could not even contemplate.

After four long years and many disappointments, the gamble had eventually paid off – professionally at least. As the *Hindenburg* turned into Rosyth, among the crowds ashore was a Pathé news crew shooting above the many heads of off-duty sailors, businessmen, and women with young children. Cox, Jenny Jack and Bunty were on the *Hindenburg*'s bridge as she sailed under the Forth Bridge. The sun shone and the people cheered. It was his finest hour.

Chapter 13

Von der Tann

The *Hindenburg* was sold to Metal Industries Limited (or 'Metals' as they were more affectionately known), formally the Alloa Shipbreaking Company. She was not put in the Admiralty dry dock like the other ships, but moored alongside the quay and systematically stripped down to a bare hulk. Breaking her up was a scientific process. Before work commenced, metal samples had to be taken and tested in Metal Industries' laboratories and carefully analysed to see exactly what she was made of. The *Hindenburg*'s guns and deck structures were the first areas to be broken up, as well as her remarkably well-preserved teak decking, which was also carefully removed.

Her many alloys and other valuable metals were piled on the dockside into their various grades and types before the gutted battle cruiser was towed to nearby Charlestown, beached and stripped in a similar way to the warships back in Mill Bay. Metal Industries faced an immense job when they agreed to buy the *Hindenburg*. They required so much oxygen to run enough burners to break up all the ships simultaneously, that they needed their own oxygen-making plant. Oxygen was fed at pressure from the plant directly to batteries of cylinders. These led to pipes along the quayside to which the burners could be connected at regular intervals. Their plant was the second biggest in the world, producing $1^{1}/_{2}$m.ft^{3} of oxygen per week. Breaking up the *Hindenburg* alone used two-thirds of its entire output. When she was reduced to usable pieces, much of the *Hindenburg*'s steel was exported to the Clyde. Her gunmetal and precious alloys went to Birmingham, Canada and, ironically, back to Germany. Lighting for the Metal Industries' site was supplied from three generators, one of them coming from the *Hindenburg*. After its extraction from the hulk, the reconditioned machine was in perfect working order even after eleven years under the sea.

Jenny Jack and Bunty wanted Cox to retire and perhaps rest a little, and enjoy some peace with his family away from the madness of Scapa Flow. He did have other scrap metal interests, which were prospering, so raising the sunken fleet was no longer as necessary to aid his recovery as it was back in 1924. After the *Hindenburg* salvage there was nothing left to prove, either professionally or financially, to his critics. But Cox was still only forty-seven, fit, razor-sharp mentally and bursting with more energy than a man half his age. Cox still owned two warships, the 20,000-ton battle cruiser *Von der Tann*, and the 25,000-ton battleship *Prinzregent Luitpold*. He had paid £1,000 for each vessel. After seven years' salvage experience neither warship presented any real problem to raise. Should he succeed, then Cox could turn over more than £70,000 on his £2,000 investment in both vessels when they, too, were sold to Metal Industries. 'Just one more year,' he said.

Where the *Hindenburg* was the last of the great German battle cruisers, the *Von der Tann* was the first, and the oldest in the High Seas Fleet. She was built to rival the dreadnought HMS *Invincible*, but the *Von der Tann* was a far superior warship. Following the German philosophy of preservation over devastation she had slightly smaller guns than the *Invincible*, but a vastly increased armour protection. On sea trials, her engines produced almost double their expected output. The *Von der Tann*'s combat career included involvement in bombing raids up and down the British east coast and, like most German warships, front-line action at Jutland. During the first engagement between British and German battle cruisers, the *Von der Tann* was pitched against HMS *Indefatigable*. Twenty-seven minutes later the *Von der Tann* scored a direct hit on the *Indefatigable*'s fore turret, penetrated her magazine spaces and blew the ship in half, killing more than 1,000 men. Only four survived.

When the *Von der Tann* was scuttled three years later, she settled on the seabed less than 500yds from the *Hindenburg*'s original position, completely submerged with a 17° list. On paper she was another textbook job and looked to be very much like the *Kaiser* operation. Recovering the *Von der Tann* began properly in August 1930 and steadily progressed to late in the year. One major difference with the *Von der Tann* was that her airlocks had to be 60ft long on the low port side, which allowed the workers to decompress at the 40ft mark.

The first airlock went on in September and once the oxy-acetylene cutter had burned into her bottom plates, the men descended down into the foul smell of rotting debris that would be their working environment for the next four months. The venting power was at first doubled and then trebled in an attempt to improve the working conditions, while avoiding the risk of flash fires like those experienced aboard the *Bremse*. The revolting stench of decay remained even after excessive airing. Venting alone was never going to solve the problem because the gas from the rotting matter continually mixed with the oil vapour and dry coal dust to create a deadly and explosive combination. As each airlock was positioned on a new section, the hull was breached. The next job was to spray the internal compartment with fluids to neutralize the volatile cocktail, but to the men's chagrin, the smell of the chemical agents was worse than the foul-smelling gas. Once the gas was successfully dampened down, flame cutters could be used freely.

The careful fitting of airlocks and spraying of each section took six weeks. In addition to the filthy working conditions, the weather was also now going against them. At one point, a squall was so bad that the tugs had to cast off twice in one day. During another storm, the fixing of one of the airlocks had to be abandoned. When the workers returned the following day, the airlock had been torn clean off the *Von der Tann*.

Eventually she was divided up into six cross-sections to trim her fore and aft. A further four sections, two down each side to control any port or starboard list, completed her division. The *Von der Tann*'s depth was greater than that of any other ship they had yet raised. Men worked inside her at pressures of more than 20lb/in^2.

After a long exposure at high pressure, gradual decompression is absolutely essential if harmful effects are to be avoided. The main harmful effect was the bends and compressed air workers were as likely to be affected as divers working outside at the bottom of the sea. McKenzie's many years' experience as a diver allowed him to explain clearly what actually happens inside the body when compressed air is breathed in and back out:

Here we are dealing with a gas under pressure in contact with a fluid. The lungs become saturated with nitrogen at the existing pressure in the air. The blood passing through the lungs picks up the nitrogen. When passing on it reaches the capillaries and then it will diffuse out and the blood return for a fresh charge, this process being repeated until at length the tissues are fully charged.

Safe decompression is that which will so decrease the pressure of the air breathed by the worker as to permit the nitrogen to come out of solution, but not to expand in such large bubbles that they cannot pass through the capillaries. The longer the exposure in relation to the depth the greater the saturation and, consequently, the longer it will take to desaturate.

The bends is an excruciating condition, which even in its mildest form can best be described as a thumb being pressed harder and harder into a sensitive pressure point until a diver can hear and feel his own heart pounding. Without treatment it can lead to paralysis, blindness or even death. The bends, or caisson disease, was first studied during the construction of the Brooklyn Bridge in the 1870s and 1880s. At least three men died of the bends, ascending too fast from the pressurized caissons that were dug out to build the foundations for the bridge's two central granite towers. The project's chief engineer, Washington Roebling, was left paralyzed, partly blind, deaf and mute from the bends after ascending too fast from a caisson 78ft beneath the East River. A constant air pressure of about $33lb/in^2$ had to be maintained to hold back the river, a very similar pressure to that in which Cox's men worked.

Fashionable women in New York during the 1870s adopted a posture called the Grecian bend. They simultaneously forced out their breasts and buttocks by wearing tight corsets, a bustle, shoes with the highest heels they could manage and walked, swaying their hips in an exaggerated manner as their spines curved outwards. The effect has been called the most erotic style of the nineteenth century and certainly accentuated their curves as the young ladies sauntered down a boulevard. The term 'bends' was first used by Brooklyn Bridge workers to describe decompression sickness and is rather derogatory for the unfortunate sufferer who was said to resemble one of these ladies of fashion as the agony from nitrogen bubbles trapped in his blood stream contorted his body.

Cox had no decompression chambers for his divers, so to avoid the bends they used the stage decompression technique. A diver decompressed 'on the line', meaning he had to stop at specific points on his shot rope and wait for set amounts of time to ensure he did not get the bends. Throughout the eight years Cox operated in the Flow there was not one single case of the bends reported from either the divers or the men working under compressed air conditions deep inside a ship.

The inner and outer patching of the *Von der Tann* went through its normal routine of making small and large wooden covers, pouring in cement patches and repeating the process in the next section. By early November she was airtight and ready for a test raise. But just when all the new safety precautions were in place, the incessant unpredictability of marine salvage overshadowed what was supposed to be an easy lift.

At 8.00 am on 11 November, thirty men were working inside the *Von der Tann*, spread around many of her ten compartments. Work had been proceeding steadily for three months and the sealing process was nearing its end. Thomas McKenzie had been working in an after section all morning along with his assistant Jim Southerland, burner Robert (Bob) Kelday and diver Sinclair (Sinc) Mackenzie. About half an hour before lunch only a few more holes needed to be plugged in their section before the area could be safely pressurized. Cold, fresh winter air had been pumping into the space for some time and there was no trace of gas. Men had been using oxy-acetylene burners to cut through pipes all morning.

Deep down a ladder in a cramped after section waist deep in icy water, Bob Kelday found one of the last pipes to be sealed. It ran from the port stern section through the bulkhead to the other side. The pipe was big, heavy and made of steel. It was obviously leaking air into the next section and if they did not cut and plug the end, the pipe would act as a big enough conduit to push air into the next section and cause a substantial loss of compression. Normally such a pipe would be cut by hand and immediately plugged, but it was almost lunch-time. The job would be long, laborious and tiring. With no gas in the area they decided to burn through the pipe.

Kelday's piercing orange flame roared as a match ignited the gas. He turned the small air valve to mix the gas with oxygen, changing the flame to violet and making it much hotter. Within seconds the flame's centre was white-hot, crested in deep blue. Kelday stroked the flame over the pipe, which smoked and crackled as the rust and old paint disintegrated. Within minutes the pipe glowed bright red and started melting like hot butter under the flame. The red-hot

132

droplets hissed and spat as they ran down the ever blackening side of the pipe like molten bubbles and dripped into the water. While the men were finishing off, McKenzie had been making one of his many inspection tours. He could hear the cutters at work and see the bright flashes and shadows that the cutting actions were making as he returned to the compartment. He reached the section and stuck his head in to see how Kelday was doing.

Sandy Robertson was working nearby when the whole ship groaned and juddered as a whoosh of compressed air rushed passed him, racing through the ship, sweeping men off their feet. Inside the compartment, the piercing flame and hissing had abruptly stopped as the entire section lit up bright white. An ear-splitting sound hit the steel plating all around, causing a compression wave that temporarily deafened Kelday, Southerland and Sinc Mackenzie as they were blown around the space like rag dolls. The blast forced Thomas McKenzie back the way he had just walked. His head ploughed into the hatch coaming so hard that he was knocked unconscious. Inside the compartment Sinc Mackenzie was knocked hard against the steel bulkhead face first, crushing his nose to pulp. Southerland was suffering from painful facial injuries and Kelday could not be found. Sandy Robertson remembered:

> We were on the high side and they were on the low side. We saw this man floating in the oil. We grabbed him, hauled him up and turned him over. The oil on his face had to be scraped off and we did not know who it was until we saw his collar and tie. 'God! It's McKenzie,' someone said.

A deep-red stream from a nasty gash behind his left ear was slowly mixing with the black oil. Alive, but unconscious, he was minutes away from drowning in the oil and water mix. He was carefully taken up through the airlocks and carried into the fresh air. Once outside McKenzie came to a little, but he was dazed and incoherent. A tugboat came alongside to take him to a waiting ambulance and away to Balfour Hospital in Kirkwall.

Three workers were still unaccounted for, in total darkness, and deafened by the contained shock wave within the compartment. Southerland did not realize what had just happened until he was involuntarily spitting out sea water. He instinctively pulled himself upright to get away from the inrush. Unable to see anything, he felt someone next to him and grabbed the wet clothing. Sinc Mackenzie screamed out. His leg and nose were badly broken.

'Where's Bob,' Southerland shouted.

'I think I've broken my back,' said Bob Kelday's weak voice somewhere in the darkness. Although all three were injured Southerland knew they had to get out of the compartment fast or drown. He felt his way around the rapidly filling space to get a precise mental picture of their surroundings – and locate the exit. The water was rising by the second. He felt around the wall foot by foot until he found the door. It was jammed by the blast. There was no way out.

The explosion had blown against the 2in bulkhead and buckled the door out of alignment. By now their ears were clearing from the blast and Southerland heard hammers banging on the other side. Southerland, Kelday and Sinc Mackenzie searched by touch to find anything to reply. He and Southerland could not find anything. As a precaution the oxy-acetylene bottle Kelday used was outside the compartment and his rubber lines fed into the working area. Kelday grabbed his burner line and traced it to the end, hoping to use the metal cutting torch to bash on the bulkhead. He found the end, but the force of the blast had blown the torch off and the rubber line was hopelessly ineffective in signalling through armour plating. In utter frustration, he tugged on it as hard as he could, but it just stretched and retracted, making no noise whatsoever. There was no way of indicating that anyone was still alive in the compartment.

Considering the mental and emotional pressure they were under, it is remarkable how calmly they waited for the end. To give some idea of what they faced, during the First World War when submarine combat became an established attack method several had been salvaged after sinking. On more than one occasion salvers reported seeing scratches down a submarine's internal bulkheads where, as the water rushed in, some trapped submariners tried to claw their way out. Sinc Mackenzie, Kelday and Southerland, all injured, freezing, and having had plenty of time to think about what was happening, were now in the same situation.

Their plight was made worse by knowing that safety was only 2in away through the armoured bulkhead. On the other side their co-workers were slowly coming to the conclusion that maybe no one had survived the blast. If they had, surely they would return the hammer bangs. Cutting through the bulkhead could cause another explosion and the water in the lower compartment might rise up and engulf anyone who survived a second blast. Or they could walk away and leave their friends to drown in the most appalling conditions. 'We saw a pipe shaking and we knew there was life on the other side,' continued Sandy Robertson. 'One of the chaps dashed up and got another set of gear to burn through the bulkhead.' Without hesitation they automatically mounted a rescue operation. The cutter was brought down to burn through the armour plating. The inrushing water and lost compression were beaten back by pumping more compressed air into the hull to give the burners enough time to get Southerland, Kelday and Sinc Mackenzie out. The rise in water-level was slowed, but not stopped.

As the flame cutter melted through the bulkhead and a shower of sparks danced across the black water, there was no secondary explosion. When the hole was cut wide enough a worker jumped in with his torch shining in every direction. His beam soon caught the three men huddled together at the higher end to make use of the list and to capture the last few gulps of air.

Southerland, Kelday and Sinc Mackenzie swam and crawled as best they could towards the hole. Too exhausted to heave themselves out, their colleagues pulled them to safety. They all had to be carried carefully out of the airlock and taken by stretcher to an ambulance and then on to Balfour Hospital. Kelday, who thought his back was broken, was severely bruised, lacerated and black from his waist to his shoulders. He would walk again. All three were badly burnt on their faces and hands – but alive.

On further inspection it was discovered that the explosion had wrenched the bulkhead so badly that it had to be condemned and the next one along sealed, but the men were reluctant to go back into the area and finish the job. There was no explanation for the explosion, which had come so close to killing four men. What if it happened again? And next time perhaps the workers unfortunate enough to be trapped might not survive. The job had to be finished, or the *Von der Tann* with her possible £35,000 turnover would remain on the seabed, not to mention the loss of the many thousands of pounds Cox had already invested in her recovery. To give his men confidence, Cox went down into the compartment himself and continued the job. His bold move worked. The men soon followed to seal the new bulkhead.

135

The repairs took another two weeks before she was ready. Her fore and after ends were lifted alternately several times to test air pressure and to gauge how she might rise. On the morning of 6 December 1930 the *Von der Tann* was ready to lift. Cox decided to start with the stern. He would balance the compressed air pressure between the sections and counter the list while she was coming up. The lower starboard side was pumped full of air to a pressure of about $35lb/in^2$. The higher port side was kept at a much lower pressure of around $25lb/in^2$. The two forward sections were pumped full while the remaining three amidships and after sections were left at negative buoyancy.

By midday her stern was coming alive slowly, gradually picking up speed as the air expanded with the dropping water pressure. At about 3.00 pm the tip of the rudder and four propellers burst through the surface, spraying plumes of dirty white water up around her as surplus air escaped from underneath. Within minutes the rest of the stern section was afloat and settled fully 20ft above the sea. A reading with a lead and line showed a zero list. Although her bow was still submerged, the operation had been a complete success. Cox was too close to claiming the *Von der Tann*. With many of his workers about to knock off for some well-earned weekend leave, he cancelled their break to make the most of the following day's low tide and thereby increase their chance of final success.

Squads of men worked all through the night, making the myriad final preparations before the bow could be raised, mainly trimming for the final push. By Sunday afternoon the bow was fully inflated and coming alive. Later that same day the bow broke the surface. She was up, trim, and apart from some trapped superstructure the *Von der Tann* was ready to be towed to Cava, like the *Kaiser*, to capitalize on the island's deep water where the trapped upper structure could be blasted off. Unlike the other ships, the *Von der Tann* was not covered with tons of lush weed or marine life. What weed had grown over her was shrivelled up or dead and very few shellfish clung to her hull. The time of year and her depth were largely the reason. Many of the other ships were raised during warmer months or from shallower water. The summer marine plant life thrives in warmer weather much the same as vegetation on land. Likewise, as the vegetation withers in winter so the same happens beneath the sea. The timing meant a great deal less backbreaking work for Cox's men and less financial outlay, trying to cut, scrape and hack the weed off.

The following day bollards were welded on to the *Von der Tann* and she was slowly towed towards Cava and secured opposite the beach. The air pressure was reduced to only 8lb/in^2 and made common throughout keeping her high enough in the water to guard against possible bad weather. Much of the bridge section, both masts, and a large derrick had sticks of gelignite lashed to them by divers. The explosives were electrically detonated from aboard the ship. Assistant salvage officer McAusland said:

> These operations were very successful and when relieved of this encumbrance the *Von der Tann*'s bow was swung round by the strong wind, and the whole vessel floated very much nearer the shore. The gear all lies on the bottom now, but is hardly worth lifting.

The weather was too uncertain to chance towing her across to Lyness especially as she proved to be a little too unstable during rough weather. By 18 December the *Von der Tann* was firmly anchored just off the beach. All obstructions were blown away and she was floating perfectly trim. Cox then closed down operations for Christmas and everyone scattered from Scapa Flow to their homes throughout the country until the New Year.

Due to his head injury, McKenzie spent Christmas in Balfour Hospital and did not return to work until 4 February 1931, more than two months after the explosion. The day after he arrived, the *Von der Tann* was towed, bow first, to Lyness Pier in a choppy sea by the tugs *Lyness* and *Ferrodanks,* as well as an Aberdeen trawler and the SS *Hoy Head*. While she was being prepared for the voyage to Rosyth, Cox decided not to send her south. The New Year also brought in a massive slump in scrap metal prices. The *Von der Tann* would never reach the £35,000 she was worth and remained in Lyness for more than two years without earning Cox a single penny.

Chapter 14

The *Prinz*

The 25,000-ton *Kaiser* class battleship *Prinzregent Luitpold* was, like her sister ship, one of the first turbine-powered battleships in the Imperial High Seas Fleet. She had a pretty uneventful combat career, having shadowed the battle cruisers on their hit-and-run bombing raids on the English east-coast, and she made several unsuccessful deployments in the upper North Sea. Although she fought at Jutland, the *Prinzregent Luitpold* was one of the few ships to leave the battle theatre completely unscathed.

The men returned for work after their Christmas break and set about preparing and sealing the *Prinzregent Luitpold*. She soon let the men discover her own particular quirks, the first and most important being her great depth. To a less experienced salvage engineer the *Prinz* represented a nightmare recovery scenario. Her low port side was 60ft below the surface. The high starboard side was submerged at nearly 45ft and her overall bottom upward attitude came to rest in 108ft of water with a 20° list. No vessel at that time had ever been recovered from such a depth, let alone a 25,000-ton battleship.

Being the *Kaiser*'s sister ship, Cox was already well aware of her internal structure. Her resting position on the seabed was similar to the *Von der Tann*, so he immediately had two good examples to help him understand position, weight, size and salvage capability. Knowing the *Kaiser* also meant that Cox could see exactly where to place the airlocks and could go directly to every valve, vent and cable route without a trial-and-error, time-consuming search. All his start-up costs had by now been covered and the successful raising of the *Prinzregent Luitpold* would bring him into a reasonable profit.

The explosion aboard the *Von der Tann* was another constant reminder that however much a salvage is planned and every safety aspect covered, the predictable stages of each operation must never be taken for granted. Cox almost lost four good men in the *Von der Tann*'s oily blackness. One of the greatest problems those trapped men had faced was being plunged into sudden darkness. Controlling spatial perception in a well-known area quickly falters once light is removed. In a sunken, capsized battleship the scenario is made much worse, due to an individual's surroundings already being reversed. To avoid a repetition, Cox provided torches to all the men working below decks. Perhaps he should have done this from the beginning, but although light had been lost before, such a drastic, life-threatening situation had certainly not occurred.

The *Von der Tann*'s biggest airlock was taken from her upturned hull and became the first of eleven to be fixed on the *Prinz*. Once her hull was breached she, too, was found to have a large gas build-up from her oil-fired generators and full coal bunkers mixing together over the previous twelve years. Further safety procedures were employed to avoid a repeat explosion. Thousands of cubic feet of fresh spring air were pressed into her hull to create a safe working environment. All electricity for the interior lighting was generated from machinery on the floating docks and fed by wires into her interior to avoid the possibility of a spark. Each section was sprayed with gas neutralizing chemicals, even in areas the workers would not visit. Cutting was done by hand because all naked flames were absolutely forbidden throughout the ship. Once all the airlocks and equipment were in place, the men took the long climb down the narrow steel tubes and entered the filthy hull to start their eight-hour shifts. But it was not long before the first accident occurred.

Just before lunch-time on 2 May 1931, labourer William Boyd, his rubber boots and hands smeared in thick, slimy oil, reached the upper ladder in an airlock and was about to hand a heavy bag of tools over to the man above him. He let go with one hand to pass the tools over his head to his colleague. As Boyd took a deep breath and heaved the bag above his shoulder, both his rubber-soled boots slipped off the steel rung. His one oily hand gripped the rung above his head, but could not take the weight and his fingers slid off. Plunging through the air, he tried desperately to grab at pipes or the ladder as they hurtled past him, but his oil-smeared hands just slipped off. He struck a platform halfway down and hit the bottom of the airlock nearly 40ft below. His colleagues clambered down the ladder expecting to find Boyd dead but, when they reached the bottom, he was on his knees trying to stand up. Attempting to grab the pipes and hitting the steel plate had broken Boyd's fall and, apart from severe bruising to his back, he was unhurt and very lucky to have survived. Towards the end of May another accident occurred that would make a mockery of all the safety features Cox and McKenzie had put in place.

Once the airlocks were in place and the internal water had been pressed down to negative buoyancy, the process of dividing the *Prinz* up into eleven sections began. Venting the gas was the next important stage. The first deck was immediately vented through the airlock, but this method did not allow the other decks in a section to release any possible gas content. Two holes about 7/8in in diameter were drilled through the armoured deck, level by level, and repeated until the bottom deck was reached. At each level the driller gave instructions for the air pressure to be dropped to allow the water to rise, thus pushing any gas out of the section and eventually out through the airlock. The method was simple and effective.

On the afternoon of 27 May, James McAusland left the ship's fore end (FE), giving orders to labourer Robert Johnston, carpenters Robert Mowat and William Tait, diver William Hunt and driller Harry Donally to drill venting holes to clear the FE section on the starboard bow. Drilling, releasing gas and re-plugging the holes went on all afternoon. At about 4.30 pm, Donally had drilled two holes and was waiting for a signal from Hunt to put his two plugs back in the openings. A short distance away, Tait was following the same procedure. Once water reached the holes he had drilled, Tait was to plug them and inform Donally.

McAusland had been up on deck in the fresh air for less than fifteen minutes when a vibration ran through the whole ship. McKenzie had also just come up from within the ship. At the same moment both men saw a plume of water shoot more than 40ft into the air around the ship's starboard bow. McKenzie commented:

I had just come up from another compartment and Mr McAusland, my chief assistant, had come up from the FE section when the explosion occurred. I went to the airlock immediately and instructed two divers to see what the blow was.

Below decks in the FE section, moments before the blast, twenty-four-year-old Johnston was sure he saw the lights flicker before they

140

went out. Twenty-nine-year-old Donally had just seen a flash, followed by a bang.

> I would not say it was a blinding flash. The flash came to where I was standing, passed me and went through another opening. After the explosion it was a case of getting to the nearest airlock as quickly as possible.

Donally had to scramble up a 12ft ladder to reach the main FE compartment, and with his portable lamp beam bouncing round the space, his only thought was to reach the airlock and get out.

The FE airlock's pressure gauge had dropped by as much as 3lb/in^2. This may seem an insignificant spread over a 25,000-ton battleship, but each pound of pressure loss equated to a water rise of 2ft. McKenzie continued:

> When we got to the FE airlock, Donally and Johnston were coming out. They said there had been an explosion. All the lights were out, but they did not know very well what had happened as they were very excited and could give nothing very clear. McAusland immediately went down the airlock and I rushed extra air pipes and power into the section.

Three men were still unaccounted for and the air pressure kept falling, meaning the water was still rising.

McAusland climbed down the airlock and into the FE compartment. Hunt and Mowat were slumped at the foot of the ladder. The blast had blown Hunt more than 6ft up and along before he landed on the hard steel plating. If he had been any nearer the blast, Hunt would have been squeezed like a diver by the sudden pressure shift, or trapped and drowned. Both were badly burnt, dazed and suffering from shock. Even in his burnt and shocked state, Hunt wanted to go back into the compartment to find his friend, Tait, who was still missing. McAusland would not hear of it:

> He [Hunt] is a little fellow with a big heart. As I saw I could do nothing myself, owing to the fact that smoke and fumes were getting into my eyes and throat, I set about getting them up the airlock. I was expecting them to collapse any minute, but with difficulty we managed to get up the 50ft to the surface.

The two men were bandaged and taken to Scapa Pier by the *Ferrodanks*. As they disembarked, Hunt and Mowat looked more like two Western Front war victims rather than 1930s salvage workers. They were filthy, smeared in blood and oil, with their clothes in rags. Both their hands and heads were completely covered in bandages except for an air hole to breathe through. They had to be led by colleagues holding their arms, explaining every step the men had to take, to get off the tugboat and into a waiting ambulance for the 2-mile or so run to Balfour Hospital.

McKenzie and McAusland climbed back down the FE airlock to find Tait, but the compartment was thick with dense, black, choking smoke and sulphurous gas. After only a few steps they had to retreat back up the ladder. Smoke helmets were needed to venture any further and precious minutes were lost donning the cumbersome equipment. By the time they returned, the ship's internal air pressure had dropped a further 5lb. The water level in the compartment was now up to nearly 11ft.

The explosive force had been so great that many rivets in the ship's hull plating around the FE starboard section had been blown out like bullets from a gun. Divers were sent down to plug the many holes as fast as possible in a bid to slow the inflow. As more plugs were rammed into the rivet holes so the air pressure increased, the incoming water slowed, stabilized and then gradually began to recede. The compressors forced 1,000ft³ of air back into the FE section every minute for nearly an hour before Tait could be reached. At the time of the explosion, forty-nine-year-old diver William Peterson was working in the aftermost section. He immediately climbed back up to the ship's bottom and made for the crowd of workers clustering around the FE airlock. When the level was low enough, McAusland and Peterson re-entered the section to rescue Tait.

The dense, black smoke blotted out any chance of light from the lamps as they gingerly felt their way around the compartment. The only light came from flames crackling and popping from a worker's smouldering clothing once worn by Mowat. McAusland recalled:

I searched the only available places I thought Tait would have used in an attempt to reach the airlock, but I was met with water to a depth of 14ft. I took off my smoke helmet and shouted across to the only place where Tait could be alive and I got no reply, so I turned back.

McAusland hurriedly replaced his helmet in the choking fumes before he and Peterson left the FE section.

'Perhaps I have overlooked something,' McAusland thought. 'What if Tait was lying unconscious, or trapped?' He went back into the FE compartment by himself to try one more time.

When I was in the ship a second time, and at the point furthest from the airlock, Peterson came along without any smoke helmet. It was a very gallant act, but I don't think a very wise one. I mention this to show there are a few of those among us who did not mind taking more than an ordinary risk in trying to find Tait. It really was a very gallant act.

The smoke and sulphur fumes were burning and stinging Peterson's eyes, nose and throat and the longer he was exposed the more pain he had to endure.

We were able to wade through this section up to our necks in water until we came to the place where Tait had been working. It would seem that Tait, when he was waiting for the water to rise through the hole from which the gas had been escaping, had sat down on a shelf, and when we found him he was in a sitting position. I think the origin of the explosion was where Tait was actually working; the damage done to the section points to that.

Tait was not found until about 7.00 pm that evening. McAusland and Peterson slowly lifted him off the shelf and half floated, half carried him out of the small, compartment to the FE airlock where he was carefully hauled up and out on to the ship's bottom. The short journey took the men until 9.00 pm that night. Dr Cromarty, the village physician from Stromness, had already arrived. He examined Tait and confirmed that he was, indeed, dead. His opinion was that Tait died through 'asphyxiation following upon the mouth and nostrils being submerged in water during a period of insensibility arising from shock'. Finding the cause of the explosion became paramount. It should not have happened. Every possible safety precaution was in place and Tait was, McAusland insisted, 'doing an operation which we had done almost every day for years'.

McKenzie thought there were only three possible reasons for the blast. The fusing of an electric wire, a naked light or spontaneous combustion. And he thought that putting them in that order would be about the way they would happen. Much of the wiring was destroyed and every fuse had been blown in the blast. Spontaneous combustion was a thousand-to-one chance. Tait did smoke, but he was also a capable man who was fully aware of how dangerous the gas could be. Most of the workers kept their cigarettes in their caps. Tait's was blown off, but Donally insisted Tait kept his cigarettes in his pocket. None were found.

Donally was asked if he knew whether workers had the occasional smoke in a compartment while they were working. He said that they never did. From the time Tait drilled his hole, until the blast, was a little over an hour. Sitting in a dark, damp space with nothing better to do, did he chance a quick smoke? There was no reason to even suspect gas was building up. Normally workers could smell its noxious fumes. On 27 May they smelt nothing.

A court of inquiry was held to consider all the evidence, most of which was really inconclusive. Lights had flickered, which was known to happen just prior to a fuse blowing. It was no secret among the workers that, contrary to the rules, men often did smoke below decks. Like other workers in the FE section, McKenzie still insisted Tait would not have been smoking. Hunt and Mowat were too ill to attend the inquiry. McKenzie did visit them in Balfour Hospital the night before the inquiry to gauge their opinion of what might have happened. McKenzie sat by Hunt's bed and asked him what his views were, but Hunt claimed to know nothing. 'He asked me several questions about Tait and asked if I found matches and cigarettes in his pocket, but I found none', said McKenzie, 'Hunt said they should have been there. From that I gathered Hunt thought Tait had cigarettes and matches.' The verdict could have gone either way.

The truth will never be known, but after all the evidence had been heard, Kirkwall's Sheriff George Brown turned to address the jury:

The least possible way was by spontaneous combustion. The next was by lighting a match – a match lit by one of the workman in order to smoke, which was against the rules and regulations. The third was the fusing of an electric wire. Mr McKenzie had no hesitation in saying that in all probability it was not the act of the workman, but the fusing of the wire that caused the explosion. If you accept the third reason as being the real one, it would be one from which no one was to blame, and therefore the accident was a pure accident.

If that is your view, I would suggest the following verdict. 'The jury unanimously find that the accident through which the deceased, William Brock Tait, met his death occurred at Lyness on board the ex-German battleship *Prinzregent Luitpold*, was caused by an explosion of gas, which occurred at the place where deceased was working. And blew a hole in the side of the said vessel, which thus caused an inrush of water by which the deceased was engulfed and asphyxiated while in a state of unconsciousness caused by the explosion. And there was no person to whose fault the accident is attributable.'

The jury unanimously accepted the verdict and the twenty-six-year-old carpenter's death was officially recorded as an unavoidable accident.

McKenzie summed up the feelings within Cox & Danks towards their lost colleague, 'Tait was one of our best men, respected alike by officials and workmen, and his loss was deeply regretted.' Ironically Tait had been studying to become a diver to earn more money. He had already made two or three successful dives and was well on the way to achieving his goal when the very water he was learning to survive in so ably, claimed his life.

'He was a cheery soul,' remembered Sandy Robertson.

A few days after the gas explosion, work resumed to lift the *Prinzregent Luitpold*. Her depth meant that air pressure between 20–30lb/in² was needed to bring her alive. On 9 June, exactly two weeks after Tait's death, Scapa Flow had a monochrome appearance as thick, grey drizzle and haze enveloped Orkney. All through the morning, air was pumped into each of the eleven sections from two floating docks, one on either side above her upturned hull. A workman wearing a life-jacket was stationed on top of each airlock, constantly monitoring the pressure in his section.

Cox knew that each compartment had to vary if he was to correct her 20° list. Some compartments were compressed more than double that of others, such as port-side Airlock Number Six, which had

31lb/in^2 on by midday, whereas her corresponding starboard-side Airlock Number Five had only 15lb/in^2 on. By lunch-time her bow had crept up a few feet when the siren sounded for half an hour's break. While the men tucked into their lunches, the black-backed gulls, herring gulls, kittiwakes and guillemots feasted on clusters of mussels that were being exposed as the bow rose out of the sea. After their lunch break the men continued their task. By mid-afternoon the drizzle had increased and Cox suspended all work until the following day when he would attempt to trim her as she came up higher.

Intensive pumping went on all Wednesday morning until she was fully 12ft above the surface. All efforts were then concentrated on correcting the list. The workers in their life-jackets were ready on top of each airlock as Cox slowly released air on the high port side, which screamed out as if protesting at the unnatural pressure it was put under. The gauge readings were scribbled on boards and held up, the air delivery was constantly fine-tuned. Air was also pressed into the low starboard side and, ever so slowly, the *Prinzregent Luitpold* began to correct. This time there were no sudden surprises, no bulkheads failed and no air leaked. Cox had reduced marine salvage to a technical exercise.

He had to test raise the stern before she could be brought up and secured. Then on Friday evening the pumps were kept running all night. The following afternoon two rudders and four gigantic propellers broke the surface amid plumes of spray and the sun glinted off the water as it streamed down the bronze and steel, back into the sea. The stern rose 20ft above the sea as the escaping air blew into the surrounding water, forcing it high into the sky. This spectacular event should have lasted for a few minutes as the surplus air blew out, but half an hour later the air was still escaping. The loss eventually reached a critical mass and with all the pressure being forced into the stern it slowly sank back below the waves.

Although raising the stern had failed, Cox had enough experience to know what was wrong and how to correct it without any undue fuss. Quite simply, when the divers had plated over the portholes and other external apertures, they had not gone deep enough. This was not their fault, but Cox's orders. Judging how far down a ship's side one should go, plugging and sealing, had always been pure guesswork. The amount of a ship forced above water by the expanding air volume could never be gauged accurately because each ship was different. He now knew how far her stern would rise, so a week's further work lower down each side of her hull should then be enough to claim her for the breaker's yard.

While the work progressed a sudden loud buzzing like a giant prehistoric insect was followed by the sight of a huge, black shape, which cast a shadow right across the *Prinz*. The German civil airship LZ 127 *Graf Zeppelin* was en route from Friedrichshafen, near Biberach in Germany, to Reykjavik in Iceland with twelve passengers and some mail. The airship dropped to about 300ft to get a good look at one of their country's former great battleships before slowly turning north and droning away over the horizon.

After another four days plugging, Cox decided that the divers had sealed the *Prinzregent Luitpold* far enough down her hull to attempt another lift. He made a test raise of the bow and managed to correct the remaining list before she was lowered back down on an even keel, carefully ensuring that her new trim attitude was not lost. Not until Thursday, 9 July did he attempt to lift the stern, which should now come up level. At 3.00 pm the stern was 20ft above sea level and trim.

The men were due to stop for the day, but there was still more than twelve hours work left to bring the bow up and secure her once and for all. The wind was calm and conditions were favourable to press on. 'Just another hour', he thought, 'to make some final preparations for the following day and get a few more pounds on.' They started pumping air into the bow sections while others scurried around the floating docks. 'The successful culmination to the feat came somewhat as a surprise to everyone,' Cox said. 'The hull was rising steadily, though ever so slowly, but there came a sudden development.' Just as he was preparing to wind down operations for the day a rumble was felt below the floating docks. The sea surged and boiled green-white as the bow came prematurely shooting out of the sea. To everyone's surprise, the bow broke the surface and settled perfectly trim. For once a miscalculation had worked in Cox's favour and the *Prinz* was his.

She was immediately towed and beached on a sandbank off Rysa at low tide. On 10 July she was towed off at the morning high tide and taken to Lyness by the *Ferrodanks* and the *Sidonian*. Cox now held two world records. Overall, the *Hindenburg* was the biggest ship ever raised for which he used the pumping-out method. And the *Prinzregent Luitpold* was the deepest and biggest ship ever raised using compressed air. 'She could be commissioned again as a warship in one year. If she could, I could make two million pounds out of her,' Cox remarked. But under the Versailles Treaty, and its attempt to achieve international peace and security, she had to be scrapped.

The Press called Cox 'Britain's brainiest bulldog', but for all his ingenuity and dogged determination, the scrap metal market was still in a slump. The *Prinzregent Luitpold* joined the *Von der Tann* in Mill Bay. More than £70,000 was floating idly at Lyness, failing to make him the money he had hoped for. All the other warships were in much deeper water and would be more costly to salvage. For the first time in eight years, Cox had to accept that his days in the Flow might be coming to an end.

Chapter 15

Selling Out?

One of the floating dock sections and a pontoon were towed out to the *Kaiser*'s former wreck site in late summer 1931. Preparations were then made to lift the massive 400-ton gun turret that had dropped off her more than two years earlier. This represented only a fraction of the tonnage Cox was raising just a few months before, and once the turret was towed to Lyness and strung between the two platforms, there was nothing left to scavenge. Thirteen warships were still on the seabed. Nine were over 20,000 tons and four over 4,000 tons, representing a considerable amount of ferrous and non-ferrous metal, should the price of scrap improve. Publicly, Cox was saying that his scrap firm had every intention of continuing with operations, but in private his actions told a different story.

Rumours were beginning to appear in the Press that Cox no longer wanted to operate in the Flow. Towards the end of the year from his head office at Ulster House, 168 Regent Street, London, Cox leaked a story to a reporter who went to interview him for one of the many articles then appearing about how he raised Germany's once mighty fleet. Sitting behind his desk, Cox informed the surprised journalist:

> We had practically decided to abandon our activities up there. Meantime it would be more correct to say we have simply postponed our operations. But things have altered to some extent since we gave the order to halt. If the price of steel scrap improves, as there is now every prospect of it doing, there is no reason why we should not carry on again.

Nearly four months before he gave the interview, and within a few weeks of raising the *Prinzregent Luitpold*, Cox had already begun trying to sell his Scapa Flow operation to the biggest buyer of his recovered scrap, Metal Industries. He was adamant that deeper wrecks could not be raised, although, with proper financing and a full replacement of all the tired equipment, McKenzie was convinced they could. McKenzie wanted Cox & Danks to continue, with him as their chief salvage officer, but Cox was not interested.

Scrap metal prices did begin to show some signs of gain. Some experts claimed the market would improve due to expected duties being placed on imported steel. Others claimed an increase was imminent due to better conditions in the British metal industry But there were more than 10m. tons of obsolete shipping laid up around the world. Two liners had just been sold for breaking. The 11,000-ton *Demosthenes* had been sold to a small breaker in Rothesay, Scotland and the 12,000-ton *Corinthic* was steaming up from New Zealand on her last voyage before being scrapped. These vessels, like many others, had the advantage of incurring no salvage costs, so were more easily disposable. Despite hopes for a rallying in the scrap metal market, the price continued to drop steadily. Over the next two years the price fell from about 70 shillings per ton in 1929 to only 30 shillings per ton by 1932.

Cox gave the order to halt work, keeping just seventy men from his workforce of up to 200 to maintain the plant. Several ideas have been put forward as to why he wanted to quit the Flow after such a staggering eight-year success. Some said that the death of William Tait affected Cox much more than he would admit openly. The lack of an explanation for the fatal explosion meant that another might happen and Cox's rigid pragmatism did not allow for the lack of a causal reason for such an accident. He was, indeed, sorry for Tait's death, but not as upset as many have believed.

His workers had been whispering for some time that Metal Industries and other ship breakers had been manipulating the price of scrap metal to force Cox & Danks out of business. There is evidence to show that when Cox successfully raised some ships, from the *V.70* in 1924 right up to the *Von der Tann* and *Prinzregent Luitpold* in 1931, the market did drop considerably at the same time. But by the time the *Prinz* and the *Von der Tann* were ready to be broken up, Metal Industries were only producing about 50 per cent of their normal scrap output compared with the previous two years, and had recently declared their first financial loss. No doubt Cox was also under pressure from Jenny Jack and Bunty to take life easier. He was now nearly fifty years old and had worked harder than most of his peers ever since he was a seventeen-year-old apprentice engineer. Cox's true reasons for quitting were twofold, the first dating back to 1926.

His first attempt to raise the *Hindenburg* was clearly made too soon in his salvage career. Cox's impetuous cavalier attitude failed him and the desperate attempt he made to hang on to her, only to lose the wreck to a storm, burnt his soul. Another facet of Cox's character was a sudden lack of interest in a subject, which came as quickly and as keenly as his initial complete absorption. Through the *Hindenburg* he lost his temper with himself and in doing so Cox sowed the seeds of his separation from Scapa Flow. His grandson, Jon Moore, recently recalled:

> Grandpa was very proud of what he did at Scapa. He was also very disappointed. He was hailed as a hero everywhere he went. He loved it. But even he knew in his heart of hearts that he lost his temper with the *Hindenburg*. He should have been more careful, but the word 'prudence' never came into his vocabulary.

By the time the *Prinzregent Luitpold* was secured Cox knew his salvage equipment was getting old. The fun had gone out of Scapa Flow and all his available funds were frozen in the two hulks floating idly in Mill Bay. His stubborn pride had already proved the experts wrong on every count and Cox was truly the world master of salvage, which nobody now denied.

Sitting back in his chair, Cox remained unfazed at his feelings regarding his motives and quite rightly stressed his successes in the Flow. He told the reporter:

> One way or another, I suppose our feat in raising no fewer than thirty-two men-of-war from the bed of Scapa Flow has been rather a wonderful achievement. Without boasting, I do not think there is another man in the world who could have tackled the same job. Before I undertook this formidable task, I had never raised a ship in my life. Quite frankly, experts thought me crazy, but to me these vessels represented nothing more than so much scrap of brass, gunmetal, bronze, steel etc., and I was determined to recover this at all costs.

151

He had first offered his Scapa Flow interests to Metal Industries for about £5,000, which they refused. There was very little they could use profitably should they wish to continue salvaging ships. In addition, although Metal Industries were expert at breaking up and selling wrecks, they lacked Cox's experience, and that of his men. This was a vital component for anyone willing to take over successfully. Cox then turned to another scrap metal company who looked at buying the operation, but they too turned it down. He even considered financing the towing of the two hulks to Rosyth and taking a chance by putting them up for auction to the highest bidder, to claw back at least some of his outlay. But he decided to hold on to them, should Metal Industries reconsider.

Meanwhile, Cox was assuring his remaining workforce at Lyness that after six weeks, 'some' work would be resumed. The six-week lay-off turned into a few months and in the spring 1932 he paid off the remaining workforce and predicted work would cease for at least a year. The compressed air that had been keeping the two capsized warships afloat for so long without a buyer was finally released. As the air vented, the metallic screaming was heard all over Lyness, as if the two ships were going down in pain. Eight years of prosperity for the Orcadian men and many others from around the United Kingdom, finally and officially came to an end.

Cox concentrated on his scrapyards, which had multiplied throughout the United Kingdom with one in London, Sheffield, and Manchester, and two in Birmingham. Without the costly outlay of raising whole ships and paying hundreds of men, the scrapyards did prosper. By the mid-1930s Cox & Danks, or 'C & D' as they were more fondly known, were well established as one of the top three scrap metal companies in the country. Cox settled into a routine of running his fledgling scrap metal empire out of Acton, London, when to his surprise, the Admiralty contacted him.

On 8 June 1931 the 25,000-ton *Iron Duke* class dreadnought HMS *Emperor of India* arrived in position off the south coast British town of Bognor, where she was to be used as target practice for secret firing trials. Early the following morning a strong south-westerly wind blew up. Her stern wire and starboard cable parted, forcing her to run aground on the nearby Owers Shoal. Two days later the trials went ahead as scheduled. The first ten shells rained down on her without causing any serious damage. The next two shells had a somewhat different effect. The first shell penetrated her 12in armour plating above the water-line, punching a small hole less than 2ft². The shell then pierced her 2¹/₂in sloping inner middle deck and passed through her bunkers, tearing away bulkheads as it travelled. In a matter of moments the shell tore into her 'B' boiler room and detonated, blasting outwards from the confined space, immediately blowing a 20ft² hole in her side below the water-line. The second shell was just as devastating; after bursting close to her starboard engine room it blew a hole about 56ft² inwards below the water-line. Although she was grounded, thousands of tons of water poured in through the two gaping holes, making any attempt to tow her clear of the Owers Shoal useless.

The following day the Admiralty mounted their salvage operation. As Cox did for the *Hindenburg* they, too, opted to patch the holes and pump her dry. Altogether more than sixty skilled shipwrights, acetylene burners, mechanics and electricians from Portsmouth Dockyard and a further sixty unskilled men built and fitted the patches and commenced pumping. The more they sucked the water out, the more she seemed to flood. Successive diving surveys found small openings. Each one was plugged, but she still failed to rise. With every tide the *Emperor of India* was rubbing her bottom along the seabed, puncturing it in numerous places. Any amount of pumping was futile. Then another storm on 9 July carried away one of the two patches, rendering many days of work useless. After nearly seven weeks of fruitless effort the Admiralty contacted Cox.

He must have chuckled at the irony of the Admiralty now calling on his services after their experts had considered the arrogant scrap dealer 'crazy'; a man who could not possibly succeed where they had failed in the Flow. He took the job. But, unlike with the *Hindenburg*, he was unable to carry out McKenzie's straight 'pumping job'. The only option was his revolutionary compressed air method, but this time on an upright ship with her superstructure above the high-tide mark – now that was a challenge! Along with his third officer, Ernest McKeown, Cox took a few hand-picked men and some equipment down south to get the job done. Upon his arrival at Portsmouth all the Royal Naval personnel were put under his personal supervision and the new salvage operation began at once.

Although one of the patches was now gone and there were many other openings along her bottom, the use of compressed air meant that none of the gashes caused by the tide, or the gaping shell hole, needed to be covered. All that was required was to force in compressed air sufficient to lift her clear of the rocks and then tow her to Portsmouth Dockyard. However, time was now against him. The next available spring tide was between 13 and 17 August, only a month away. Cox immediately began his standard plan for a compressed air lift. The *Emperor of India* was divided into sections and all bulkheads sealed. All her trunk, gland and pipe openings on deck were also sealed and all hatches between the superstructure and below decks were closed. Airlocks were built to gain access through the main deck where men entered to plug any small holes as the level dropped. Within a week the first pound of pressure was on.

All was going to plan when by chance Cox realized that there were not enough explosives available to blast off some of the battleship's jagged metal below the water-line. He flew into one of his famous rages. Cox did not intend to lose precious time because of such an oversight. The Navy's bureaucratic minefield, which had to be negotiated every time the slightest job had to be done, made him livid. Trying to buy and deliver explosives through the paperwork chain was simply not fast enough. After all, his professional integrity, or more likely his pride, was at stake. The fastest way to get the explosives was to drive out of Portsmouth Naval Dockyard, buy it commercially and smuggle it back through the dockyard's maximum security system then out to the battleship. Cox got into his car, started the engine and drove out towards the security gate. The guards had got to know the strange man salvaging the old target ship quite well over the weeks, and waved him though without a second thought. Several hours later he returned. The back seat of his car was piled high with gelignite – only hidden by a rug.

He approached the gate as if nothing was wrong and coolly waved and smiled to the guards. They waved him on without as second glance and he drove through the dockyard carrying enough explosives to be arrested for suspected treason. He pulled up to his motor launch and hastily transferred the gelignite before steaming out to the *Emperor of India*'s wreck site. Again sheer nerve had got Cox through, and the Admiralty was none the wiser. The *Emperor of India* was eventually raised on 14 August 1931, right in the middle of his three-day spring tide deadline.

Royal Navy Lieutenant H. E. Guerrier worked with Cox and was full of praise for his compressed air method. A few months later he wrote an article giving detailed information on how she sank and how much better Cox's compressed air system was compared with contemporary salvage practice. According to Admiralty procedure, Guerrier had to apply for permission to publish his article, which immediately ruffled the Admiralty over what they perceived to be detailed coverage of the secret trials. Regarding the shell damage they stated:

> It is considered that the less the *Emperor of India* trials, and their results, about which all foreign countries are endeavouring to obtain information, are advertised, the better.

Guerrier said:

> The subject of the secret trials has been studiously avoided, and that far from the cause of the damage being divulged, the major injury, from the description given of it, might well be attributed to a torpedo.

Although Cox had raised many warships using compressed air, the Admiralty curtailed Guerrier's enthusiastic comments on this new method.

'This paper', they continued, 'is not a suitable one in which to discuss the use of compressed air in salvage operations.' Still, a heavily edited version of Guerrier's article was published, but with very little mention of Cox and the use of compressed air in marine salvage.

The prediction of another year until the sale of the *Prinzregent Luitpold* and the *Von der Tann* became two years. However, by early 1933 scrap prices had crept back up to a more respectable 50 shillings per ton and in February he sold both ships to Metal Industries for £68,500 out of an original value of about £75,000. Cox, though, was still responsible for getting the warships safely to Rosyth. The Lyness yard was once again staffed and prepared to ready the ships for their last journey south. The *Prinzregent Luitpold*, the last ship raised, was the first of the two to be delivered. Again, 2m.ft^2 of compressed air was forced back into her hull and the final preparations were made to secure her for the open sea.

Two huts were erected on the upturned hull. The one nearest the bow was the self-contained power station. Two compressors were installed to supply enough compressed air through an arrangement of lines to any section, should a massive leak occur while in transit, and a dynamo was fitted to provide electric lighting. Two lifeboats and a life raft were also secured in case the *Prinz* was lost.

Eight years' experience had taught Cox the best method for building towing posts strong enough to take the pulling and steering power of the tugs in all weather conditions. The usual towing method for all ships consisted of one smaller tug on each side of an upturned hull and one bigger tug secured at her bow. About 200ft back from the bow, a bollard was bolted on to both the port and starboard sides, with a 2-ton hand winch secured behind them to help manoeuvre the lines from the smaller tugs. A similar bollard-and-hand-winch combination was fixed about 50ft ahead of these for the tow-lines from the main tug. Four hollow 10in fairleads were sunk deep into the ship's bow section to help guide the tow-lines. Cement was poured into the space to help strengthen the joint and railway lines were rammed into the hollow bollards before they, too, were filled with cement. The overall effect allowed the main tug to act as the ship's new engine and the two smaller tugs as her new port and starboard rudders.

By early May she was fully fitted out and seaworthy. Fourteen men comprised the runner crew and they made every attempt to make the upturned rusty hull as homely as possible. Their sense of comradely humour could be seen everywhere. A rough corrugated kitchen was erected and named the Hotel Metropole. The mess-room and bunkhouse for the men was called the Apartment De Luxe and one of the compression chambers was named the 'Cocktail Bar'. They even had a carved, wooden bird in a cage as a pet. James McAusland led the crew, which included foreman Jim Southerland and James Lewthwaite, a *Daily Mail* reporter.

The three German tugs, *Seefalke*, *Seeteufel* and *Parnass*, all flying the tricolour of the new German republic, fixed their tow-lines and heaved the *Prinz* out of Mill Bay, into Gutter Sound and south towards the Pentland Firth. As the procession passed Rattray Head on one of the most north-easterly tips of Scotland, the fog became so dense that for a short time the *Prinzregent Luitpold* and her tugs disappeared in the gloom. The crew aboard her could not see the tugs for many hours and only heard the constant booming of their sirens to alert any other vessel in the same area that a large tow was underway. Speed had to be increased fractionally so as not to put too much strain on the tow-lines. The top speed then reached was only 2½ to 3kts at the very best.

Cox travelled down with his crew as far as Wick on the north-east Scottish coast and left in the tugboat *Ferrodanks* to join Jenny Jack and Bunty who were following the procession by car down through the Highlands. The *Seefalke* was instructed to leave wireless messages at each coastal town they steamed passed so Cox could be fully informed of his ship's progress. Meanwhile on board the *Prinz*, reporter James Lewthwaite was enjoying being part of the ship's crew. He later wrote:

> Jimmy Black is our cook. A great sailor. If it is fog, wind or rain, Jimmy just goes on cooking. Through all the turmoil of the Pentland Firth, Jimmy concentrated on boiled beef and carrots, with rice pudding to follow. Bill Hunt, our chief diver, a short cheerful man, walked about the deck with a proprietorial air.

Hunt had been the first man to enter the *Prinzregent Luitpold* when the first airlock was attached to her upturned hull nearly two-and-a-half years earlier. 'He was most cheerful when the swell was heaviest and our compressed air was escaping from underneath the ship in twenty-foot bubbles,' continued Lewthwaite.

Just before the *Prinzregent Luitpold* arrived at the Firth of Forth, Cox rejoined her to make his penultimate triumphant arrival at Rosyth. The usual crowds of interested spectators were there to welcome her arrival, with Cox, as always, at her bow taking the glory. Among the cheering crowds, British sailors aboard a recently returned destroyer flotilla shouted him on. But among the myriad small pleasure craft was a German naval training cutter with boys of their new navy learning how to row. As the once mighty battleship passed by their cutter, the boys stopped rowing and solemnly held their oars upright in a final salute to the shattered image of their once Imperial High Seas Fleet.

On the night of 11 May 1933 the *Prinzregent Luitpold* was towed into the Admiralty dry dock at Rosyth a little before 5.00 pm on the high tide and secured in place for the breakers to take her apart. Bunty was on the quay to wave encouragement to her father along with her mother. They had both dashed from nearby Edinburgh to be in time for the *Prinz*'s arrival. Once the gangway was in place Cox's twenty-four-year-old daughter was among the first on board the floodlit ship to welcome her father to Rosyth. One of the first men she met was Lewthwaite. She laughed as she saw the reporter and said:

> We have certainly kept well in touch with your progress. We have dashed about a little in following you, but now that it is all over I feel very proud for Father's sake. I think one might be proud of a father who handles old battleships so successfully!

Scrap metal prices held and within three months the *Von der Tann* was pumped full of compressed air and fitted out for delivery with her thirteen-man crew taking Cox's last warship out of the Flow. At 11.00 am on the morning of 5 July 1933 she was towed out of Mill Bay on a half ebb tide and through Cantic Sound to catch the flood tide into the Pentland Firth. The procession set out in stormy weather and turbulent seas that plagued the *Von der Tann*'s final four-day voyage. Finally they arrived in the Firth of Forth, two miles from the Admiralty dry dock, and anchored for the night. Cox went out to her on a pilot cutter the following morning for his last moment of glory.

The first sunshine for many days shone down on Scotland's east coast as the *Von der Tann* was towed the last couple of miles. As she passed under the Forth Bridge in the mid-afternoon heat, a passenger train lumbered overhead like summer thunder. The rumbling vibrated through the bridge's steelwork and briefly drowned out the horns and sirens from the motor launches, cabin cruisers, pinnaces, sloops and yachts that weaved and dodged in and out of the procession. Cox stood proudly on his last prize in the bright sunlight, facing for the final time the throngs of spectators who had come to pay homage to the end of his great salvage achievement.

After the *Von der Tann* was secured, he gave an interview and stated that he was glad the eight-year adventure was now all over. But he had formed an élite crew of the best salvage experts in the world. Men who began their working lives as crofters, stewards, shipwrights, electricians and merchant seamen were destined, ironically, to become an asset to the very Government who once scoffed at the amateurs in the Flow.

A sinister hint of things to come was seen aboard one of the tugs as she helped steer the *Von der Tann* to Rosyth. A few months before

Cox was ready to take her south, Adolph Hitler's National Socialist Party came to power and this tug had swapped its German Republican flag for the Nazi Swastika. The crowds who had flocked to see Cox's arrival were among some of the first British people to see this new and menacing German emblem, which six years later would be a common symbol of evil throughout the free world.

With the *Von der Tann* safely delivered to Rosyth, Cox was keen to sell his salvage operation, even if this meant dropping his price. Cox said, 'I am sorry to leave my men, but I have taken risks for ten years and I can no longer continue to take them.' Metal Industries were still reluctant to buy without the guarantee of experienced workers in the deal. With the threat of unemployment, re-recruiting most of Cox's ablest men was not thought to be a major obstacle. But the key figure was McKenzie who convinced Metal Industries' managing director, the portly Robert McCrone, that with a considerable cash injection into the project and of course his own unique experience, all the remaining ships could be raised. The scrap metal market was coming out of its slump. Very shortly there would be a great demand for all forms of metal for rearmament as Britain again prepared to go to war with Germany.

Metal Industries were by now the biggest shipbreaking firm in Great Britain and if they could gain access to the highly prized German steel on the bottom of Scapa Flow, they could make a tremendous profit. About a month after Cox delivered the *Von der Tann*, Metal Industries offered him only £3,500 for his entire operation at Lyness. Although considerably less than his asking price, Cox agreed to the offer and finally severed all his ties with Scapa Flow. McKenzie was made chief salvage officer for Metal Industries and the first task at Lyness was to break up most of Cox's plant that had served them both so well for so long.

One half of Cox's unique floating dock was towed to Rosyth and broken up. His little tug, the *Ferrodanks*, was also scrapped and replaced with the 487-ton cargo ship *Bertha*, which had previously been used to carry Channel Island tomatoes from Guernsey and Jersey across to England's south coast. With McKenzie's new budget, she was fully fitted out as a state-of-the-art self-contained salvage vessel with her own decompression chamber, compressors, powerful winches and a variety of different workshops to cover the day-to-day salvage operational duties. The compressors alone were ten times more powerful than those operated by Cox.

McKenzie believed that to have the compressors and workshops on a ship would be far more beneficial than having them built into the side of a floating dock. When the *Bertha* was finished, she housed everything needed for a successful salvage operation, including 20 tons of old stones from the streets of Glasgow as ballast. She eventually became the home of sixty men, including divers, carpenters, electricians and catering staff.

Each time Cox had travelled up to Scapa Flow, he had taken a train up to Scrabster on the north coast of Scotland and then taken his own launch, the *Bunts*, across the Pentland Firth to Orkney. She was named after Cox's daughter and had been his own personal runabout while working in the Flow. He also owned von Reuter's pinnace, which he had sometimes used in the Flow when the sea was calm enough. Metal Industries' senior personnel always flew up to Kirkwall in a fraction of the time. In late January 1934, McKenzie flew into Kirkwall ahead of the *Bertha*'s arrival to begin his new salvage career under a new master. Cox's old depot at Lyness was ready and fully staffed, mainly with his old employees. The *Bertha* was still in Rosyth, taking on coal and provisions, and was due to arrive in the first week of February when work would immediately begin on the battleship *Bayern*.

Meanwhile Cox ploughed all his efforts into his growing chain of scrapyards after selling out to Metal Industries. He took all kinds of metal, from major factory break-ups to domestic scrap such as old bedsteads and pots and pans from members of the public. To achieve such success he doggedly and personally ran everything, from each branch's office stationery to international consultancy work, by repeatedly travelling between each outlet to oversee what his men were doing. His work ethic succeeded because the C & D staff were always alert to his presence or imminent arrival. The end result was a considerable personal fortune out of what many people considered to be nothing more than old rubbish. Six years would pass before McKenzie and Cox met again, but this time their combined salvage experience was needed to try to rescue nearly 100 men trapped in a foundered submarine at the bottom of Liverpool Bay.

Chapter 16

HMS *Thetis*

Salvage work progressed slowly for McKenzie aboard the battle cruiser *Derfflinger* on the morning of 1 June 1939. At the same time, about 500 miles further south in Liverpool Bay, Lieutenant Commander Guy 'Sam' Bolus of His Majesty's Submarine *Thetis* was climbing down from her conning tower and firmly securing the bridge hatch. She left Liverpool at about 9.30 am to start her first diving trials before formal delivery to the Royal Navy two weeks later. If all went well, she would be back alongside in Liverpool by 10.30 pm. The sea was calm and a blistering heat prevented any mist from obscuring a crisp horizon. It was a good day for her first official trial dive. The tugboat *Grebecock* was acting as escort, but from the moment the dive commenced, at 1.30 pm, her crew realized something had gone wrong. The *Thetis* lumbered, almost as if bouncing along the surface, and failed to dive.

Aboard the *Thetis* her ballast report showed that two of her six tubes were flooded to act as dummy torpedoes, but still the bow had been too light, meaning that perhaps the ballast report was wrong. One tube, Number Six, was checked by cracking a small inlet valve and was found to be flooded. Number Five tube was also checked by opening its inlet valve. No water escaped. Each tube should have carried 100 gallons, adding more than a ton to her overall crucial diving weight. To make doubly sure, the torpedo officer, Lieutenant Fredrick Woods, ordered a rating to open the dry tube, knowing that the outer bow cap was sealed. The rating slowly eased open the inner hatch. At first it refused to move then, suddenly, a solid circle of green water poured into the torpedo room. For reasons that have never been fully explained, the outer bow cap door was wide open. The pressure of a 1,500-ton *Triton* class submarine struggling to get below the surface, which was already steaming at 5kts with her hydroplanes at 10°, meant that the open sea was now gushing into the *Thetis* with colossal and unstoppable force.

Only 45 tons of water were needed to fill the compartment, which poured in at a rate of 2 tons per second. In the twenty or so seconds Woods and his men had to assimilate what had happened. All they could do was to struggle against the incoming freezing torrent and abandon the compartment at once. She could surface with one section flooded, but not two. The second compartment was nearly twice the size, giving them only about forty seconds to get through and close the door. They made it through, but because the hatch opened forward, the submarine's increasing angle made it hard to pull the door's weight up rather than close it in the normal manner. As they struggled to pull up the heavy steel door the lights went out. Fumbling in the dark, hand over hand, they fought to secure the eighteen hasps and butterfly latches around the door. In the darkness and confusion one of the hasps jammed between the hatch and its coaming. The second compartment had to be hastily abandoned. The third compartment housed the submarine's batteries and if the sea water came into contact with them, chlorine gas would fill the *Thetis* in minutes and kill everyone on board. The third compartment's hatch was quick-closing, having a central wheel that could be rapidly spun, thereby shutting all its latches at once.

Far from being too light, her flooded bow section now pulled the *Thetis* towards the seabed at a 40° angle. As the forward end bumped and scraped along the shingle, the submarine began to level off. HMS *Thetis* was now stranded on the seabed. The standard complement aboard a *Triton* class submarine was about fifty-nine officers and men. For her dive trials the full complement numbered 103, including technicians, engineers and observers all taking part in the many and varied tasks needed to pass a new submarine for active duty. The normal air supply for her crew was estimated to be about thirty-six hours. With nearly double the men exhaling carbon dioxide into their already cramped living space, and two compartments flooded, the air supply was now a drastically reduced unknown quantity.

On the surface, nearly three hours passed before observer Lieutenant Richard Coltart aboard the *Grebecock* contacted Britain's submarine base at Gosport, Hampshire, to ask how long the *Thetis*'s dive was due to last. Even then his message did not reach Gosport until after 6.00 pm. Gosport had already been trying to contact the *Thetis*, transmitting the same signal every ten minutes without an answer. Still no action was taken to launch Operation Subsmash (the Royal Navy's crack submarine rescue programme) until Coltart's message fuelled concerns that there might, indeed, be a problem.

After a brave, but failed attempt was made aboard the *Thetis* to pump out the flooded compartments, Bolus was left with few choices. His men could escape through the Davis escape hatch, wearing special breathing apparatus designed for submariners in just such a situation. But very few men aboard, including professional submariners, had been trained in how to use the escape system. Or he could wait for rescue from above. The water depth was 160ft and the *Thetis* was 275ft long. Bolus knew he could re-ballast her to put part of the stern above the water, thus giving their exact location and making escape a simple task. This procedure would take some time so he followed procedures and launched an indicator buoy. As the sun set, he fired a smoke candle and twenty-one indicator lights. With the *Grebecock* circling above, he thought rescue would only take a few hours.

With the *Thetis* more than four hours overdue, Subsmash was ordered at around 7.00 pm that evening. The Navy's duty destroyer HMS *Winchelsea* was in Portsmouth and would take nineteen hours to arrive. The deep-diving vessel HMS *Tedworth* was in the Clyde Estuary with no coal and would take about twenty hours to reach the scene. Four Avro Anson aircraft were dispatched from Glasgow at 7.40 pm and arrived at the search area at exactly 9.00 pm. That night the sun set at 9.04 pm. The few ships in the area, including the destroyer HMS *Brazen*, and the aircraft were expected to find a black submarine or a black oil slick in total darkness. To make matters worse, Captain Godfrey aboard the *Grebecock* could only give an approximate last position for the *Thetis*. This eventually proved to be hopelessly inaccurate, meaning that all available air and sea craft were searching in the wrong area anyway.

The *Thetis*'s men were already nearly six hours into their limited air supply. Carbon dioxide poisoning is notorious for having a wide degree of effects, often in healthy people, let alone those perhaps a little more out of condition. Lethargy was already setting in among the less fit and older men. Some were wheezing and complaining of headaches. As time dragged on there was no sign of rescue from above. Although attempts had failed to pump out the two compartments from within, it was possible to execute the plan from outside. This required a message being delivered by hand to the surface. A plan was formulated to send a fit man up through the escape airlock with a detailed account of what had happened and a sketch of how to force the water back out. The plan relied on fresh air being pumped in, while another hole allowed the toxic atmosphere to be blown out. This second hole was essential. If compressed air was forced in with no outlet, the carbon dioxide would pressurize and asphyxiate the men at a much faster rate. But with night falling, Bolus considered it folly to send men up only to break the surface in darkness and probably never to be found. Instead he concentrated on getting the *Thetis*'s stern above sea level.

Early the following morning Captain Oram, who was an observer aboard the *Thetis*, volunteered to take the message up to the surface, attached to his arm. Hopefully he, or his body, would be found and action taken before the submarine's air ran out. Lieutenant Woods was chosen to accompany Oram. Just before 8.00 am, with the *Thetis*'s stern now about 18ft above the water, the two men entered the after chamber wearing their Davis escape apparatus, closed the door, flooded the chamber and prepared to open the outer hatch to the sea. While they were preparing to leave, the *Thetis* shuddered with the impact of several small charges from HMS *Brazen*. They had been found. Just as the *Brazen* radioed their position to the Admiralty in Plymouth two heads broke the surface amid cheers. Captain Oram and Lieutenant Woods were hauled aboard a boat and rowed to the safety and warmth of the nearby warship. Oram unfastened their plan from his arm and offered it to the assembled senior naval personnel while giving a detailed account of the desperate situation oxygen starvation was causing within the *Thetis*. An urgent message was sent to Mersey Docks and Harbour Board requesting cutting gear with compressors and all the necessary equipment to effect a rescue. Meanwhile, no attempt was made to approach the *Thetis*. With two men up, the rest should now follow at twenty-minute intervals. If too many ships were near the stricken submarine, ascending men could be badly injured.

The time was now a little after 10.00 am. The trapped men had been submerged for nearly twenty hours. At twenty-minute intervals it would take another seventeen hours to get them all out, with the air quality diminishing every second as the internal atmosphere slowly became toxic. Aboard HMS *Thetis* the combined euphoria of the two men's successful escape and the certain knowledge that they had been found raced around the boat. Three men drained down the escape chamber ready for the next two to escape, but one opened the door too soon. Due to the *Thetis*'s now 60° angle, a low wave of sea water poured into the compartment, hitting a switchboard and some motors. Fire broke out instantly. Amid a cloud of choking white smoke the fire was extinguished, but precious air had been sucked into the flames.

What if their rescue plan could not be executed in time? What if another accident added to their already dire situation? Many breathing sets were lost in the flooded compartments. Others were used up trying to pump out the flooded area and for men to fight the fire. The increasing carbon dioxide levels were also taking their toll. Some men were involuntarily coughing and visibly becoming confused as their ability to concentrate degraded along with the air quality. Pulse rates were going up as the poisoning increased. Sweat drenched their clothes and men could be heard hyperventilating. Bolus knew time was running out and any attempted rescue from above was happening far too slowly.

Although the chamber was only designed for two men, four at a time were put in to get them to the surface as fast as possible. At least if some men could escape then precious air could be saved for those who were too unfit to chance what was becoming such a demanding exertion. The first four men were packed into the tiny chamber wearing their Davis breathing sets. The inner door was closed and the compartment filled. Outside the chamber their comrades waited for the shaft of light to shine in a spy hole, meaning the outer hatch was open and the occupants were free to swim up to the surface: it failed to appear.

After twenty minutes the chamber was drained and the door opened. Four twisted bodies jammed the space. Three were already dead and one was almost gone. The outer hatch was jammed. Each panic-stricken man had ripped off the others' breathing sets as they fought, clawed and bit to survive in the black, freezing water-filled compartment. Looking down on the white faces frozen in the men's final agonizing moments, any morale left among the living was shattered.

Immediately two more volunteers were asked for, probably to show that this was still a good form of escape. Leading stoker Walter Arnold and Cammel Laird engine fitter Frank Shaw agreed to go. Shaw was already suffering from bad carbon dioxide poisoning. He described the air as 'very thick' and could hardly speak due to a choking feeling around his throat. They entered the chamber, the door was closed, and the chamber was again flooded. Icy water once again hissed into the tiny space and gradually worked its way up their bodies, passed their knees, hips, chest, and over their heads. Arnold reached up to open the out hatch. It was jammed. He calmly withdrew, waited a few minutes to allow the pressure to equalize and tried again. This time the door opened and the two men were free to swim to the surface.

News of the submarine accident became known nationwide by mid-morning. In Scapa Flow McKenzie had heard the news at around 10.00am and his first thought was to offer the full use of his men and their expertise. He immediately contacted both the Admiralty and the Birkenhead-based builders of the *Thetis*, Cammell Laird. Two-and-a-half hours later he received a reply, thanking him for the kind offer, but McKenzie was told that the submarine had been found and all aboard were reported safe. He then returned to the immediate problems of trying to raise the *Derfflinger*. When Cox heard the news he was at his new head office called Scapa House in Park Royal, London. He immediately telephoned both the Admiralty and Cammel Laird to offer his services as a salvage expert. His offer, like McKenzie's, was politely refused.

There were now sixteen vessels in a circle around the *Thetis*. Slow carbon dioxide poisoning was having a serious effect. Some men's eyes were constantly watering and they were also panting. Many had no idea that they were going into pre-renal failure, the stage just before their kidneys would stop functioning altogether. Some were involuntarily twitching, vomiting and shaking. Others suffered from blinding headaches and even carbon dioxide-induced depression. Thought processes and actions were starting to happen in slow motion, as the effort to concentrate on the simplest tasks was becoming impossible. In theory the lucky ones would remain lucid enough to effect an escape for about twenty-four hours. After about thirty hours none were thought to be capable of the elementary tasks needed to operate the escape chamber.

On the surface still little was happening. Everyone was expecting more heads to appear. There was still no sign of the rescue equipment from Liverpool, which did not leave aboard the tugboat *Crosby* until nearly midday, nearly four hours after being requested. Meanwhile, Bolus could see that an increasing number of men were looking less

166

and less likely to have the strength to leave. He knew he must still get as many out as possible. The chamber was prepared for the next two men. When it was flooded, the men attempted to open the outer hatch. It moved a little then jammed again. The men hammered on the hatch to free it, but had to admit defeat, drain the chamber and go back into the *Thetis*'s toxic interior. Two more men tried. Once the chamber was flooded they, too, managed to open the hatch only a few inches before it again jammed. The ninety-nine souls aboard the *Thetis* were now trapped. There was no alternative but to wait for rescue from above.

By now the deep-diving vessel, HMS *Tedworth*, had arrived. The tugboat *Grebecock* was also standing by along with the destroyer HMS *Brazen*, three Sixth flotilla destroyers and HMS *Winchelsea* from Portsmouth. At least seven Royal Navy vessels were now in attendance. McKenzie, having resumed his salvage operation for the *Derfflinger*, simultaneously received two more telegrams. One was from the Admiralty stating, 'Grateful for your assistance, request you start immediately to submarine.' The second telegram arrived from the King's Harbour Master at Scapa Flow. '*Thetis* position is desperate. There is aeroplane waiting at Longhope to take you and 3 or 4 divers to Liverpool, changing at Inverness to be at Speke Aerodrome at 5pm.'

McKenzie's senior diver Sinc Mackenzie (who had survived a similar fate aboard the *Von der Tann* a few years before), along with two other divers, Peter Taylor and James Thomson, was about 140ft below the surface working on the *Derfflinger*. McKenzie telephoned down an emergency message for the three men to return to the surface at once. He explained the gravity of the situation as they were taking off their diving gear aboard the launch to Lyness. A car took them to the plane in nearby Longhope. The plane was only designed to carry five people. McKenzie, the three divers, two diving attendants and an assistant salvage officer greatly overloaded the tiny aircraft. Seven people now had to squeeze into a space for five, and hope the plane could get off the ground and safely to Inverness. The pilot turned into the wind and opened up the throttle as the plane bounced along the runway before becoming airborne.

Two hours before they were due to arrive in Liverpool, the tugboat *Crosby* arrived at the wreck site with the cutting gear that had been urgently requested nearly six hours before. (The steaming time from her mooring to the wreck site was only two-and-a-half hours.) The tide was dropping and *Thetis*'s stern began to move. Before burning commenced, a 3½in wire was strung under her stern between two ships to secure it from the possibility of sinking. At first the plan worked well. Then, without warning, the *Thetis* tilted and started to sink once again. This put too much strain on the wire, which parted with explosive force. The razor-sharp ends flailed about the *Thetis* as she disappeared under the waves.

At Inverness, the Admiralty's chartered plane took the rescue party down to Speke Aerodrome where a car rushed them to Liverpool's Princes Landing Stage, normally used to embark and disembark passengers from Cunard and White Star liners. From there they were taken out to the *Thetis* wreck site aboard the *Tribal* class destroyer, HMS *Matabele*. They arrived at about 10.00 pm, two hours before whatever breathable atmosphere left within the submarine was due to expire. A conference was held aboard the Sixth flotilla leader, HMS *Somali*, between McKenzie and his men, naval officials and Cammel Laird executives.

Since early in the morning the internal temperature had been dropping aboard the *Thetis* as the batteries began to fail and the cold from the water outside soaked through the hull. Lethargy had become rife. Men were lying down or slumped against bulkheads. Mental confusion was becoming worse. Some were probably already dead. About the time McKenzie and his men left Scapa Flow, a few men still had enough sense not to give up and yet another escape attempt was made. Two more men dragged themselves into the escape chamber. The door was shut and the chamber flooded. Then one of the two men tried to open the hatch, but not up to freedom. Through confusion or exhaustion he opened the watertight door leading back into the *Thetis*.

The two escapees were sucked back into the submarine on a wave of inbound water pouring in from the open sea. One man was snagged by his belt loop and pinned to the hatch as the water poured over him. The massive inrush had the same effect as pumping in compressed air with no outlet. Before the flood had its chance to drown whoever was still alive, the pressurized carbon dioxide brought on rapid asphyxiation. Although death was swift, it was far from painless. The men gagged and wretched like fish out of water. As the seconds passed and the carbon dioxide continued to pressurize, some primeval desire to live induced others to suck the foul air into their lungs, causing their eyes to bulge as they bit their own tongues. Others curled up or hugged each other in a last bid to gain what comfort they could as the dense carbon dioxide levels brought on welcome death. But for some their agony was not yet over.

When McKenzie was told that no men had reached the surface for more than twelve hours he was shocked that no other action had been taken between the nine or so Royal Navy vessels now in the immediate vicinity. He ordered Sinc Mackenzie to dive immediately and see if there were still signs of life. He was not ready to dive until about 1.00 am on 3 June, nearly one hour after the last of the air was estimated to be gone. He dived down to the wreck and hammered hard against her side. The vibration travelled through the *Thetis*. Bang! Bang! Bang! Then came a faint but distinct reply from the vicinity of the control room.

There was still life on board, but because the tide was turning, Sinc Mackenzie could only stay down for about fifteen minutes before returning to the surface and reporting his good news. The strong tidal current meant it would not be possible to safely attempt another dive until 6.00 am the same morning. Just before sunrise McKenzie's two other divers descended to the submarine. For nearly an hour they walked around her hull hitting it with a hammer as hard as they could. There was no reply. At about 5.00 pm, the Admiralty formally announced that all life was lost. The *Thetis* had now been submerged for fifty hours. With nothing more to be done to save her crew, McKenzie and his men returned to Scapa Flow.

A month later they were summonsed to give evidence at the public inquiry. The question arose about whether there was cutting gear present. Under oath McKenzie said, 'I cannot say whether there was any gear to do the work. There was oxy-acetylene gear, but whether there was a full apparatus I do not know. I rather think there was. Any ordinary oxy-acetylene apparatus would have done the job if operated by an expert cutter.'

'Is that a thing you could have done on the *Thetis*,' asked King's Counsel Geoffrey Hutchinson.

'Yes,' replied McKenzie.

'Should you have drilled a hole just above the water, and would it have been a good thing?'

'Very definitely. Two pipes would have been needed – one to pump in air and another to let foul air escape'.

'What about the gear, was it there?' asked Attorney General, the Right Honourable Sir Donald Somervell.

'The gear was aboard the destroyers,' replied Hutchinson.

'Quite right,' commented Somervell. In fact the destroyers had arrived at the wreck site around mid-morning when the men still had a maximum of fourteen hours air left.

While working as a young diver in 1917, McKenzie was involved in the *K.13* 'Killer' submarine rescue attempt in Gareloch. A similar plan to Bolus's was adopted. After her stern was flooded the *K.13*'s bow was raised above the surface by her captain to give their position and effect an escape. Once above the surface the bow was burnt into with oxy-acetylene torches to allow forty-six men to successfully escape. McKenzie told the inquiry that he wanted to adopt a similar procedure for the *Thetis*:

> I could have cut a hole into 'Z' tank [aft] and another through the tank into the pressure hull. It would have taken five to seven minutes to cut each hole big enough to get a man out. In view of what Captain Oram had said about the condition of the men, I should have treated it as a matter of extreme urgency and cut a hole inside the ship to get the men out. I would have waited an hour or an hour-and-a-half before assuming that the men in the submarine could not escape, but I would not have delayed any longer taking the measures I suggested.

During the weeks following the loss, Cox had plenty of time to think through what had happened. The failure of simple procedure and sound common sense angered him greatly. A day after the inquiry opened he wrote a lengthy letter to Mr Justice, Alfred Townsend Bucknill, the chairman of the *Thetis* inquiry, to explain how *he* could have saved the men and the submarine in only a few hours. His rescue plan was similar to McKenzie's, but Cox went one stage further to show how the *Thetis* could have been salvaged and how such a tragedy could be avoided in future. In his characteristically blunt, working-class way he had no time for subtlety:

> When the *Thetis* was found with her stern out of the water the ship, as we would say in salvage language, was a gift. All that was required was someone with salvage experience, to take charge and direct salvage operations.
>
> The first thing was to get out on the spot with compressors and tools, and drill a hole in the stern of the submarine. This

would have been child's play as we have done similar jobs hundreds of times in worse conditions, and my divers have done the job underwater. The time at the very outside should have been fifteen to thirty minutes. The hole would then be tapped and a three-quarter bend or straight piece of pipe screwed in same, and a check valve, if one has been thought of but it's not very essential. I am positive compressed air could have been put into the ship within one hour after the arrival of the tug or ship with a compressing plant. If this had been done, there is no question that everyone in the submarine would have been saved, also the submarine itself.

The letter impressed Bucknill who suggested to Somervell that he invite Cox to give evidence. The Attorney General agreed to hear him and Cox was formally invited to attend. As McKenzie stepped down from the witness box, Cox was next to give evidence. They passed very closely and nodded to each other before Cox took his former colleague's place in the witness box. 'I am positive the disaster to the *Thetis* could have been avoided if proper precautions had been taken previously,' he said. 'I feel so positive that I could suggest alterations which would prevent similar disasters, that I would be prepared to pay for the necessary alterations to one submarine to prove my conviction.'

He reiterated the contents of his letter before the court, adding, 'Even with only one compressor, they would have been able to build up the pressure and displace all the water in five hours.' He then declared emphatically, 'It sounds extremely easy, and it is as easy as it sounds, if salvage men with experience of compressed air are on the spot.' He was adamant that the stern should not have been tampered with. 'That was one of the biggest errors, which cost the men their lives.'

To prevent a similar accident happening again, Cox suggested that all submarines should have valves to pump oil to the outside and alert rescue vessels to a submarine's position. Along the lines of the warships he had raised at Scapa Flow, he added that each submarine compartment should be fitted with connections to pump in compressed air and outlets to release the water. Attorney General Somervell then informed Cox that the fore hatch, which Woods and his men struggled in vain to close, was not of the quick-closing type. Director of Naval Construction, Sir Stanley Goodall, had already informed the inquiry that although a quick-closing door was specified, Admiralty policy decided not to fit it due to space restrictions and the necessity for quick and unhindered access between the two compartments. Cox paused for a moment as if stunned, 'Then the whole of my evidence is of no use. I am more staggered than ever. It does not give the men a chance. My plan of salvaging the *Thetis* would have been a wash out in view of this terrible disclosure.'

'You are not entitled to make an observation of that sort,' cut in the Attorney General before Cox had time to finish his sentence.

'I am entitled to my views,' Cox replied defiantly.

'I do not think you ought to take advantage of your position in the witness box to condemn anything. A phrase like "a terrible disclosure" is not justified, and does a certain amount of harm to uninstructed people.'

Cox suddenly and calmly gathered up his notes along with a small piece of machinery he brought along to back up his plan, stepped out of the witness box without instruction and walked out of the stunned court without looking back. Somervell adjourned for the day.

From the *Triton* class of the 1930s right up until today's *Vanguard* class nuclear-powered submarines, every rear torpedo tube hatch is opened fractionally with the aid of a swing bolt to ensure the tube is not flooded. Although the design of the swing bolt has changed over the years with the evolution of the submarine, its job remains the same. Another aspect of the swing bolt has not altered through the years; its other name – the '*Thetis* clip'.

Although they were world leaders in the use of compressed air, Navy procedure and sheer bad luck meant that Cox and McKenzie could do nothing to help avert what is still the worst peacetime disaster in British submarine history. Both men felt bitter at the outcome. No one was officially blamed for either the loss of the submarine, or her crew. More than seventy women were widowed and ninety children orphaned.

In the aftermath, many questions were asked regarding the conduct of the Royal Navy and Cammel Laird. The *Thetis* cost £305,000 and took eighteen months to build. War was about to be declared. Gossip around the streets and pubs of Liverpool suggested that the Admiralty wanted the submarine more than the men, and that cutting into the inner pressure hull would render her useless. Eventually HMS *Thetis* was salvaged and re-fitted. Almost a year later she became HMS *Thunderbolt* and went on to complete six impressive tours of duty, eventually transferring to the Mediterranean.

On her seventh tour, the *Thunderbolt* successfully attacked an enemy merchant convoy bound for Italy. One of the convoy escorts was an Italian corvette commanded by an ex-submariner. Using his skills, he doggedly chased the *Thunderbolt*, eventually tracking her down and launching a depth charge attack on her near the Messina Strait between Italy and Sicily. He scored a direct hit. The *Thunderbolt* broke the surface stern-first for the second time in her life before nose-diving 3,000ft to the seabed, taking her entire complement of sixty-one officers and men with her. By the time she hit the bottom, HMS *Thetis/Thunderbolt* had claimed the lives of 162 British civilians and military personnel during her unlucky six-year life.

There is no known record to show whether Cox was allowed to 'pay for the necessary alterations to one submarine' to prove his conviction that minor changes could be made in submarine design to prevent such a waste of life from ever happening again.

Chapter 17

Salvage Heritage

Cox's salvage heritage has left behind many direct and indirect consequences leading right up to the present day. One of the greatest contributions his men and his expertise made was during the Second World War when marine salvage played an integral role in recovering merchant ships for North Atlantic convoy runs. Before, during and after D-Day, the salvage work undertaken by McKenzie and other Scapa Flow men greatly helped the Allied advance on Germany. Today, marine salvage is a highly specialized business that has advanced beyond all recognition since Cox and his men threaded their first steel wire under the *V.70* in 1924. But as the salvage business goes into the twenty-first century, the basic principles he laid down at Scapa Flow remain the same.

When Cox set out to strip Scapa Flow of her rich metal deposits, he had no idea of how he would change marine salvage. For him the enterprise was solely a means to make a great deal of money as quickly as possible. After he had been paid for delivery of the *Prinzregent Luitpold* and the *Von der Tann*, he could finally measure his salvage operation profits. The final costs for the outlay on wages and materials, as well as the initial purchase price for the ships, amounted to £500,000 (about £24m. today). More than £300,000 (or about £14m. in real terms) of this sum was spent on the men's wages alone. The remaining £200,000 covered initial vessel purchases, machinery and insurance premiums. The actual declared earnings for Cox & Danks's salvage business amounted to only £490,000, most of which went straight back into the business. In 1939 he wrote in a personal letter:

I only gave up the salvage work at Scapa Flow in 1933 because I was, at that time, only getting £30,000 for a battleship delivered into Rosyth Dockyard when the cost of lifting the ship was at least £45,000.

He was never really disappointed at his £10,000 loss, which seems small by twenty-first century figures, but in 1933 the amount represented £300,000. He had always maintained that the risk was solely his and that if it was a foolhardy one, he alone would lose by it. Cox openly admitted that his financial reserves were greatly harmed by errors he made in the early years, such as trying to use anchor chains when raising the *V.70*, and the many mistakes he made during the first attempt to raise the *Hindenburg* in 1926. But what he lost in financial reward Cox certainly made up for in prestige and worldwide acclaim for his somewhat head-strong, but extremely successful, approach to marine salvage. If, indeed, after all the final accounting was considered, he really did present a complete picture of his profit and loss.

Cox was a very astute businessman who continued to raise ships at a time when the price for recovered metal was low and labour costs were high. His pride and ego definitely played a part in his limitless professional drive, but would he really have persevered for so long had he known that ultimately he would perhaps have to face bankruptcy and the whispered 'I-told-you-so' comments from the established salvage community. Cox's grandson, Jon Moore, said:

Because of the falling price of scrap he did not make as much money as he should have. As to whether he physically made a numerical loss, I have been led to believe that is the case. I think nobody in the family dared ask or delve to actually find out what was the case, and probably it is now far too late to find out.

Whatever the truth really was back in 1933, the media called Cox's achievement a 'triumph of individual effort', which was the sort of adulation he loved. But his very individuality contributed greatly to his not making the profits that were readily available and were eventually reaped by others. Metal Industries was clearly in a more powerful position to buy the wrecks at a much cheaper price than Cox could ever negotiate. By fostering contacts within the Admiralty over many years they were able to get advanced information on internal Admiralty policy and thus secure much more competitive rates. Although considered an unethical and perhaps even illegal practice today, in the 1930s such a strategy was considered fair – especially by those who had the advantage. Metal Industries was established as the biggest shipbreaking firm in Britain when they undertook to salvage the *Bayern* in 1934. Through their Admiralty contacts she was purchased for only £750, which was almost a quarter of the price Cox had to pay for some of his capital ships. The price of scrap metal was also climbing as demand for steel escalated with the possibility of another war looming.

When the *Bertha* was ready to leave Rosyth bound for Lyness to commence salvage work, Cox's former depot was already fully modernized and fitted out with all-new plant necessary for breaking up the many tons of scrap in which Metal Industries had invested. The firm also put a great deal of time and money into making life as comfortable as possible for their new and specialized workforce. The island of Hoy, on which Lyness forms the main harbour, is very remote today with only 400 residents. During the 1920s and 1930s life was even more isolated. The men's ex-Navy barracks were refitted and a badminton court was built as well as a football club to occupy their leisure time. Every second Saturday a tugboat took them across to the nearby island of Pomona to visit the cinema in Kirkwall. They were also given a week's paid leave each year and had a pension scheme.

The new salvage team was hand-picked out of the many men McKenzie had worked with under Cox. Only the best were considered and those more than forty years old were rejected. Their new working conditions were to be much more dangerous, with divers regularly working at depths in excess of anything they had experienced before. This required a much higher fitness level to work both inside the wrecks and on the seabed. To compensate for the added danger, the men were paid higher than the average daily rate. They were also allowed to bring their wives and children to live with them on Hoy, and before long a happy, albeit small community flourished.

Work on the *Bayern* began in January 1934 and by the end of July she was afloat and ready to prepare for the breaker's yard. McKenzie successfully raised six capital ships under his new masters, thanks to their more modern equipment. His eight years working for Cox proved to be an invaluable experience. Three of the deeper warships were of the 24,000-ton *Kaiser* class, the *Kaiserin*, the *Konig Albert* and the *Friedrich de Grosse*. Allowing for the normal technical difficulties every salvage operation brings, these three battleships were the same class as the *Kaiser* and the *Prinzregent Luitpold*. He knew the ships well, so finding and sealing the necessary internal bulkheads was a relatively speedy operation. McKenzie also raised the 25,000-ton battleship *Grosser Kurfurst*. Between 1934 and 1939 he salvaged one battleship each year. McKenzie was so confident he could do the job he took a low salary for a high bonus on each ship delivered. Often his bonus was as high as £5,000. On 29 April 1938 he surprised his new employers by raising the *Grosser Kurfurst* exactly a year to the day after the *Friedrich der Grosse*. By today's inflation rates the two wrecks earned him a little under £500,000 for twelve month's work. Metal Industries made about £58m. by today's buying power.

The next choice was the 26,000-ton battleship *Derfflinger*, which was a particularly difficult ship to raise. McKenzie was reluctant to even try and voiced his views to the Metal Industries Board. She was down twice the depth of the *Moltke*, with men having to work at pressures of nearly 65lb/in² inside her. The board pressured him into raising her and he reluctantly agreed to at least try. McKenzie eventually succeeded, but always maintained that the *Derfflinger* was the deepest and most difficult of all the wrecks he had raised. The depth and pressure were so great that the divers could only work for a one-hour shift instead of the normal eight. They then had to decompress for a full ninety minutes after each work session to avoid getting the bends.

By the time Metal Industries had established themselves in the Flow, the political situation had changed considerably in Europe. Adolph Hitler said publicly that it was too humiliating for the German people to know that tugs from the Fatherland were being used to tow the remains of their once mighty navy to be broken up for British profit. He formally recalled the tugboats and they were never again allowed to undertake the work. The *Seefalke*, being the most powerful tug in the world at the time, was sorely missed, but the Dutch firm, Smit, took over the contract and safely delivered the remaining hulks to Rosyth. Through McKenzie's experience, Metal Industries were then able to raise a capital ship, break it up into ferrous and non-ferrous scrap, and sell the metal with an average clear profit in excess of £60,000 per vessel for all six they recovered – something Cox dreamt about but never achieved.

Ironically at this time the British Government allowed UK companies to sell scrap armour plate from both the German ships scuttled in Scapa Flow and the scrapped British warships, back to Germany. Some of the steel armour plate was turned into scissors, then re-exported back into Britain to supply the consumer market. In the United States, knives, forks and spoons for American dinner tables were pressed out of German armour plate. Many of the gramophone needles and razor blades used throughout Europe and America during the 1930s had once been part of one German warship or another.

However, a great deal of the scrap was exported to Vereinigte Stahlwerke, or United Steelworks, who were one of the main suppliers of raw materials to Germany's secret armaments programme in the latter 1920s and early 1930s. Germany was desperately short of key materials like manganese, chromium, nickel and copper. A great deal of these metals came from the scrap salvaged by Cox and later by Metal Industries, and found their way back into enemy warships. It is interesting to note that while thousands of tons of valuable metal were being exported from Scapa Flow to rearm Nazi Germany, there were shortages for Britain's own naval armament programme. Vereinigte Stahlwerke were also one among many companies who financed Adolph Hitler's meteoric rise to power.

The new Nazi Government even offered to buy a small number of the complete guns that had been removed from the salvaged ships. Germany approached the British Government, claiming that the guns were needed only for coastal defences, and experimental and metallurgical purposes. On 21 October 1936, Prime Minister Stanley Baldwin's Cabinet informed the German Embassy that there would be no objection to export licences being granted, allowing Germany to buy the guns they wanted. The steel manufacturer Messrs Stern of Essen, also made an independent bid for the guns directly to McKenzie's new boss at Metal Industries, Donald Pollock. He was unwilling to sell them without written authority from the Admiralty or the Government. Quite why Baldwin's Cabinet were willing to sell the guns the year after Adolph Hitler admitted to Germany's secret arms race is a mystery, but Pollock's confidential letter of concern to the Admiralty sheds some light on Germany's request and Britain's compliance. Pollock wrote:

I may say that in conversation with Mr Le Band, who is I believe an agent for Messrs Stern, we were led to understand that the German Government had been able to do some favour to the British Government. And that, consequently, the latter were desirous of doing something to oblige the German Government. Also that there would be no doubt about the necessary request being forthcoming.

Whatever favour Baldwin's Government did to 'oblige' the Nazi regime has never come to light, but when the Foreign Office received Germany's licence applications they immediately became suspicious. Germany wanted 12in and 6in guns numbering eighteen units altogether. The quantity went beyond coastal defence and experimental use. A full Admiralty survey of the guns found that although they had spent about fifteen years on the seabed, they were in remarkably good condition. They could easily be fitted with new breech blocks, mounted and fired. The Admiralty advised the Government that the guns should not leave Scotland even in a mutilated state and Germany's export licences were consequently denied. Using the weapons for coastal defences was still considered a good idea. The Foreign Office did flirt with the idea of using them for defence purposes in colonies such as Hong Kong or dominions like South Africa, but the plan never materialized and they were broken up in Rosyth.

Marine salvage in British waters had been mainly a private commercial enterprise. The Admiralty's first salvage department was formed in 1915 after private companies could not cope with the shipping casualties caused by Germany's unrestricted U-boat activity. In its infancy the department was underfunded and ill-equipped for the task, but by 1918 it had grown to fifteen salvage ships, operating between the United Kingdom and the Mediterranean, and had returned 400 ships to active service.

At the end of the First World War the department was disbanded and its equipment sold off, most of it being purchased by Cox to begin his Scapa Flow operation. The Admiralty's experience during the First World War proved that marine salvage was an integral component of modern naval combat. A few days before the Second World War began on 3 September 1939, the Admiralty Salvage Department was re-formed. With no time to set up an effective operation, the six major commercial salvage firms were taken over. The Liverpool & Glasgow Salvage Association, who won the contract to salvage HMS *Thetis*, covered Britain's west coast. The Southampton firm Risdon Beasley Ltd worked along the south coast and three smaller firms shared the east-coast region. Finally Metal Industries were responsible for the whole north coast, including the Shetland Islands and Orkney.

The transfer to Admiralty control was very fast indeed. Diver Sandy Robertson recalled, 'I can remember war was declared on a Sunday, and we were all working for the Admiralty by the following Thursday.' McKenzie, Sandy Robertson, Sinc Mackenzie and many other men who had originally worked and trained with Cox were now about to give their expertise to the war effort. Almost immediately Britain's marine casualties rose dramatically through sustained U-boat activity. McKenzie said:

> Within a few weeks ships were being torpedoed, bombed and mined in all areas around the coast. Salvage vessels, lifting craft, tugs, lighters, and other craft suitable or capable of being adapted for use on salvage work were requisitioned and put into commission with the least possible delay.

Convoys of ships arriving in or departing from British waters were particularly vulnerable. During the remainder of 1939 a few ships were saved, but over the next few years the department's success rate all around the British coast was phenomenal. In 1941 alone the combined efforts of all Britain's salvage companies totalled 213 merchant ships saved and able to continue convoy duties, and seventy-nine damaged Royal Navy ships returned to active duty. In 1942, as the U-boat threat reached its peak, a similar number of ships, although considerably more Royal Navy vessels, were saved after being mined or torpedoed off the British coast. As the Battle of the Atlantic was slowly being won in 1943 through improved tactics and technology, the number of ships requiring salvage dropped significantly. However, during the summer of 1944, Allied shipping casualties rose steeply and once again the Admiralty Salvage Department played a vital, but largely unknown role, this time in Operation Overlord and the invasion of France on 6 June 1944.

As D-Day approached, McKenzie was appointed Principal Salvage Officer for the Allied invasion and joined the staff of the Naval

Commander in Chief, Expeditionary Force, Admiral Sir Bertram Ramsey. One of the Salvage Department's first tasks was to refloat the Phoenix Units, purposely sunk off the south coast of England, and then tow them across to Normandy where they formed an integral part of the two floating Mulberry Harbours. The hollow cement caissons ranged in weight from 2,000 to 6,000 tons. They averaged 180ft long, 75ft high and about 50ft wide. Towing the units took two large tugs, steaming at an average speed of 3kts.

At dawn on 6 June 1944 eighteen out of fifty salvage ships crossed the Channel with the Allied armada of more than 2,000 vessels. The rest of the salvage craft followed at intervals during the next few days. Before too long, Salvage Department personnel were repairing what craft they could and towing them back to England. The number lost through enemy action during the initial invasion and in the few weeks thereafter was much lower than anticipated, but two weeks later a severe gale greatly disrupted the latter stages of the Allied invasion. McKenzie recounted:

> Over the first whole month of the invasion, including the initial assault phase, only 241 ships and craft (excluding minor landing craft) were destroyed or seriously damaged by enemy action, against a total of over 600 as a result of the gale and adverse weather conditions generally.

Mulberry Harbour A was fixed at Omaha Beach, in the American Sector, and was destroyed in the storm. Its loss occurred partly because the Americans changed the original design specifications to increase its size. The changes involved sinking the harbour deeper in the water. When the storm hit, water poured into the Phoenix Units causing many of them to disintegrate.

Mulberry Harbour B, at Arromanches in the British Sector, was damaged but repairable. McKenzie and his men were heavily involved in getting the harbour operational again. It became the only main entry point for vital supplies into Europe until the Salvage Department could clear several ports blocked by ships, which had been purposely scuttled to disrupt the advancing army's supply network. Both Mulberry Harbours were designed to land 12,000 tons of supplies a day between them. Once Mulberry Harbour B was fully operational the floating port was able to clear 10,000 tons of food, guns and ammunition each day to support the Allied advance.

The salvage men worked in shifts delivering a twenty-four-hour service, repairing the harbour and clearing the Normandy bridgehead of war debris. Altogether, McKenzie and his men salvaged more than 800 vessels from the Normandy beaches, often using techniques learnt and developed while working with Cox. And, in the spirit of Scapa Flow, they adapted the techniques or developed new ones as and when needed.

As the Germans retreated back across Europe, the Salvage Department accompanied the Allies, mainly undertaking port clearance duties. Every major inlet or port was jammed with scuttled ships in a bid to slow down the march on Berlin. Dieppe had only twelve ships to clear, but Le Havre had sixty. At the approaches to the port of Rouen and the Seine the number jumped up to more than 160. Along the main waterways from Boulogne to Amsterdam another 321 ships were cleared. When the Allies reached Germany, 787 ships were cleared from the River Elbe, Hamburg and Kiel alone. Often unarmed and, by the very nature of their job, working in exposed positions, salvage personnel were sometimes subjected to sustained *Luftwaffe* attack as the enemy tried to ensure that a scuttled ship remained in place, blocking a particular seaway or harbour entrance.

After only eighteen months the Marine Salvage Department cleared 1,700 ships from more than fifteen European ports. Many were raised intact, but some were so badly damaged that for a speedy removal they had to be blasted to pieces. McKenzie's contribution to such an astounding success was a direct result of his work in Scapa Flow. Although Cox's salvage heritage is still very much evident to this day in the way ships are raised, the salvage work McKenzie achieved in the latter years of the Second World War was among some of the greatest. He was finally made a commodore and awarded the CBE in 1941 and then made a CB in 1945 for all his work in Northern Europe. The Marine Salvage Department changed its name to the Marine Salvage Service in 1946. That same year McKenzie returned to Metal Industries.

Shortly after the war against Germany ended, the defeat of Japan pushed the world into the atomic age and Scapa Flow steel became highly prized for more than its quality scrap value. On 16 July 1945 the United State's Manhattan Project detonated its first relatively small 21-kiloton, plutonium implosion bomb in New Mexico. A few weeks later the slightly smaller, but no less deadly 15-kiloton bomb with the harmless sounding code name, 'Little Boy', was dropped on

Hiroshima with devastating effect. Four days later another plutonium bomb was released over Nagasaki. Between 1945 and 1992 nearly 500 above ground and more than 2,000 underground atomic explosions for experimental purposes followed. They ranged in size from 18 tons to 15 megatons, contaminating the atmosphere forever.

Steel production requires vast amounts of oxygen to purify the molten mass. Although only fractional, all steel produced after 1945 is to some degree contaminated. This is harmless to organic life, but the production of sensitive instruments such as radiation monitoring equipment, atomic medicine, and even the American space programme demand radiation-free steel. The Scapa Flow warships, having been built and sunk prior to 1945 and then protected from the atmosphere by nearly 100ft of water, are the only significant source of steel with such qualities.

Seven warships are still at the bottom of Scapa Flow, the 25,000-ton *Konig* class battleships, *Kronprinz Wilhelm*, *Markgraf* and *Konig* and the 5,600-ton *Dresden II* class light cruisers *Cöln* and *Dresden*. The *Brummer*, the 4,400-ton sister ship to the *Bremse*, and the 5,500-ton *Konigsburg II* class light cruiser *Karlsruhe* were also left behind. More than 90,000 tons of radiation-free metal is still sitting on the seabed. Although no more complete ships were salvaged, demand for uncontaminated metal certainly grew, and became greater as industrial developments increased during the postwar years.

From 1956 to 1972 a local Orkney firm called Arthur Nundy Metals stripped some of the remaining warships down and brought the metal to the surface, piece by piece. The work carried on until 1977, under different management, until another scrap metal market slump halted any profitable means of raising the metal. However, in 1979 more than sixty steel companies showed a keen interest in Scapa Flow steel. *Time* magazine reported a new plan to resume salvage operations. The seven remaining warships were valued at $16m. with the salvage costs estimated at $7m., but the plan never materialized and the warships are still where they lay in 1919. Organized dive trips were offered for the first time in 1980. Today more than a dozen charter boats take about 3,000 divers around the main wreck sites each year; between them they make more than 20,000 dives. Scapa Flow is one of the few places in the world where recreational divers can visit warships because, having all been scuttled, none of them is designated as a war grave.

183

Most of the ships are now in a sorry state, like the *Karlsruhe*, which is in an advanced state of decay. Others, like the *Dresden*, are some of the best examples to be seen. Divers can swim through the hulls and even into some of the ships and get an idea of what it must have been like for Cox's men to clump around on the seabed on a daily basis in such freezing and inhospitable conditions. The remaining ships are protected and no more artefacts can legally be removed from the site.

Marine salvage today is more concerned with protecting the environment from oil and chemical spills, and the removal of wrecks is for safety reasons rather than for their scrap value. But accidents still do occur. Some of the operations make worldwide news and often echoes of Cox's legacy can be seen in modern salvage stories. One recent salvage operation was similar to Cox's raising of the battleship *Emperor of India* in 1931 and also relied on compressed air technology for its success. On Good Friday evening, 23 March 1989, the Very Large Crude Carrier (VLCC) *Exxon Valdez* sailed with her 200,000-ton cargo of crude oil from the Valdez Oil Terminal in Prince William Sound, Alaska, bound for Long Beach, California. Just after midnight she ran aground on Bligh Reef, immediately spilling more than 20 per cent of her cargo (about 258,000 out of 1,263,000 barrels) or roughly 11m. gallons of oil into the sea. Underwater damage extended for nearly 700ft of her nearly 1,000ft length. She was cracked right across her hull and threatened to snap in half, dumping her entire cargo into the Sound.

Eight of her eleven cargo tanks were breached and oil was continuing to leak. In addition, the forepeak tank and two starboard wing segregated ballast tanks, each designed to carry sea water were either holed or had suffered internal or bottom plate damage. Like the *Emperor of India*, the *Exxon Valdez* was stuck fast in an upright position on a reef and as every day passed the damage increased through wind and tidal action. Patching her breached hull for a salvage operation was also impossible. The first stage was to empty the remaining 80 per cent of her cargo, or about 45m. gallons, into three smaller tankers, making the *Exxon Valdez*'s deadweight only a little more than the battle cruiser *Hindenburg*.

The tanks were purged with inert gas and then pressurized to create sufficient buoyancy to raise the ship during a rising high tide – a far less complicated plan than the complex bulkhead sealing process needed for salvaging the warships in Scapa Flow. Cox had to raise a sunken warship as much as 100ft from the seabed to the surface, the *Exxon Valdez* only needed to be lifted 3ft to be removed from Bligh Reef. Twelve days after running aground she was refloated. Due to concern that she might capsize after breaking free, several salvage tugs were positioned ahead of the vessel and to either side and were used to pull the *Exxon Valdez* clear. On the morning of 5 April the VLCC gradually came alive. Fully supported on her giant air bubble she remained completely upright and smoothly floated clear, nearly four hours ahead of schedule. Regarding her surprise early departure from Bligh Reef, Exxon oil spill response team member Gary Gorski repeated a phrase so often quoted by Cox. 'You know, this is not an exact science.'

She was towed to an anchorage off nearby Naked Island to be made as seaworthy as possible for the voyage to dry dock about 2,500 miles away in San Diego, California. The *Exxon Valdez* is now called the *SeaRiver Mediterranean* and has been used to transport foreign-sourced crude oil to many destinations around the globe. Without compressed air technology it is unlikely that her salvage and continued service would have been such a success.

One of Cox's lifting methods from the 1920s was not used again until the early twenty-first century, which perhaps gives some indication of how far ahead of his time Cox really was. On 12 August 2000 the 18,000-ton *Oscar* class Russian nuclear-powered submarine, *Kursk*, was taking part in a naval exercise in the Barents Sea where her mission was to fire a training torpedo. After successfully firing the dummy round, the *Kursk* was travelling at only 6kts when an unstable torpedo detonated in her bow section. Due to her depth, the water pressure prevented the blast from naturally going outwards as it would do on the surface. Instead, the explosion blew into the torpedo room and continued into the control room compartment because a connecting hatch had been left open. Many men in the two compartments were killed instantly or in the ensuing fire. Her command centre was also dead as she took a bow-down attitude and headed for the seabed.

Those left among her original crew of 118 men began immediately to do what they could to save her. But only 135 seconds later the entire torpedo compartment exploded, shattering her bow section and sending a fireball through the submarine. Some men survived the inferno and the inrush of water as she plummeted to the seabed. A few of them even had time to write messages to their loved ones. An officer's burnt corpse was found with a note pressed against his chest and with his arms protecting it from the flames. Another crew member sealed his farewell in a mineral water bottle. Within twenty-four hours all life aboard the *Kursk* was thought to be lost, to either fire or water. Poor Russian rescue procedure and their unwillingness to accept help from the West are blamed for the remaining submariners' horrible fate.

The *Kursk* had to be salvaged for three reasons: first, to prevent her two nuclear reactors from leaking into the Barents Sea; second, to recover her twenty-two cruise missiles; and third, to exhume the remains of her crew. The Dutch salvage firm Smit (who later towed the German warships to Rosyth after Cox left), and Mammoet won the contract to raise her. Smit were to carry out all the underwater work and Mammoet were to do the actual lift. Several options were discussed and Smit finally opted for a winching system. The *Kursk* was twenty times the weight of an average destroyer raised by Cox and she was six times as deep. But although Cox's gear was primitive and basic compared with Smit's twenty-first century design, both salvers had to overcome the physical characteristics of raising vessels off the seabed, and their equipment even looked strikingly similar.

Initial preparations followed similar lines to those for a destroyer. First, any extraneous metal that might hamper her ascent was removed. This meant cutting off the *Kursk*'s entire shattered bow section by literally sawing it off with a hydraulic chain cutter, using a new diamond-like material called *widia*. She would then be winched up and suspended under a single lifting pontoon capable of holding eight times more deadweight than Cox's floating docks. The pontoon would then be towed into a dry dock, lowered, and the *Kursk* detached.

The unpredictability of marine salvage had also not changed since the 1920s. The underwater cutting wire was a completely new invention and to cut a huge vessel like the *Kursk* at this depth was extremely difficult. But after overcoming some technical problems the removal of the *Kursk*'s 1000-ton bow section was a complete success.

Smit's salvage pontoon was about the same length and breadth as Cox's two floating docks combined. Twenty-six hydraulic winches were fitted into her main deck in two rows of thirteen. Each cable consisted of fifty-six smaller cables for added strength, making each bundle capable of lifting 900 tons. Instead of running the cables underneath the wreck like Cox had done, each bundle was plugged into the *Kursk*'s main deck at intervals to help spread the load. The technique involved cutting holes into the submarine, lowering the plugs through into the inner hull where they sprang open like massive cavity wall bolts, locking the plugs in place. Once they were all fitted, the lift could begin.

With all the modern technology available for the raise, the same fundamental problem that Cox had to allow for in 1924 faced Smit. If an uneven load causes one wire to part then it is only a matter of moments before the rest will go. If this happened, the *Kursk*, like the first *V.70* attempt, would nose-dive to the seabed and probably become irrecoverable. Cox's man-operated winches were finely regulated by a keen eye and orders yelled through his megaphone. Smit used a central computer to read and adjust the slightest degree of uneven load. This meant installing massive hydraulic rams to help counter anything up to about 9ft of swell on the surface, thus independently balancing the ever-changing load on each wire bundle. Without this control many, if not all, of the twenty-six wire bundles would have parted as if made of cotton.

The computer system lifted her a few inches at a time, again and again as the *Kursk* sucked out of the bottom mud. The hiss of hydraulic rams and the whir of computer fans replaced the sound of men grunting at the winches as they pulled a destroyer to the surface. The method resembled Cox's 'heaving twenties' as they lifted a destroyer a few inches, took a short rest and started again. Eventually Smit's salvage pontoon safely delivered the *Kursk* into dry dock. She was stripped of her nuclear reactors and cruise missiles before being scrapped at the Nerpa shipyard in Murmansk. The *Kursk* tragedy shares many similarities with HMS *Thetis*, highlighting particularly inadequate rescue methods and crucial time wasted when men could have been saved. The most eerie similarity was that both submarines lasted exactly six years before killing their own crews. Smit had no idea that the technique had been pioneered nearly eighty years earlier in Scapa Flow, albeit in a more primitive fashion. Altogether, between 1924 and 1926, Cox's men heaved and pulled 21,500 tons of shipping to the surface using his crude but effective version of the original salvage-by-winch system.

Chapter 18

Family Man

Cox settled into the steady life of a managing director at the head of his scrapyard empire. His accountant, John Moore, later became the firm's managing director, but Cox remained the sole shareholder. Just as Cox met Jenny Jack through frequent business and social occasions with her father, so both Bunty and John Moore met in the same manner. Before too long they looked forward to seeing each other, their friendship turned into love and they eventually married in 1935. In June the following year Bunty gave birth to Jon and then in January 1938 came Peter.

Not having any sons of his own, Cox doted on the two boys. From an early age they saw their grandfather as a magical figure who was able to produce rationed food in abundance throughout the Second World War and through continued rationing thereafter. Jon recalled:

> He pulled up at our house, honk, honk honk, would go the horn. 'He opened the car boot of whatever new car he was then driving and it was full of fresh fruit, at a time when it was really rare. Why he wanted to give us fruit, we never found out, but it was all part of his largess. He always wanted to arrive with presents and appear to be bountiful.

When they were still quite young, Cox sat the boys on his knees. 'Well, what have you been doing?' he used to say. The two frightened little boys had not been doing anything constructive and honestly told him so.

'He used to get irate about that,' Jon remembered.

The outbreak of the Second World War brought with it a renewed hunger for scrap metal and Cox & Danks, Cohen's, and T. W. Ward were the only three scrapyard chains licensed to supply the war effort. Cox & Danks continued to grow and at the company's zenith there were fourteen branches throughout Britain.

Most of the metal came from three main sources: industry, demolition and people's own homes. In Sheffield alone, lorries, carts and barrows jammed the Cox & Danks yard daily to unload their precious cargoes of obsolete guns, shells, machine tools, bedsteads, tin cans and even pots and pans. When waste scrap metal was becoming exhausted Winston Churchill's War Cabinet demanded people's railings. Thousands of tons of the cast iron ended up in Cox & Danks scrapyards, including those from Hyde Park, which somehow found their way up to Sheffield.

Although Cox lost in excess of £10,000 on his Scapa Flow operation, the money was now flowing in and the prestige of what he had achieved was not yet over. His work in Scapa Flow was even discussed in Parliament, which must have greatly appealed to his vanity. As the only civilian to own a navy there had been frequent Parliamentary debates to discover his buying price. The Admiralty's contractual stipulation to keep the figure confidential was first attacked two months before Cox was even near to raising the *V.70*. In June 1924, Conservative MP Sir Fredrick Wise asked Parliamentary Secretary to the Admiralty, Labour MP George Ammon, to make the figure public. Ammon began:

> Contracts for raising some of the ex-German vessels sunk in Scapa Flow, have been given to Messrs Cox & Danks and the Scapa Flow Salvage and Shipbreaking Company, Ltd. As the operations are very speculative it is not possible to say whether the contractors will profit by them, but the vessels have been sold at fixed prices.

Less than a week later Sir Fredrick Wise asked Prime Minister James Ramsey MacDonald what prices the warships were sold for, and who received the proceeds? Ammon was directed to answer the question – or not, as he skilfully avoided giving the figure away. 'The Reparation Commission have not been consulted,' he began, 'The proceeds will be appropriated in aid of Navy Votes.'

Wise changed his tack. 'Has the Honourable Gentleman carefully considered what effect this will have in regard to the metal trade of this country.'

'Yes,' replied Ammon. 'All those facts have been taken into consideration.'

Most of the metal was then, and was for many years afterwards going straight back out of the country, so Wise's concerns were groundless. But Wise, spurred on by the insistence of other MPs to know more of the financial dealings between Cox and the Admiralty, made sure that the issue would be raised again. Not until two months before the Second World War commenced did Irish MP and Sinn Fein member John Francis McEntee press the new Parliamentary Secretary to the Admiralty, the Right Honourable Sir Geoffrey Shakespeare. McEntee demanded a full account of the salvage operations: How long had they been in operation? Were they ongoing? And most importantly, who profited by their salvage and sale? Shakespeare gave a potted history of the salvage operations, claiming them to be a private enterprise, 'I have no information as to the value of the ships raised, or the cost of the salvage operations carried out, nor whether further attempts at salvage are to be carried out'.

McEntee continued to press his point. 'If this is done at the expense of the contractor, what happens to the ships when they are brought up?'

'That is not our business,' replied Shakespeare, 'but I presume he sells them for scrap.'

Liberal MP George Rennie Thorne stood up, cutting into the debate, 'Do I understand that these ships belong to the people who have raised them and not to the Government?'

'We sold them outright,' replied Shakespeare.

Conservative MP for Argyll, Scotland, Fredrick Macquisten then stood up. 'Could not these people raise the *Thetis* without the slightest difficulty, seeing they have raised these battleships without accident of any kind?'

McEntee, Shakespeare and Thorne ignored the comment. McEntee finally and categorically demanded, 'Can the Honourable Gentleman say for what price they were actually sold?'

Shakespeare had no more lines to spin or facts to hide behind. 'They were sold,' he finally admitted 'I think for about £24,000 at the end of the War.' Finally after fifteen years Cox's buying price was no longer a secret.

In 1941 Cox took part in his last salvage venture. The 5,000-ton merchant ship *Stella* had been bombed by the *Luftwaffe* and sunk in

190

the Manchester Ship Canal. Cox opted for a compressed air raise. She had one large hole, measuring about 20ft by 30ft, which was patched up in the normal way. The routine operation came to an abrupt end one evening when the night shift took over at the same time as another bombing raid commenced. Although no shells hit the *Stella*, all her power was knocked out, stopping the compressors and causing her to flood rapidly. Six men had to scramble out with only candlelight to guide them. There were no casualties. The following day, work resumed and before too long the *Stella* was raised, repaired and again shipping cargo for the war effort.

Where Cox had once cleared the war debris from Europe's battlefields, he was now collecting peacetime scrap to be forged back into armaments. And for the first time in his adult life he had time to spend with Jenny Jack, Bunty and her two boys.

The end of the Second World War brought another scrap market for Cox to exploit. Thousands of corrugated Anderson air raid shelters had to be cleared from back gardens all over the country. So many were delivered so fast that floodlights had to be erected in the scrapyards to process the metal around the clock. Many shelters became linings in the galleries of coal mines. During the immediate postwar years, Cox was again approached by the Government, but not so much for his marine salvage expertise.

Four months before Germany surrendered, the Allies held a conference in Yalta, Crimea, to decide Germany's postwar fate. Destroying her war potential was paramount. This meant prohibiting all arms production, including aircraft, shipping and related machinery, metals or chemicals, which could lead to any form of weapons manufacture. The Allies were again going to demand reparations for the cost of the Second World War, which were incurred by the victors, just as they had done in 1919. Britain, the United Sates and Russia were going to demand $20bn dollars from Germany, the greatest share going to the country that bore the biggest loss. Russia was deemed to have suffered the most and was allocated 50 per cent.

The Crimean Conference's protocol ensured that Germany would deliver within two years:

equipment, machine tools, ships, rolling stock, German invesments abroad, shares of industrial transport and other enterprises in Germany etc. These removals to be carried out chiefly for the purpose of destroying the war potential of Germany.

Many experts were drawn from all walks of life in all three countries and they visited Germany on behalf of their governments to advise on what material should be removed. The Ministry of Supply invited Cox to join the British delegation. He was given the honorary rank of major and sent to Germany as a salvage adviser, where he selected material that could be officially liberated under the agreement and returned to Britain.

After his return to England, Cox took life a little slower. He was now in his early sixties and wanted to spend more time with his loved ones. As life slowly returned to normal in the postwar years, Jon Moore recalled Cox's continued generosity towards his two grandsons. Sweet rationing eventually came to an end and their grandfather took the boys to a sweet shop where he told them that they could have whatever they wanted. Looking at all the sweets, the two little boys were overwhelmed. There was too much choice for what was, for most of their young lives, forbidden by cost or availability. 'Both of us had just one Mars Bar each,' recalled Jon. Cox was a little dismayed by their lack of enthusiasm.

'But you can have whatever you want,' he said.

So many years of not having sweets whenever they wanted had made its mark.

It was something we could not get our heads around, but we were perfectly happy with our one Mars Bar each. In fact Grandpa bought a whole load of sweets anyway, which we subsequently devoured at home.

The boys often visited Cox at his Acton scrapyard on Saturday mornings. He used to let them test pieces of steel to assess the metal's quality through either magnetism or 'spark'. Two desirable types of steel that came into the yard were high-speed steel and the cheaper stellite. The better and more expensive metal contained tungsten carbide and was used for drill bits. Testing was a simple process of putting a grinder on the scrap chunks. If they gave a long spark, they were the cheaper metal. If the spark was short and orange, the steel was of a higher quality. Cox walked around the filthy yard immaculately dressed as always. Once the boys had finished a fair morning's work he allowed them to play amid all the scrap. Acton had a large crane that could reach over the whole yard, including the nearby railway sidings. The sorted metal was dropped by magnet or grabs into 12ft long semi-circular skips, craned over the sidings and tipped into a railway carriage. 'One of our biggest treats was to be put in one of the skips and spun around the yard a couple of times,' remembers Jon Moore. Cox stood there, looking pristine amid the mud and dirt, watching them. 'Grandpa thought it was terrific.'

Cox continued to cash in on the postwar scrap metal boom until 1949 when, one Sunday, he arrived home late for his lunch with a stunning admission. Jenny Jack, Bunty, his son-in-law and managing director, John, and his two grandsons had already started. As they sat eating, he breezed in and announced to his MD, 'Oh Jack, I just sold the Company.' He casually sat down and filled his plate, adding that Metal Industries was the new owner. Everyone stopped eating and watched him in disbelief. The firm was his life, but he treated its sale just like another scrap metal transaction. Cox & Danks was also John Moore's life. In a matter of moments he lost everything without any prior warning or discussion.

Many of Cox's decisions were based on gut feeling and it is highly likely that his resolve to sell out was no different. He was getting older and his grandsons were too young and inexperienced to take over. But the decision greatly affected his managing director. 'As a young man, I did not recognize what was the matter with my father,' said Jon, 'but my mother had to put him to bed. He was devastated.' John Moore loved the scrap metal business and tried to set up his own yard, but without too much success.

After living in London and various towns along the south coast of England, Cox and Jenny Jack eventually settled down in Torquay, where he used to delight in telling people of his days in Scapa Flow. He even had a housekeeper. His sister-in-law, Peggy Miller, or Aunt Peg, lived opposite his house on Broadpark Road. When asked how he managed to achieve what he did in Scapa Flow, Cox always quoted his favourite phrase. 'There's no such thing as can't, only won't and shan't.' Quite often he was invited to give lectures around the country. He loved the opportunity to once again get before an audience and describe what he had achieved.

The Coxes frequently took cruises, often in the same ships to the same places three or four times. Cox's dominance even exerted itself over the other passengers. Knowing the best places to visit ashore, he rallied the other passengers into groups for where he thought they 'ought' to go. When passengers feigned interest he used to say, 'Why the bloody hell aren't you going when I tell you to?' Aboard ship, Cox acted as a self-appointed entertainment's officer. He arranged teams for deck sports like quoits.

By the late 1950s he was still dashing up and down the country, giving talks and going on long, expensive holidays, when he began to have pains that affected his back, pelvis and hips. He probably put it down to old age or simply being tired, but as a result he began to spend more time on his hobbies. He was a keen freshwater fisherman and purchased a section of the River Dart above Totnes, Devon, which he surrounded with ex-Army barbed wire so that he could fish in peace and keep out poachers who would wade across the river from the opposite bank. He often took his grandchildren with him and although Cox was becoming an old man, he still had a sharp and unforgiving tongue when anyone, including his grandsons, dared to argue a point with him. Cox once took Jon for a day by the river in his barbed wire haven. While they were waiting for the fish to bite, grandfather and grandson discussed which way a hacksaw blade should be fitted into its handle. Cox quite rightly said that the blade should be fitted with its teeth facing away from the handle so it would cut, pushing downwards. That way, he explained, made the blade stronger and far less likely to snap. The young Jon disagreed. He was adamant that the blade's teeth should face towards the handle.

> Grandpa gave me three attempts to agree with him, then he let loose with a volley of insults and expletives and shouted 'just do it my way will you' and the matter was closed.

The war had been over for more than ten years and Britain's economy was rapidly improving. Many modern, time-saving consumer products for the home were appearing on the market. Cox loved gadgets and bought every new item whether it was a new kind of radio, a television, a or vacuum cleaner. He had also been an ardent supporter of Wolverhampton Wanderers since being a young man and later supported Torquay United. Whatever he was doing on a Saturday afternoon at 5.00 pm he would stop, open a bottle of Whitbread beer with its distinctive sweet smell, and switch on his latest radio to hear the football results.

As the months passed, the pains were getting worse and he began passing blood. When he eventually sought medical help, prostate cancer

194

was diagnosed. In the 1950s treatment was not as well developed as it is today and he most definitely knew his illness was terminal. He spent much more time at home in Torquay with Jenny Jack until eventually on 17 February 1959, Cox died. Jenny Jack, Bunty, John Moore and his two grandsons were at his side.

Cox had worked in many fields during his life. When he was only a teenager he had an illustrious career as an electrical engineer. Next he was a salver of ships, before working for the Government after the Second World War. Throughout most of his life he was one of Britain's most successful scrap merchants, but in his declining years Cox always considered himself a salvage engineer, 'retired'.

He lived and worked in a golden age for men of his type. With no labour laws and no health and safety rules governing workers' rights he frequently sacked men on a Friday and re-employed those he liked, but not necessarily the best for the job, on a Monday morning. The men worked in filthy and inhuman conditions; after an eight-hour shift, they thought nothing of coming out of a ship and walking into the freezing sea to wash before going back to their barracks at Lyness. But because of his success, he was hero-worshipped by his men. Quite simply he got the job done and gave them an immense feeling of pride at a time when mass unemployment and its psychological effects were rampant elsewhere in Britain. Cox was very generous to his men, often to the annoyance of his family. If his workers asked him for help, usually financial, Cox always obliged without a second thought. But if the same worker did not do what he was told when he was told to do it, Cox was just as likely to have him thrown off the job. More often than not Cox would physically do it himself.

Metal Industries abandoned all salvage work once the *Derfflinger* was raised, but continued for many years as ship breakers. As well as their scrap metal interests, Metal Industries also developed a successful electrical engineering division, which in the late 1960s was taken over by Thorn Electrical Engineering (later to become Thorn EMI). Cox & Danks was retained by Thorn until being absorbed into British Steel in the 1970s. Metal Industries lasted another ten years before being sold once again. By 1988 no trace of Cox & Danks or Metal Industries existed.

Today, salvage companies like Smit form part of an alliance called the International Salvage Union (ISU), which has been in existence for fifty years. Even with the advent of satellite navigation, and radar and maritime regulations, shipping casualties through collision, fire, grounding, structural failure and even terrorist attack still occur relatively frequently. The ISU's primary role is to act as a voice between salvage firms worldwide and within the maritime community as a whole whether they are political, financial or legal issues. They also work to foster cooperation between their fifty members, spread throughout twenty-nine countries. Such collaboration is essential to ensure safe and effective maritime salvage operations with all their legal and practical complexities.

The result is a highly effective worldwide organization whose members can reach a marine casualty anywhere in the world at very short notice. Today the business is split between 'dry salvage' and 'wet salvage'. Dry salvage is the recovery of ships and their cargoes while still afloat and accounts for most operations like the *Exxon Valdez*. Wet salvage is wreck removal. When oil tankers like the *Erika* and the *Prestige* go down they make worldwide headline news, mainly for their environmental damage. The *Prestige* polluted more than fifty miles of the Spanish coastline and is still on the seabed in two pieces. With improved salvage methods and coordinated response, ISU members have between them recovered more than 11m. tons of oil and chemicals from shipping casualties during the past decade. Putting the figure into perspective, this amounts to 143 spillages the size of the *Prestige*, which never got into the environment – and never received media attention. Salvage also involves raising ships from the seabed, such as the *Herald of Free Enterprise* after she capsized off Zeebrugge, Belgium, in 1987 and the *Kursk* in 2000. Smit salvaged both vessels. Altogether in the past twenty-five years, ISU members have salvaged nearly 5,000 vessels. The amount of cargo and shipping saved has grossed $27.4bn.

Had Cox been a salvage expert, one wonders if he would have succeeded. Being a novice and not knowing the boundaries meant that his pioneering spirit could push on and transcend the established limits making it possible for others to ride in his wake, which they did. The approach to, and success of, modern marine salvage is truly staggering, but Ernest Cox still holds the world record for raising the biggest and deepest ship in history when he pumped out the *Hindenburg* in 1930. In total more than 200,000 tons of shipping were salvaged, using cut-down boilers, makeshift pontoons and the stubborn, pig-headed attitude of a self-obsessed genius.

Sources and Bibliography

Bakker, Alexander & Walder, Lars, *The Salvage of the Kursk*, Smit, Rotterdam, 2003

Barnes, Brian, *Coast and Shore*, The Crowood Press, Wiltshire, England, 1986

Bowman, Gerald, *The Man who Bought a Navy*, Harrap, London, 1964

Brassey's Naval Annual 1911, J. Griffin & Co., London, 1911

Brassey's Naval Annual 1914, William Clowes & Son, London, 1914

Brassey's Naval Annual 1915, William Clowes & Son, London, 1915

Brown, Malcolm & Meeham, Patricia, *Scapa Flow*, Allen Lane, Penguin Press, London, 1967

Buxton, Ian, *Metal Industries: Shipbreaking at Rosyth and Charlestown*, World Ship Society, 1992

Campbell, N. J. M., *Jutland*, Conway Maritime Press, London, 1986

Cousteau, Jacques-Yves & Frédéric Dumas, *The Silent World*, Hamish Hamilton, London, 1953; Penguin Books, 1958

Davis R. H., *Deep Diving and Submarine Operations*, Siebe Gorman, Eighth Edition, Gwent, Wales, 1981

George, S. C., *Jutland to Junkyard*, Birlinn, Scotland, 1999

Grosset, Harry, *Down to the Ships in the Sea*, Hutchinson, London, 1953. Reprinted with permission of The Random House Group Ltd

Hough, Richard, *Great War at Sea*, Oxford University Press, Oxford, 1983

Jane's Fighting Ships 1914, Sampson Low, Marston, London, 1914

Light, Michael, *100 Suns*, Jonathan Cape, London, 2003

Lipscomb, Commander Frank W. OBE, RN, *Up She Rises*, Hutchinson, London, 1966

Masters, David, *The Wonders of Salvage*, John Lane/The Bodley Head, 1924

Masters, David, *When Ships Go Down*, Eyre & Spottiswoode Ltd, London, 1932

Peeke, Jones, Walsh-Johnson, *The Lusitania Story*, Pen & Sword Books, Barnsley, England, 2002

Roberts, David, *HMS Thetis: Secrets & Scandal,* Avid Publications, Liverpool, 1999

Scott, David, *Seventy Fathoms Deep*, Faber & Faber, London, 1931

Truscott, Peter, *Kursk: Russia's Lost Pride*, Simon & Schuster, London, 2002

Van der Vat, Dan, *The Grand Scuttle*, Birlinn, Edinburgh, Scotland, 1997

Von Reuter, Rear Admiral Ludwig (translated by Lieutenant Commander I. M. N. Mudie), *Scapa Flow: the Account of the Greatest Scuttling of all Time*, Hurst & Blackett Ltd, London, 1940

Warren, C. & Benson, J., *Thetis: "The Admiralty Regrets..."*, Avid Publications, Liverpool, 1997

Whyte, A. Gowens & Hadfield, Robert L., *Deep Sea Salvage*, Sampson Low, Marston & Co. Ltd, London, 1933

National Archives, Kew
ADM 116/2074
ADM 116/4115
ADM 116/4342
ADM 116/4429
ADM 116/10368
ADM 1/8562/172
ADM 1/8571/296
ADM 186/84
ADM 1/8762/251
ADM 1/8766/77
D035 187/12
TS 36/259
T 116/91

Organizations
BAE Systems, Submarine Division
Economic History Services
Exxonmobil
General Register Office
General Register Office for Scotland

House of Lords Library
Institution of Mechanical Engineers
Institution of Engineers and Shipbuilders in Scotland
International Salvage Union
ITN Archive/Stills
Meteorological Office
Ordnance Survey
Orkney Museum and Archive, Kirkwall and Stromness
Proudman's Oceanographic Institute
Reed's Nautical Almanac
Smit Salvage, Rotterdam
United Kingdom Hydrographic Office
United Salvage, Hull
University of Liverpool
Wolverhampton Archives

Newspapers, Magazines & Periodicals
Daily Mail
Guernsey Evening Press
Hansard
The Illustrated London News
M I News
The Orkney Herald
Time
The Orcadian
The Times

Index

Index

Aberdeen, 66, 97, 137
Aberdeenshire, 66
Acton (London), 152,192
Admiralty: acceptance of submarine *K.13*, 82;
    amount Cox pays for German warships
    from, 189–90; appointment of independent
    salvage experts, 16; asks Cox for help to
    recover the *Emperor of India*, 152–4;
    bigger warships for convoy escort, 114;
    charters plane for McKenzie and divers, 168;
    Cox buys equipment from, 22; Cox buys
    German dry dock from, 18; Cox contact
    with re. *Thetis* loss, 166; dry dock in Rosyth,
    94, 126, 128, 157, 158; export licence for
    German guns, 178–9; invitation to private
    salvage firm, 17; involvement in *Lusitania*
    design, 27; lowering of German ensigns, 8;
    Marine Salvage Department, 28, 179–80;
    Metal Industries' contacts with, 175–6;
    official observer for *Hindenburg* arrival in
    Rosyth, 123; permission to publish article
    on salvage of HMS *Emperor of India*, 155;
    base in Plymouth, 164; pilot for *Moltke*, 93;
    public announcement that all life aboard
    Thetis is lost, 169; proposing naval base
    at Scapa Flow, xiv; purchase of remaining
    fleet from, 41; sheds on Lyness Pier, 50;
    suggestion that *Thetis* worth more than
    crew, 172; taking of German ships by force,
    13–14; takes possession of German
    floating dock, 18; telegram to McKenzie
    for help to save *Thetis* crew, 167; theft of
    metal from, 38; *Thetis* design policy stuns
    Cox, 172
A. G. Vulcan shipbuilders, 56
Ajax, tugboat, 126
Alloa Shipbreaking Company, 93
America (see also American & United States):
    American Sector, D-Day, 181; as Britain's
    ally, xvi; division of German warships
    among Allies, 9; naval power concerns,
    xv; space programme, 183; transport of

arms aboard Lusitania, 26; use of scrap
    metal in, 178
Ammon, George (Labour MP), 189–90
Amsterdam (blocked by scuttled ships), 182
Anderson (shelter), 191
Armada (Spanish), xiv
Armistice, xv, 5, 8, 10, 16
Arnold, Walter (submariner), 165–6
Arromanches (France), 181
Arthur Nundy Metals (Orkney salvage firm), 183
Atrocity List, 16
Audax II (British tugboat), 66

B.112 (German destroyer), 66–7
Baldwin, Stanley (Prime Minister), 67, 178–9
Balfour Hospital (Orkney), 133, 135, 137,
    142, 144
Ballymore (Ireland), 118
Barents Sea, 185, 186
Battle of Dogger Bank, 95
Battle of Jutland: action of *Von der Tann*, 129;
    attack on *Kaiser*, 106; attack on *Moltke*, 83;
    attack on *Seydlitz*, 96; clash of British and
    German fleets in, xv; *S.36* veteran at, 51;
    Hindenburg built too late for, 70; *Prinzregent
    Luitpold* unscathed in, 138; strength of
    German warships at, 20
Battle of Skagerrak, xv
Battle of Trafalgar, xv
Bayern (German battleship), xiii, 160, 176
Beaty, Admiral Sir David (Admiral of the Fleet), xvi
Belgium, xv, 5, 196
Berlin, xv, 9–10, 16, 95, 182
Bertha (British salvage vessel), 159–60, 176
Biberach (Germany), 147
Birkenhead (England), 166
Birmingham (England), 128, 152
Bligh Reef (Alaska), 184, 185
Blohm and Voss (shipbuilders), 56
Blue Riband, 106
Board of Trade, 67
Bognor (England), 152

206

upturned *Seydlitz*, 103–5; increases safety features within sunken warships, 140; involved in rescue aboard submarine HMS *K.13*, 170; lied to by two divers, 46; made chief salvage officer for Metal Industries, 159; makes 'pumping job' of *Hindenburg*, 72, 153; meets Cox at *Thetis* inquiry, 160; mounts rescue operation after explosion aboard *Prinzregent Luitpold*, 141–2; nearly drowns in *Von der Tann* explosion 132–3, 137; new bosses offered money for German guns, 178; offers divers to help in *Thetis* rescue plan, but rejected, 166; offer of divers to help in *Thetis* rescue accepted, 167; plays leading salvage role in Battle of the Atlantic, 180; position within salvage team, 63; ready to raise *Hindenburg*, 119; recalls loss of *V.70* while raising her, 32; re-floods *Hindenburg* to allow trapped diver to get free, 122; shocked at lack of sound rescue plan for *Thetis*, 169; successfully raises six capital ships under Metal Industries 176–7; takes part in conference on *Thetis* rescue, 168; takes part in first airlock operation aboard *Moltke*, 86; talks of faulty lighting aboard sunken warships, 75; talks to trapped diver by telephone, 43–4; thoughts recalled on raising *V.70* by collegue, 35; tries in vain to help locate life aboard *Thetis*, 169; tries to revive Hall, 112; wants Cox to continue salvage work, 150; works aboard *Derfflinger* while *Thetis* is on her trials, 161

McKeown, Ernest (salvage officer): thoughts recalled on raising *V.70* by colleague, 35; present when Henderson was killed, 58–9; gives evidence at Henderson's inquest, 60; hired by Cox, 22; position in salvage firm, 63; tows *Bremse* to Lyness, 117; takes part in salvage of HMS *Emperor of India*, 153

Medway, River (England), 55, 95

Mersey Docks and Harbour Board, 164

Messina Strait, loss of HMS *Thunderbolt* near, 173

Metal Industries Ltd: abandon all salvage work after raising *Derfflinger*, 195; biggest ship breaking firm in Great Britain, 159, 176, 177; buys *Hindenburg*, 128; buys *Prinzregent Luitpold*, 155; buys Von der Tann, 155; convinced to carry on salvaging in Scapa Flow, 159; cover Scotland's north coast during Second World War, 180; Cox plans to sell *Prinzregent Luitpold* to, 129; Cox plans to sell *Von der Tann* to, 129; Cox sells Cox & Danks to, 193; Cox's workers feel Metal Industries control scrap price, 150; Cox tries to sell salvage operation to, 150, 152; disappeared by late 1980s, 195; employ McKenzie as chief salvage officer, 159;

established as salvage firm, 177; finally buy Cox's salvage interests, 155, 159, 160; McKenzie returns to after Second World War, 182; modernize Cox's salvage plant, 176; negotiate better prices for wrecks, 175; personnel fly to Orkney, 160; Pollock becomes new boss at, 178; presses McKenzie to raise *Derfflinger*, 177; profit made on salvaged warships, 177; raise deeper warships, 176–7; reluctant to buy Cox's scrap interests, 152, 159; salvage *Bayern* 176; scrap exported back to Germany, 178; sells out to Thorn Electrical Engineering, 195

Mill Bay (Orkney): *G.38* beached in, 48; *G.39* delivered to, 63; *G.91* towed to, 47; *G.104* delivered to, 68; *H.145* bound for, 51; *S.36* delivery to, 52, 54; *S.52* on her way to, 49; *S.53* towed to 39–40; *V.70* towed to, 34; all ships follow same breaking plan in, 50; *Bremse* broken up in, 116; Cox's first dock beached in, 23; Cox's second dock altered in, 64; destroyer from, used to raise *Hindenburg* 121; *Hindenburg* stripped, similar to destroyers in, 128; *Hindenburg* towed stern first to, 125; means established to break ships in, 51; *Prinzregent Luitpold* and *Von der Tann* secured in, 148, 151; *Prinzregent Luitpold* towed out of, 156; proximity to Lyness Pier, 50; proximity to Ore Bay, 41; rapidly filling with warships, 49, 55; sixteen destroyers broken up at, 67; *Von der Tann* towed out of, 158

Miller, Robert (Cox's father-in-law), 4

Ministry of Supply, 192

Moore, John (Cox's son-in-law), 188, 193, 195

Moore, Jon (Cox's grandson), x, 151, 175, 192–3

Moltke (German battle cruiser): anchored in Scapa Flow, 12; ballasting to raise trim 90–1; comparison with *Seydlitz*, 96, 98, 99, 100, 101; Cox's first big salvage operation, 83; *Derfflinger* twice as deep as, 177; diving survey of, 83–4; finally secured in dry dock, 94; first seen by Cox, 20; influenza outbreak aboard, 90; inside of 87–9; placing of airlocks on, 8–7; position of external openings, 84; raising of first time, 85; rapid air loss from, 89; second attempt to raise, 91–2; successfully raised, 91–2; takes part in attack on British coast 95; towed to Lyness Pier for stripping, 92; towed to Rosyth, 93; tugs lose control over, 93; visit to New York, 83; wires part while in ascent, 91

Mowat, John (salvage crane driver), 49, 58–9, 60–2

Mowat, Robert (salvage carpenter), 117, 118, 140, 141, 142,144

Mulberry Harbours, 181

Mull (Scottish island), 28